MW01232846

DEVELOPING LEADERSHIP AND PERSONAL SKILLS

DEVELOPING

LEADERSHIP AND

SHARON HUNTER

Lee and Associates
Starkville, Mississippi

MARSHALL STEWART

State Agricultural Education Coordinator
North Carolina

BRENDA SCHEIL

Agriculture Teacher
New Auburn, Wisconsin

ROBERT TERRY, JR.

Teacher Educator
Texas A&M University

STEVEN D. FRAZE

Teacher Educator
Texas Tech University

PERSONAL SKILLS

Science and Technology Series

Series Editor
Jasper S. Lee, Ph.D.

Interstate Publishers, Inc.
Danville, Illinois

DEVELOPING LEADERSHIP AND PERSONAL SKILLS.
COPYRIGHT © 1997 BY INTERSTATE PUBLISHERS, INC.
All rights reserved. Printed in the United States of America.

Order from

Interstate Publishers, Inc.

510 North Vermilion Street
P.O. Box 50
Danville, IL 61834-0050

Phone: (800) 843-4774
Fax: (217) 446-9706
Email: info-ipp@IPPINC.com

Library of Congress Catalog Card No. 96-75863

ISBN 0-8134-3077-1

1 2 3 4 5 6 7 8 9 10   02 01 00 99 98 97

Preface

A new century is ahead. Success in that century will require people who have leadership and personal skills. As a student, you can develop those skills. You can be successful! You can become whatever you want to become! This book is a good beginning.

Leadership and Personal Development has been designed as a dynamic book based on modern approaches. The latest theories and research have been used to prepare this book. The ideas have been tested with individuals and groups of students.

Leadership and Personal Development is structured to make learning about leadership fun. It makes developing important personal skills come alive through the use of many student models in the photographs. The book is intended as a rich up-to-date learning tool. A student-friendly format has been followed. Sound educational practices have been integrated into the content and design.

The book is based on the fact that leadership is not hereditary and can be learned. It offers a broad look at what leadership is and why it is important. It provides the beginning leader with a guide for personal development. Tools needed to achieve personal goals are described.

Leadership and Personal Development offers an exciting look at what any leader will need to know. It does this with the use of many photographs and drawings. The sequence is logical and easy to follow.

Developing Leadership and Personal Skills is not a student organization book—it is a book about your future. The authors suggest that being active in an organization is a good way to practice leadership and personal skills.

Turn the page and start learning about the leader you are to become!

Acknowledgments

The authors of **Developing Leadership and Personal Skills** are indebted to many individuals who made contributions to writing this book. Their assistance helped the authors realize their goal.

The assistance of Sheila R. Carlson of Thousand Oaks, California, is gratefully acknowledged. Dr. Carlson assisted in conceptualizing a book on leadership and personal development for today's students.

Special appreciation is extended to the Mississippi Governor's School for providing photographs used throughout the book. Others acknowledged for photographs include Texas Tech University, Piedmont College, and Jasper S. Lee. Anita Jouppi of New Auburn, Wisconsin, is acknowledged for her assistance with line art.

The students and staff members of Newton Vocational Center and Leake County Vocational Center in Mississippi and Paxton–Buckley–Loda High School in Illinois are thanked for serving as student models. Special appreciation goes to administrators Lynn Wagner and Monte Ladner of Mississippi and teachers Doug Anderson and Mike White of Illinois.

Special acknowledgment goes to Robert D. Sommers of Ohio, Will A. Lewis of Tennessee, and Scott Stump of the National FFA Organization for reviewing the manuscript. The assistance of Carol Easters of the Future Homemakers of America and Edward Miller of the Future Business Leaders of America is acknowledged.

The authors are most grateful for the assistance of President Vernie Thomas of Interstate Publishers, Inc. His untiring efforts in producing quality materials for today's students are greatly appreciated. Kim Romine is given special appreciation for her work in designing the book.

Contents

PART ONE: DEVELOPING PERSONAL LEADERSHIP QUALITIES

PART TWO: GROWING INTERPERSONAL RELATIONSHIPS

PART THREE: NURTURING GROUP LEADERSHIP

1

LEADERSHIP: WHO AND WHAT IS A LEADER?

> *Take me to your leader.* **Anonymous**

Think of the groups you know about. Why do some get much accomplished, while others fail to do anything? Why do some grow and become popular, while others wither away? Why do some give members fun experiences, while others are not fun at all? Often, the difference between successful groups and groups that fail can be found in the leadership of the organization.

The terms "leader" and "leadership" are not new to any of us. We have heard them used and discussed often. But, can you really describe leadership? Can you readily identify what makes a person a leader?

1-1. People fill a variety of leadership roles in groups.

OBJECTIVES

This chapter focuses on defining terms related to leaders and leadership and describing what leadership is about. It has the following objectives:

1. Describe leadership

2. List traits of effective leaders

3. Explain leadership style and contrast three styles

4. List common misunderstandings about leadership

5. Contrast leadership with power and management

T
E
R
M
S

autocratic leader

charisma

conceptual traits

democratic leader

follower

influence

internal traits

interpersonal traits

laissez-faire leader

leader

leadership

leadership style

management

power

technical traits

trust

DESCRIBING LEADERSHIP

What is leadership? Many definitions of leadership are used. Books and articles have been written to help define and describe leadership. Ideas about leadership change over time because more is learned about what leaders do and how they do it.

Leadership is a relationship where influence is given to meet individual or group goals. Personal growth is usually a major part of leadership. Leadership is far more than "taking charge" of a group. It involves many important ideas and values. A *leader* is a person who helps an individual or a group in achieving their goals. This person is not always the president or elected leader. It may be a person who is an active member of a group or one who reaches out to help another person. For individuals to be leaders, they must have followers.

A *follower* is an individual who follows the ideas, goals, or tasks of a leader. Followers conform to or accept the ideas of leaders. Every successful leader must have good followers. Followers are developed by working together to identify goals and strategies for achieving the goals.

Understanding leadership by studying the concepts involved is easier. To help, several are described here.

LEADERSHIP IS A RELATIONSHIP

If there are no followers, there is no leader. If both leader and follower do not understand their roles, the group will not operate effectively or accomplish its tasks.

The relationship between a leader and followers must be one of respect, consideration, and caring. Group members will not be eager to follow a leader who puts them down and treats them as if their thoughts and efforts do not matter. Likewise, a leader who is not respected will not have the power to influence the group in any direction.

At the heart of the relationship between leaders and followers is trust. **Trust** is having confidence that an individual will try to do the right thing. It is the foundation of any positive human relationship. If you think about the friends and family members who are closest to you, you will probably find mutual trust between them and you.

Trust is not given freely. Trust must be earned over time and through many tests. However, when leaders and followers trust one another, their group will accomplish its goals and enjoy working with one another.

LEADERSHIP IS A PROCESS

Leadership demands a trusting relationship. Because this takes time to develop and because leaders have definite duties and tasks, leadership should be thought of as a process.

A person does not become a leader just because of a position they hold in a group. Instead, leadership comes from gaining experiences, applying special skills, and developing credibility with a group. Over time, group members will learn to rely on the insight and guidance of the leader.

LEADERSHIP IS INFLUENCE

One primary job of a leader is to provide influence to a group. In leadership, **influence** is when a leader motivates a group to take action—to do something. The leader provides opinions, experiences, and advice that are important to group members.

A leader can influence a group in many ways. Some are negative, such as using power or authority to threaten or punish followers who do not perform. Other ways are positive, such as providing incentives and rewards for excellent work.

Whatever methods are used, negative or positive, the leader is responsible for influencing the group to take action. The leader's influence has an impact upon the group as a whole and each group member as a person.

LEADERSHIP IS SERVICE

Some people think that leadership is an honor, an award. It is service. Because of their many different roles in the group, leaders are required to do much extra work. When you get right down to it, the leader is a servant to the group.

Leader responsibilities include providing structure and developing positive relationships in a group. Because of these duties, leaders must devote extra time and effort to group activities not required of other members. Sometimes, leaders must be flexible and willing to sacrifice their desires to make sure the group functions properly.

While some very pleasant rewards come from being a leader, there are also many unglamourous, difficult aspects.

1-2. Leaders have traits that allow them to fulfill their roles.

TRAITS OF EFFECTIVE LEADERS

Leaders must have certain traits if they are to fulfill the role of leadership. Leadership traits can be taught and learned. Leadership traits are useful in many different situations. Leadership traits and characteristics can be placed into four categories.

INTERNAL TRAITS

Internal traits might also be called "personal characteristics." They are probably the most difficult characteristics to develop, but are the most important. Until people have well-defined internal traits, they cannot expect others to follow their lead. Listed below are some internal traits of effective leaders:

- ⇨ *Knows strengths and weaknesses*
- ⇨ *Creative*
- ⇨ *Driven*
- ⇨ *Perceptive*
- ⇨ *Moral*
- ⇨ *Hard working*
- ⇨ *Self-confident*
- ⇨ *Flexible*
- ⇨ *Responsible*

TECHNICAL TRAITS

Technical traits are called "how to do it" skills. They are the easiest of all leadership traits to master. Some technical traits are directly related to a task. For instance, a conductor of an orchestra needs to know a great deal about music. Other technical traits are more general and apply to many situations. Here is a list of some important technical traits:

- ⇨ *Follow directions*
- ⇨ *Conduct meetings*
- ⇨ *Speak effectively in front of groups*
- ⇨ *Lead discussions*
- ⇨ *Organize events*
- ⇨ *Write well*

CONCEPTUAL TRAITS

Conceptual traits are called "thinking" skills. While they are a little more difficult to learn than technical traits, they are just as important. Leaders need to be able to use their mind to evaluate situations and come up with new ideas. Here are a few interesting conceptual traits:

⇨ *Think logically*

⇨ *Analyze situations*

⇨ *Anticipate problems*

⇨ *Visualize changes*

⇨ *Recognize opportunities*

⇨ *Combine different, complex ideas*

⇨ *Solve group and individual problems*

⇨ *Make decisions*

INTERPERSONAL TRAITS

Interpersonal traits are commonly called "people" skills. These characteristics help a leader to work with others and develop good feelings within a group. These traits are not difficult to learn. In fact, they come from simply liking people and wanting to help them. Here are a few valuable interpersonal traits:

⇨ *Be trustworthy*

⇨ *Meet people with ease*

⇨ *Communicate clearly*

⇨ *Listen effectively*

⇨ *Have a positive attitude*

⇨ *Accept other views*

⇨ *Understand needs of others*

⇨ *Respect people of other backgrounds and cultures*

These traits are important. Some people are better at them than others. Understanding personal strengths and weaknesses is important for leaders. It is also important for leaders to recognize and value the talents and abilities of others to make the group strong. A good balance of internal, technical, conceptual, and interpersonal traits among group members makes it easier to be effective.

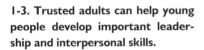
1-3. Trusted adults can help young people develop important leadership and interpersonal skills.

LEADERSHIP STYLES

Leaders vary in many ways. How they go about fulfilling their roles may be quite different from one leader to another.

Leadership style is the way individuals act in their roles as leaders. It is how a leader relates to other people. Three common kinds of leadership styles are:

■ Autocratic style—An *autocratic leader* is directive and makes decisions for an individual or group. Being autocratic does not mean the leader is coercive or a dictator. Leaders using the autocratic style realize that they have a responsibility to provide direction and make decisions.

■ Laissez-faire style—A *laissez-faire leader* gives others a major role in making decisions. These leaders recognize that involving the group in the decision-making process is important. With laissez-faire, it may appear that the leader is no longer the leader. Laissez-faire leaders are not shirking responsibility. They realize that the members are often in a better position to make a decision. A laissez-faire leader interferes very little with the affairs of individuals or groups.

■ Democratic style—A *democratic leader* selects a style between autocratic and laissez-faire. Democratic leaders recognize the importance

1-4. People are not born leaders—they develop leadership skills.

of participation by members, but retain part of the decision-making responsibility. A democratic style is different from the democratic principles of government or a political party.

Leaders vary in the styles that they use. The same individual can use different styles, depending on the situation. If people in a group are well informed, they can make good decisions. If the leader is far better informed than the followers, an autocratic approach may work best if used properly.

More information on leadership styles is presented later in the book. Chapter 17 describes how to select the style to use.

MISCONCEPTIONS ABOUT LEADERSHIP

Leadership is sometimes misunderstood. One reason for this difficulty is that many misconceptions about leadership exist. Many people think a leader has to look, dress, or sound a certain way. There are also many misunderstandings about the leader's job and how it should be done. Perhaps the best way to understand what leadership is all about is to understand what leadership is not!

MISCONCEPTION #1: LEADERS ARE BORN, NOT MADE

Have you ever heard someone say, "That person is a natural born leader"? Statements like this imply that certain people are born with special traits that make them leaders. Some people associate looks, height, hair color—even gender—with leadership ability. Nothing could be further from the truth.

No physical traits characterize leaders. Such misconceptions come from early ideas about leadership, called the "great person" theory. This theory

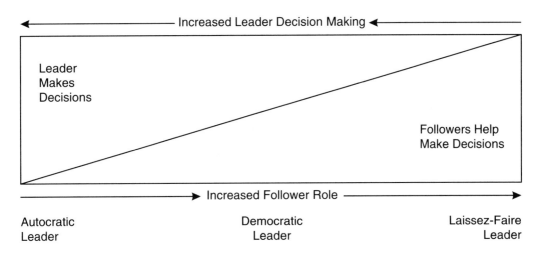

1-5. How roles of followers change with style of the leader.

stated that leadership traits, just like physical characteristics, were inherited, especially by people of the upper classes of society. Believers of this theory even thought that certain "people" traits were genetic.

The truth is that leaders come in all shapes and sizes. Joan of Arc was a small, teen-aged woman who led troops into battle in medieval times. Winston Churchill, who was short and overweight, was a very effective leader for Great Britain during World War II. Abraham Lincoln, a tall, thin man, is considered one of our greatest presidents. President Franklin Roosevelt led our nation during very difficult times from a wheelchair. No physical characteristics can be associated with leadership ability.

"Great people" theories are wrong. Leadership traits can be taught. Otherwise, studying this book might be worthless! A person can become "great" through study and hard work. Knowledge about leadership can be learned by individuals and then practiced to develop effectiveness.

MISCONCEPTION #2: LEADERSHIP COMES FROM POSITIONS IN THE GROUP

Have you ever run for an office in an organization? Why did you want such a position? Often, people want to hold an important position in an organization because they believe that is the only way they can be a leader in the group. However, you do not have to hold an office to be a leader.

1-6. Abraham Lincoln was a noted leader.

In fact, sometimes, people with leadership positions do not have any real leadership qualities at all!

The rules of an organization, such as bylaws or a constitution, describe the responsibilities and authority for people who hold office in that group. Many times, these duties give the office holder the right to make decisions that affect members of the organization. However, just because someone has a right does not mean they can use that right. The ability to use authority and carry out responsibilities is leadership. A leader is someone who can exercise their influence.

A person does not have to hold an office or position in a group to exercise their influence. Dr. Martin Luther King, Jr., is recognized as one of the most effective leaders of the twentieth century. He never held a formal political leadership position. In fact, if you think about the groups you have been in, you can probably come up with many examples of regular members who were able to influence the group.

MISCONCEPTION #3: LEADERS MAKE ALL DECISIONS FOR THE GROUP

A mistaken idea of leaders and followers alike is that leaders make all the decisions for a group. A leader is often required to give the final approval for group action. However, the process that goes into that decision should involve the ideas of group members.

One of the most important things a leader can do is to gather ideas about issues from group members. Knowing all there is to know about an issue is impossible for one person. This is especially so when that issue affects other people. An effective leader will ask for and use the input from other people when making decisions. The effective leader will seek and value feedback from others.

By sharing decision-making power, the leader can get better solutions to problems and more participation in activities. Research shows that when decisions are shared, so are the activities associated with that decision. Wise leaders do not make all of the group's decisions; they make sure everyone in the group shares in the decision-making process.

MISCONCEPTION #4: ALL LEADERS ARE POPULAR AND CHARISMATIC

Charisma is a term used to describe personality characteristics that arouse the enthusiasm and loyalty of other people. Charismatic leaders can make group members feel motivated, happy, and self-confident. They are often able to get group members to perform at high levels and to work hard. Dr. Martin Luther King, Jr., is an example of a charismatic leader who was able to influence many people to cause change.

I-7. General Colin Powell is a leader who never held a formal political leadership position.

Does this mean that all leaders have to be popular and charismatic? Certainly not. In a study of United States presidents, researchers found that only seven of our presidents were considered charismatic leaders. George Washington was a great military and political leader, but did not exhibit charismatic traits. Likewise, there are leaders who did exhibit many charismatic traits, but failed to lead their groups effectively.

Leaders often have to make choices that are not popular with group members. Sometimes, the most effective leaders are those who cause group members to look at things in a different way.

MISCONCEPTION #5: LEADERSHIP IS POWER

Power and authority are often associated with leadership. Some leaders seem to have ways of getting people to do things they normally would not do, or even things they do not want to do. Power should be thought of as a tool of leadership rather than the same thing as leadership.

Power is the ability of a person or group to employ force on other persons or groups. In human relationships, power is often thought of as negative. Some types of power are negative. However, other types of power come from the leader's ability to make followers feel good. This earns loyalty in other ways.

1-8. Dr. Joyce Brothers is well known for helping people better understand themselves.

Positive types of power, when used for the right reasons, can help a group stay focused on their goals and devoted to each other. However, used improperly, power can drive group members away and cause conflict in an organization.

MISCONCEPTION #6: LEADERSHIP IS MANAGEMENT

Leadership and management are easily confused; however, a distinct difference exists between the two. They are often confused because, frequently, one person in a group assumes the roles of both leader and manager.

Management is controlling and directing others. Approaches vary, but management includes domination by the person who is in charge. The role of management is to get work done as it should be done.

An important function of the leader is to make sure the group *does the right things*. The leader helps define the group's mission and goals and then provides the vision to carry them out. This involves creating and communicating a clear vision of what the group is to do. Leaders work to define the purpose, mission, or primary goals of the group.

On the other hand, the function of a manager is to make sure the group *does things right*. This involves providing training, record keeping, evaluation of work, and feedback.

Perhaps the following example can clarify the differences between leadership and management. A manager would make sure people in the group know how to climb a ladder properly. A leader would make sure the ladder is leaning against the correct wall!

1-9. Marie Curie was a leader in nuclear physics.

REVIEWING

MAIN IDEAS

Leadership takes place any time groups of people get together to accomplish a purpose. For there to be leaders, there must also be followers. In those simple terms, all of us have experience in leadership situations.

Many misunderstandings exist about leadership. Knowing that leadership ability is not inherited is important. It can be learned and developed. Leadership does not come from holding an office or special job in a group, and a person does not have to be charismatic to be a leader.

When it comes right down to it, leadership is based upon trusting relationships built over time. It is a leader's job to influence a group toward certain actions, but not make all of the decisions. Leadership should not be thought of as glamorous. It really involves putting in extra service and commitment to make sure the group reaches its capabilities.

To best meet the expectations of leadership, leaders need to work to develop special traits. Internal traits, technical traits, conceptual traits, and interpersonal traits all help a leader serve the group.

QUESTIONS

Answer the questions using correct spelling and complete sentences.

1. What is the "great person" theory and why is it incorrect?
2. What are some things charismatic people do?
3. What is the foundation of all positive human relationships?
4. How does a leader influence a group in a positive way?
5. What are a leader's primary responsibilities in a group?
6. What are the four types of traits needed by leaders?

EVALUATING

CHAPTER SELF-CHECK

Match the term with the correct definition. Write the letter by the term in the blank provided.

a. conceptual traits   d. interpersonal traits   g. power
b. influence   e. trust   h. technical traits
c. leader   f. management

1. _____having confidence in an individual.

2. _____referred to as "thinking" skills.

3. _____referred to as "how to do it" skills.

4. _____personality characteristics that arouse the enthusiasm and loyalty of other people.

5. _____the ability of a person or group to employ force on other persons or groups.

6. _____to make sure the group does things right.

7. _____person who helps others achieve goals.

8. _____when a leader motivates a group to take a particular action.

EXPLORING

1. Attend a meeting of a local government or civic organization. Watch for the ways the chairperson of the group exercises influence. Look for other members who influence the group without holding a formal position in the organization. Write a short report of your findings.

2. Consider all of the organizations in which you are a member. In groups of three or four, discuss the effective and ineffective things leaders have done and how it affected you. Present a summary of your discussion to the entire class.

3. Copy the lists of technical, conceptual, and interpersonal traits found in this chapter. Rate your leadership traits on each using the following scale: 1 = need improvement; 2 = Fair; 3 = Good; 4 = Excellent. Write the number that best describes you beside each item.

4. Using the ratings from item 3 above, describe the leadership traits you have to offer a group and the traits that you need to learn more about. Write a short report.

2

DEVELOPING
PERSONAL RESPONSIBILITY

> *Do not waste a minute—not a second—in trying to demonstrate to others the merits of your performance. If your work does not vindicate itself, you cannot vindicate it.* **Theodore Roosevelt**

Leadership and personal development begin "inside" of you. You must know yourself if you are to effectively grow as a leader in your school, student organizations, and community. Your successful growth as a student leader will prepare you for future challenges you face as a student, parent, professional, and citizen. This growth begins with you getting to know yourself and understanding what makes you "tick."

As you think about what makes you "tick," think about how you would describe yourself. What kind of person are you? Are you responsible? Leadership begins with your personal responsibility.

2-1. A parent must assume responsibility for children.

15

OBJECTIVES

This chapter deals with being a responsible person. It has the following objectives:

1. Describe personal responsibility
2. Identify problems when people are not personally responsible
3. Explain how to become a responsible person

T E R M S

courage
decision making
non-negotiable limits
personal management
personal responsibility
principle
self-esteem
self-motivation
work ethic

PERSONAL RESPONSIBILITY: AN UNDERSTANDING

JEFF FACES PERSONAL RESPONSIBILITY

Jeff recently turned sixteen and would like to buy a car. He is not excited about driving his mother's station wagon on weekends. A new car would mean he could drive to school every day. Otherwise, he will be forced to ride the school bus.

To buy a car, he will need a job and has been looking for a job for several weeks. Finally, he gets his break when Mr. McNeil, the grocery store manager, calls him to say he will hire him to work in the stockroom. Jeff is very excited to get the job and tells Mr. McNeil he will do whatever is necessary to make him glad of his decision.

Jeff has been working for Mr. McNeil for several weeks and really enjoys it. He has been on time and has worked very hard.

Scenario #1

On Friday afternoon, Jeff is faced with a difficult situation. For several weeks, he has been trying to get Susan to agree to go out with him. Finally, Jeff gets his big break. Susan tells him that she will go with him to the football game tonight. Jeff quickly agrees. But, there is a problem: Jeff remembers that he has already agreed to close the grocery store for

Mr. McNeil tonight. This will keep him in the store until after 10:00 p.m.

What should Jeff do? Should he call off the date with Susan? Should he call Mr. McNeil and ask if he can get out of the commitment to close the store? Should he go out with Susan and not worry about the job (surely Mr. McNeil will get someone else to cover)?

Scenario #2

On another Friday afternoon, Jeff is faced with a difficult situation. His best friend, Chris, had a tragedy in his life early this morning when his father died unexpectedly. When Jeff gets home from school around 4:00 p.m., there is a message for him to call Chris. He nervously picks up the telephone and dials Chris's number. Chris is very upset and asks Jeff to come over to his house. Jeff agrees and immediately goes over. The time passes quickly, and, before Jeff realizes it, it is 5:25 p.m.; Jeff was due at work by 5:00 p.m.

What should Jeff do? Should Jeff stay with Chris during this very difficult time? Should Jeff immediately leave for work? Should Jeff call Mr. McNeil and tell him he is running late? Should Jeff call Mr. McNeil and ask him if he can have the night off, even though Mr. McNeil will not be able to get someone else in his place?

Scenario #3

Jeff's English teacher, Mr. West, is heading the high school's annual canned food drive for the homeless. Several weeks ago, he asked Jeff to check with Mr. McNeil to see if he would be willing to donate a case of canned food. Jeff had intended to ask Mr. McNeil, but kept forgetting. The end of the food drive is tomorrow, and Mr. West asked Jeff if he had a commitment from Mr. McNeil for a donation. Jeff quickly says that Mr. McNeil is committed to giving food, though Jeff had not asked Mr. McNeil. When Jeff gets to work, he goes in to ask Mr. McNeil, but Mr. McNeil is not there. He finds out that Mr. McNeil had to make an emergency trip out of town and will not be back in town for several days.

What should Jeff do? Should he go back to Mr. West and tell him that he had not asked Mr. McNeil? Should he take a case of food from the

2-2. Properly caring for a goldfish involves assuming personal responsibility.

store and ask Mr. McNeil after the fact? Should he tell Mr. West that Mr. McNeil changed his mind about the donation of food?

These scenarios simply point out situations where personal responsibility comes into question. How do you know what to do? Should you go on the date when you are expected at work? Should you be with your friend when you have another commitment? Should you try to save face when your intentions were good, or should you face your mistake? These questions are not new and are faced by people in all walks of life every day. However, making the best choices in situations similar to these is a part of personal responsibility, *and personal responsibility is at the heart of leadership!*

PERSONAL RESPONSIBILITY: A DEFINITION

As a young leader, you will face many challenges and decisions in the years ahead. Major challenges and decisions faced by young people include career choices, education decisions, marriage, being a good parent, and having a home. However, these are only a few of the situations you will face and do not present a real reflection of leadership.

Real leadership is shown in the day-to-day decisions made by individuals. These day-to-day decisions show the kind of character and integrity you have. In essence, these decisions are the real you. These decisions are the means by which you exemplify personal responsibility.

Personal responsibility is who you are. It is the inner you that makes you tick. It is the real test by which you are judged by those whom you may work for, those whom you may work with, and those that may work for you. Personal responsibility is shown in the principles you live by, the decisions you make, and how well you can be trusted. Others will see you

-3. Computer programs are available to help people better understand themselves and improve their ability to make decisions. Your school counselor can help with this process.

as responsible if you follow-through and complete assignments and commitments. Being personally responsible takes courage. Personal responsibility is not always easy and sometimes you may be forced to stand alone to prove you are responsible.

PRINCIPLES/KNOWING YOURSELF/SETTING LIMITS

People want respect. People want others to like them. People want to be appreciated. In truth, most people at some time in their lives would like to be thought of as a leader.

Principles

Principles guide our actions. A *principle* is a guiding rule that helps in setting limits of behavior. Principles help people establish how they will act and the decisions they will make. A person who does not behave properly is often said to lack principles. Some people refer to principles as "what makes us tick."

If you want others to think of you as a leader, you must first figure out who you are and what you believe is right and wrong. You must know your limits. You must know yourself and be comfortable with yourself if you want to move into leadership roles. You must decide what set of principles you choose to live by. Personal responsibility begins with knowing yourself and the limits to which you will go in any given situation.

So what do you look for in yourself? What questions do you ask yourself? An easy way to find out is to decide what you look for in other leaders.

More than likely, you look for people who have integrity and are honest, dependable, and can judge right from wrong. You look for people that care about others and who give of themselves. These are basic characteristics. However, they are essential to personal responsibility and at the heart of leadership.

Self-Esteem

Self-esteem is much a part of knowing yourself. *Self-esteem* is how you feel about yourself. People need to feel comfortable in who they are and what they have accomplished. People who lack self-esteem often do not set goals and go about achieving them. Much of this book deals with skills that help people develop self-esteem.

Setting Limits

As you analyze yourself, ask yourself what is non-negotiable for you. The *non-negotiable limits* are the areas of life that are definite for you. These are areas on which you will not compromise. Are you certain that you will always be honest and not lie? Are you dependable? Can someone count on you to do what you say you will do? Do you feel so strongly about some things in life that you definitely would not compromise your beliefs? Is your integrity negotiable? Are you viewed by others as a person of integrity? Are you able to know the difference between right and wrong?

These can be deep questions and can cause you to have some very interesting discussions with yourself. As you come up with your answers, recognize that these questions shape who you are. They are the core of your being. These answers help to determine how you see life and all of your thinking. The answers to these questions are YOU. Leaders must develop a clear sense of who they are and what they believe if they are to wear the mantle of leadership.

Self-Motivation

Self-motivation is the mental desire to do something. A person performs because he or she wants to and not because someone else told them to. Often, an individual directs how energy is used. We can waste time or we can use it wisely. Self-motivation is based on one's own principles.

BEHAVIOR AND DECISION-MAKING

Personal responsibility is demonstrated by our behavior. Behavior is based on the decisions we make. Will we study for the test; will we get to work on time; will we tell the truth even if we risk being unpopular? These simple decisions are reflected in our behavior and are seen by those around us. Behavior will determine how our employers, friends, and family perceive us and, ultimately, how we are treated.

2-4. Our behavior shapes the feelings our team-mates have toward us.

Decision making is selecting one choice from several that are available. People must strive to make good decisions. The direction that we choose to go is important in our lives. People can make good choices or poor choices. We want to strive to make the best possible decisions. (Other chapters of the book will also include decision making.)

TRUST

Did you ever tell a friend a secret, only to hear it later from someone else? How did you feel . . . betrayed or maybe embarrassed? No one likes to be lied to and nothing hurts like a broken trust.

How well you can be trusted helps to create your reputation. Your good reputation is a part of you that you never want to lose. Trust is at the core of your reputation, which is how people describe how personally responsible you are. Trust, therefore, becomes a fundamental component of your life that can determine your success, both personally and professionally.

FOLLOW-THROUGH AND COMMITMENT

Are you a person who will finish a job? Are you a person who prides yourself in doing quality work? A key ingredient of personal responsibility is your commitment to complete a job. Sometimes this means doing something you do not enjoy or working long hours.

Work ethic is a major part of "doing what we say we will do." **Work ethic** is the drive of an individual to begin and finish a task with high standards of performance. Views of work vary. The dominant work ethic in our nation has been that work is good and necessary. All people should work and perform at a high level of productivity.

An illustration of follow-through and commitment is reflected in a discussion that occurred between two famous painters, Renoir and Matisse. Renoir was old and crippled with arthritis. One day a young Matisse asked Renoir why he continued to paint when the pain of arthritis hurt him so much. Without hesitation Renoir turned to Matisse and replied, "The pain passes, but the beauty remains." This example illustrates the importance of following through on a task. This characteristic is essential to personal responsibility.

COURAGE

2-5. Climbing the face of a rock requires courage.

Personal responsibility often requires courage. This is especially true when dealing with peer pressure. **Courage** is the ability to face difficult situations. Sometimes pain and personal loss may result. At other times, courage involves doing what is right and living by our principles.

There are many times that your friends may try to influence you to participate in activities that you may feel are wrong. It will take courage and a tremendous amount of personal responsibility to overcome these challenges. Will you be courageous? Will you overcome the tendency to take the easy way out? Only you can answer these questions. It is up to you to determine if you will have the courage to stand alone, if necessary, because it is the right thing to do.

PERSONAL RESPONSIBILITY OR NOT

So what happens if you are not personally responsible? Does your personal responsibility really make a difference? You bet it does, and your education, career, and life could depend on it!

PERSONAL RESPONSIBILITY AND YOUR EDUCATION

Education and its importance have been emphasized to each of us throughout our lives. Many people would say that it is the ticket to success. However, we find that many students do not see education as valuable.

Over 25 percent of American youth drop out of school. Certainly, there may be legitimate reasons some young people consider dropping out as an alternative, such as crises in their homes. This staggering statistic is an excellent example of individuals not being personally responsible. If they had the personal responsibility characteristic of commitment, many of these youth could and would graduate with a high school diploma.

So, what will your choice be? Will you be personally responsible? Will you commit yourself to follow-through on your education? Will you make the decision to stay in school and complete your ticket to your future? These are questions that only you can answer. You must decide, based on your principles, what you will do. You will decide if you are personally responsible.

2-6. Getting a high school diploma and being recognized for doing a good job in school are important in success.

PERSONAL RESPONSIBILITY AND YOUR CAREER

A report by the American Society for Training and Development and the United States Department of Education listed the workplace basics that employers want. One critical factor indicated in this report was *personal management*. Personal management (i.e., personal responsibility) was defined as the grab-bag of skills related to a strong work ethic. It includes positive self-esteem, goal-setting, self-motivation, and the drive to seek personal and professional improvement.

Over the next few years, you will begin the process of choosing your career. As you make these choices, you will find that employers are more interested in you as a person. In fact, you may find that personal qualities are as important as technical skills.

A study was made by the National Council on Vocational Education to identify what people need to do to be successful in their work. Here is what was found:

Employees must be:

⇨ flexible

⇨ creative problem solvers

⇨ willing to continue to learn innovations

⇨ able to set personal goals

⇨ eager to work hard for professional and personal advancement

⇨ able to communicate and interact with their peers

2-7. Doing well in a job interview is related to showing personal responsibility.

It will be essential that you have personal responsibility, for without it, you will be unable to survive in the job market.

These facts were again reported in 1991 by the U.S. Department of Labor. In that report, the personal qualities of responsibility, self-management, and honesty were highlighted as critical qualities of a successful worker. Again, it is apparent that personal responsibility is imperative to your future.

PERSONAL RESPONSIBILITY: HOW DO YOU GROW IT?

Developing skills in personal responsibility is somewhat like growing plants. By learning how it is done, we can do it well.

PLANT THE SEED

Personal responsibility, like any other area of leadership, is learned. To learn, you must first plant the seed of personal responsibility in yourself by choosing to grow it. This seed is planted by determining what you believe in and what your principles are. Although many people and other outside forces can influence this decision, you must decide for yourself. It is up to you to plant the seed of personal responsibility.

GROWING THE PLANT

Once you plant the seed of personal responsibility, you must then water and fertilize the plant. This can be a very difficult process. You grow personal responsibility by having good behavior, making positive decisions, earning and giving trust, and showing commitment and courage. You will find it easier to grow your personal responsibility by identifying people you respect as leaders and using them as mentors by duplicating their positive behaviors and characteristics.

It is also critical that you surround yourself with friends who will encourage and support your desire to grow your personal responsibility. You must make every effort to not let others drag you down no matter how difficult.

2-8. Prisons are filled with people who did not develop personal responsibility.

You have the power within you to be a person of responsibility. However, you must choose to be personally responsible for yourself and live up to your expectations.

HARVESTING THE FRUIT

As with any plant, this plant also has fruit. The fruit you will harvest from being personally responsible include: personal satisfaction, educational excellence, career success, leadership development, respect from others, and much, much more. The best part of this harvest will be that it can be ongoing and it does not have to end. Because of your harvest, you will find your performance as a leader increase. However, this harvest will only occur if you first choose to plant and grow personal responsibility.

REVIEWING

MAIN IDEAS

Personal responsibility is the core of your leadership and personal development. It is a learned behavior and you must decide whether or not you want to be personally responsible.

Personal responsibility is critical to your future. It can be the difference in having a successful career or not. It will help decide the personal satisfaction you have in your life and the way that others see you and how much they respect you.

QUESTIONS

Answer the questions using correct spelling and complete sentences.

1. What does it mean to be personally responsible?
2. What are the characteristics of a person who is personally responsible?
3. Can a person decide to become personally responsible? Explain.
4. What are some benefits of being personally responsible?
5. How can you become a more responsible person?
6. Are leaders personally responsible? Explain.
7. How can being personally responsible affect your education?

EVALUATING

CHAPTER SELF-CHECK

Match the term with the correct definition. Write the letter by the term in the blank provided.

a. personal responsibility   d. principles   g. self-motivation
b. decision-making   e. work ethic
c. courage   f. self-esteem

1. ____ how you feel about yourself.

2. ____ the drive of someone to finish a task.

3. ____ the mental desire to do something.

4. ____ core set of beliefs.

5. ____ ability to face difficult situations.

6. ____ ability to make correct choices.

7. ____ what makes an individual "tick."

EXPLORING

1. Set up an appointment with the personnel director/hiring person in an area business. Ask this person to share with you the types of leadership characteristics they look for in prospective employees. You may want to try this with several different employers to get their ideas on the leadership skills you need to develop to get a good job in the future. Prepare a report on what you learn.

2. Select three people you admire as leaders. Write down the personal responsibility characteristics that you most appreciate about them. This provides you with a list of ideas for areas you might want to focus on for future improvement.

3. Identify one personal responsibility characteristic that you would like to improve. Share this characteristic with someone you admire and trust (friend, parent, teacher, etc.) Ask them to help you strengthen this area of your life by setting up a time each week to discuss your progress.

3

ETHICS

Decisions—life is filled with decisions. Some are easy to make; others are difficult. We can learn to make good decisions by taking into account whether we are helping or hurting others.

By having good intentions and trying to do the right thing, we are practicing ethical behavior. In addition to having good intentions, we need to show respect for other people and their ideas, even though they may differ from our own.

3-1. Ethics are the building blocks and guiding principles in our lives. We begin to learn them at a very young age.

OBJECTIVES

This chapter will help you in developing your own ethics and values. It has the following objectives:

1. Explain ethics
2. List ethical values of a good leader
3. Identify challenges in behaving ethically
4. Describe ways to have ethical values

T E R M S

credibility
dilemma
ethics
fair
honesty
intangible
love
loyalty
mentor
moral ethics
respect
self-respect
truthful
values
values clarification
virtue

ETHICS AND VALUES

Ethics is sometimes a controversial topic. This is because everyone does not agree on what makes ethical behavior. Still, there are plenty of areas where most of society is in agreement about what is right and what is wrong. Everyone will agree that it is unethical to lie, cheat, and steal. We agree that it is ethical to tell the truth and do good for others.

Ethics can be defined as the principles behind behavior or conduct that is morally correct. Ethical behavior helps other people, society as a whole, and even our earth. Unethical behavior, on the other hand, hurts the earth or its people, including the person responsible for the unethical behavior.

Values are standards that influence your life and your decisions. What values do you hold now? Can you improve your ethical values? Are you in touch with positive values? Do you always know how to respond to other people without taking advantage of them? Strong and proper values help us build a positive vision for today and tomorrow.

BEING ETHICAL

Positive, healthy ethics help people feel good about themselves. When people feel good about themselves they try harder and do better. This improves self-esteem in people.

Building Blocks

Ethics are the building blocks or principles that provide a solid foundation for our lives. They are also the guiding principles in our lives. They remind us of how we should or should not act. Ethics are identified and discussed in people's personal lives. These are known as personal ethics. Values help build our character. Our character is developed by our deeds and actions, which are guided by our values.

Influence by Others

Identify those people who are the most influential in your life. Realize that their values have an impact on you. People need to know and understand their own values. This is commonly known as *values clarification*. It can also be described as being in tune with yourself.

Requires Effort

People are not automatically ethical. Ethics and values are developed through upbringing and through time. Learning is a never-ending process. Values are found in people and their families. They are also found in our schools, religious sanctuaries, organizations, communities, and society.

We are surrounded by many alternatives. Strong ethics and values help

3-2. Our ethics assist us in making valuable contributions. We become more responsible to our families, employers, and communities.

3-3. People find that there is more to celebrate with good moral ethics.

guide people in making decisions. There are certain stages within our life when we look for a place to belong. Teenage years are a primary example. Strong values assist in making appropriate decisions. Ethical decisions impact the outcome of each day.

Many of us have responsibilities. We have responsibilities to our families, school, church, and community. Being ethical assists us in recognizing our responsibilities. Our values encourage us to make worthwhile contributions as we carry out our responsibilities.

Impacts Attitudes

Being ethical has an impact on our attitude. Attitude impacts our human relations and our productivity. Attitude, along with the right set of values, helps us work to our potential.

MORALS

Our society and our world benefit from people with good moral ethics. *Moral ethics* deals with knowing the difference between right and wrong and applying that knowledge in our daily lives.

Moral ethics include striving for responsible and dedicated citizenship. The relationships of people with other people are based on caring. They work together for a safe and healthy environment.

Being ethical means having good moral ethics. It also means developing a strong foundation for life. Good moral ethics help bind people together. Storms of life are more easily weathered together. People will find that there is more to celebrate with good moral ethics!

VALUES OF AN ETHICAL LEADER

Values influence our responses to others. They affect our goals and provide direction. Values give us borders and bottom lines. They serve as reminders of what we consider right and wrong.

Leaders demonstrate their own values through their leadership. Not only must leaders know and understand their own values, they must also live them. They must set a good example for others to follow. Leaders need to be encouragers and modelers of ethical behavior.

People are very observant of a leader's values. Therefore, it is important for leaders to have sound ethical values. What are the acceptable values of an ethical leader?

ETHICAL LEADERSHIP

Taking a close look at the values of an ethical leader helps in understanding the importance of values. It will allow an individual to see the desired kinds of behavior.

Ethical Traits

Values are like a compass that give us direction. Sound values and consistent values keep a person on the right track.

Honesty is at the top of the list of ethical values. **Honesty** means that a person has high principles and does not cheat, steal, or lie. Honesty and truthfulness are admirable qualities. Being straightforward is being honest and truthful. Being truthful earns respect and builds trust. Carrying out a pledged word through a promised and kind deed relays honesty and truthfulness.

Truthful means that what a person says and does conform to reality. What is said and done is a fact. The information is accurate. Truthfulness goes with honesty in describing the ethical behavior of a leader.

3-4. Sound and consistent values help us stay on the right trail. They serve as reminders of what we accept and do not accept.

Respect is providing the proper courtesy and acceptance of another person. The other person may be a friend, teacher, parent, or community leader. All individuals are due respect. If you want respect, you need to show respect.

Trust is also an important trait. It is one of the cherished values in our society. Trust means that a person has high integrity and can be relied on to do the right thing.

Respect and trust are not given; they are earned. We earn respect and trust by keeping a promise. It takes a long time to build up respect and trust. It takes only a short time to destroy them. Once you have lost the respect and trust of others, it is difficult to regain. How much others accept a leader depends on the level of trust. Trust enables others to act. Do not abuse or neglect the values of respect and trust.

Self-respect means that we hold ourselves in high regard. It drives away negative influences. It is always healthy to keep positive influences in our lives.

Leaders need to be *fair*. This means that they go about their roles in an unbiased and honest manner. All people and ideas receive equal consideration. Treating others with fairness and equity is important in leadership roles. Often, leaders find themselves in situations where decisions are required. These decisions need to be based on honesty and fairness.

3-5. Valuing the differences between people is important. People should help others feel needed and valued.

Loyalty is a valued ethic. Loyalty means that a person is faithful to another. Strong loyalty values assist in keeping people on the right road. We can be loyal to others as long as honesty permits. Being loyal is sharing the same strong positive values. Loyalty, within a relationship or an organization, encourages ethical behavior. Loyalty promotes hard work and caring attitudes and helps in reducing stress and tension.

Being responsible allows an individual to make valuable contributions. The contributions are to our homes, schools, communities, employers, customers, and others. Being responsible is characterized by hard work to help cultivate success. Being responsible reflects an individual's choice or decision. People choose to share their capabilities to achieve desired results.

Love is most important of all values. Love is concern for the well-being of others. It serves as a "glue" to help people hold on to what is most important.

Respecting Differences

As a leader, you need to value differences between people. Recognizing other people and their talents is essential. Taking the next step to reinforce other people for their positive inputs is a major role for a leader. People should help others feel needed and valued.

A happy environment is a valued environment. It takes fewer muscles to smile than it does to frown, as you may have already known. Smiles motivate you and others. Smiles create a happy and healthy environment.

Violence is a big concern in our society. People are working to reduce violence. Remember to hold on to the value of doing no harm to others. Avoiding physical harm to others will help prevent violence. Do not put yourself or others at risk. Physical harm to others provides no gain to the person inflicting the harm.

People need to apply past knowledge to the present. Remember the strong values that have helped you in the past. Each day is full of opportunities. Opportunities will blossom when you allow your values to guide you.

3-6. Smiles create a happy and healthy environment. Strong and ethical values help build this type of environment.

It is always helpful to have appropriate values. By living by these values you will be an example for others. People pay more attention to values that are in use rather than those that are just talked about.

That is because values are intangible. *Intangible* means that they are not recognized by touch. It is the duty of the leader to make values real to other people. This is done through the leader's words and actions. People are always paying attention to the behavior of the leader. A leader's behavior does reflect ethics and values.

Values are also recognizable through people's opinions, attitudes, preferences, desires, actions, fears, and strategies. When people interact with others, they recognize a person's set of values. They recognize values by how the individual spends their time. Values are also recognizable by what questions a person asks, how they react to critical situations, and what they choose to reward.

A leader's *credibility* is built on words and actions. Credibility means that a person is accurate and honest in what they say and do. Good credibility is based on positive ethics and values. Leaders stand up for beliefs that are good and true. When leaders live by their acclaimed values, they practice what they preach. Through living by example, leaders help show others the way.

3-7. A person's credibility is built on words and actions. Being reliable and working cooperatively with others is a part of ethical values. Improving this streambank requires the cooperation of many people.

CHALLENGES IN BEING ETHICAL

Leadership does not happen without challenges. Leadership is a challenge itself. Leaders accept challenges and are challenged. Undoubtedly, leadership is a risk-taking process. Leadership is being active and not passive. Leadership is accepting the challenge and facing the challenges.

When faced with a *dilemma* our own ethics and values guide us. A dilemma is a problem to be solved. When leaders search for opportunities, challenges may arise. Change, in itself, is a challenge. There are times in peoples lives when values may be unclear. People become confused. It is at these times when talking with others is important—especially talking with positive role models.

There are those components in society that challenge people's values. For teenagers, it is often peer pressure. When values clash, challenges arise. That is why it is important for people to have a firm grip on values. Remember that people are not perfect, but do not use that as an excuse for avoiding consequences. At times, people are pressured to get even. Remember that two wrongs do not make a right.

When faced with peer pressure, do not make a decision you will regret later. Remind yourself that people will respect you more when you stand up for your beliefs and your values.

The entertainment we select is important. Many different films and videos are available. Some have a moral message and others destroy morality. People should carefully select films that reinforce their own appropriate values.

3-8. Leadership is branching out and accepting the challenge along with facing what is involved. When problems arise, ethical values will guide us.

There are also times when people strive for success and become sidetracked. They have their eyes on a goal, but forget having regard for others. People sometimes put their values on the back burner to achieve their goal. Doing this does not lead to a successful goal. Unfortunately, materialism and selfishness overcome their values. People get wrapped up in the "think-of-me-only" realm. When this occurs, people need to stop and think about what direction they are going. People need to take time and rededicate themselves to their values.

Sometimes people fail to listen. They only hear what they want to hear. People need to be open to clear communication and clear values.

A leader is someone who is effective and motivational. Leaders are not perfect; they make mistakes. Everyone needs to be accountable for their own mistakes and then learn from their mistakes.

GAINING ETHICAL VALUES

It is important for everyone to gain positive ethical values. Positive ethical values will benefit each person throughout life. How do people gain ethical values? How do organizations gain ethical values?

Virtue, or what is known as moral excellence, is acquired and earned through time. Ethical values are gained through a variety of avenues.

People that you spend the most time with have the most influence on your ethical values. Be sure to select people who have a good influence on you. Also, try to be the kind of person that has a good influence on others.

MENTORING

Relationships that help others are often known as mentoring. The relationship is usually with an experienced person who can help in overcoming problems and providing a good model to follow. A **mentor** is an individual, like an employer or a teacher, who has much influence and helps guide us in the right direction. A good mentor takes a special interest in a person. All people can learn a great deal by identifying with a mentor who is a good role model.

Families are important. Family members are mentors who provide many examples and help in many ways. Of course, families vary a great deal, but there is usually someone in a family who can provide valuable assistance. Your family is your primary source of guidance. As an adult, you will want to have a family that functions as a good place for the people in it.

3-9. People that you spend the most time with have the most influence on your ethical values. Families are often the primary source of guidance.

LEADERSHIP TRAINING

Formal leadership training and education are available for people. It is through training and education that people may gain new values or reinforce old ones. Businesses or organizations may offer formalized training to their members that is relevant to the members' needs. Educational institutions may offer courses to people not associated with a particular business or organization.

Group values need to be identified and communicated in an organization. To accomplish this requires much discussion and time. Through this process a support network is formed. Members in an organization benefit and gain values from support and reinforcement.

MAKING A PERSONAL COMMITMENT TO LEADERSHIP

Take time to assess your own strengths and weaknesses in this area. Identifying your weak points will let you know where there is room for improvement. Knowing your strengths and building on them will help overcome your weaknesses.

People need to apply past knowledge to the present. We can gain knowledge and values from previous historical figures. Using your library will provide information on historical people and their learned values.

Seek out an elderly person to talk to. Elderly people offer a wealth of information. A person who is 80 years of age has gone through many changes and challenges in their lifetime. What kind of philosophy concerning values do they offer? What kind of ethical values can you gain from their displayed wisdom? Undoubtedly, they have clung fast to values that have withstood the test of time. Listen to them with sincerity.

Leaders create standards of excellence through their values. Remember to take time to celebrate your accomplishments. It is also important to take time to reward hard work. Doing this will reinforce ethical values that guided the success.

3-10. Mature people can provide helpful information on ethical behavior.

REVIEWING

MAIN IDEAS

Ethics are building blocks that provide a lifelong foundation. They are also the guiding principles in our lives. Values remind us how we should

3-11. Awards are often based on the ethical behavior of people.

or should not act. Values help build our character. Our character is developed by our deeds and actions, which are guided by our values.

Leaders show to others, their own values, through their leadership. Ethical values that leaders and other individuals strive to achieve include: honesty, respect, trust, fairness, loyalty, love, and responsibility.

Leadership does not happen without challenges. Leaders accept challenges and are challenged. There are many different situations that challenge values in life. Peer pressure is one example. People are respected more when they stand up for their beliefs and values.

Ethical values are gained through time and a variety of avenues. People have an influence on our values. Families are the primary source of ethical guidance. Formal leadership and training are also made available.

3-12. Ethical behavior is demonstrated by how we care for animals, such as fish.

QUESTIONS

Answer the questions using correct spelling and complete sentences.

1. Define ethics and relate three reasons why they are important.

2. Provide five examples of values and describe each.

3. How can values have an impact on reducing violence?

4. Explain how a leader maintains credibility.

5. List two examples of how people's values are challenged.

6. Define mentor and provide three examples.

7. List five values that you consider most important in your life.

EVALUATING

CHAPTER SELF-CHECK

Match the term with the correct definition. Write the letter by the term in the blank provided.

a. values clarification   d. ethic   g. fair
b. dilemma   e. honesty
c. loyalty   f. self-respect

1. _____ a problem.

2. _____ being truthful.

3. _____ a value.

4. _____ knowing and understanding your own values.

5. _____ being just.

6. _____ holding oneself in high regard.

7. _____ showing faithfulness and enabling others to act.

EXPLORING

1. Think about your previous experiences related to leadership. Record your thoughts and feelings on paper. Identify those ethical values that guided you and how they might help you as a leader. Develop a list of helpful guidelines in relation to ethical behavior and share your information with the rest of the class.

2. Interview an elderly person guided by positive ethical values and develop a written paragraph of their philosophy on life. Identify what they considered their most important guiding values throughout their life. Report your findings back to your instructor.

3. Describe your best leadership experience. Identify those values that guided you in the leadership experience or that you gained from the experience.

4. Develop scenarios where difficult choices need to be made and discuss ways in which to respond to the circumstances described in the scenarios with your classmates. Example scenario: How would you react if a member of your judging team cheated in a contest?

4

SOCIAL BEHAVIOR

> *We cannot ignore social behavior and go about life in an acceptable way.* Jasper S. Lee

What do I wear? How do I order my food? Which fork do I use? How do I greet a new person? These and many other questions have answers that are important in having good social skills.

Social behavior is how we say hello, how we act at the dinner table, or how we handle an awkward situation. Our social behavior is reflected in the topics of our conversations and how we introduce our friends. Social behavior is recognized in our daily living, on a dance floor, and at a dinner party.

Have you thought about your own social behavior? How do you react to other people's social behaviors? Why are social behaviors important? Everyone needs to know and understand social behaviors. Traditional social behaviors still exist today.

4-1. Social behavior is important in relating to others. How do you feel about this scene from a fast food restaurant? (One person is feeding another a French fried potato.)

43

OBJECTIVES

This chapter will help you find answers to important social behavior questions. It has the following objectives:

1. Explain social behavior
2. List proper guidelines for social behavior
3. Identify positive social behavior traits
4. Describe links between present social behavior and future results

T
E
R
M
S

being kind
caring
considerate
courteous
empathy
etiquette
first impression
loving person
manners
social behavior
trait
well-mannered

SOCIAL BEHAVIOR: BEING COMFORTABLE

Social behavior is an important part of personal and leadership skill development. It involves our manners and mannerisms. Social behavior encompasses our behavior around other people. It is our actions and our attitudes.

Social behavior may also be called good manners or tactfulness. *"Manners"* is commonly used to refer to a way of behaving that is polite. Following good manners helps people to be at ease around each other. They know how to respond to each other. Having appropriate social behavior provides a person the advantage of being proper, courteous, and likable. Proper social behaviors, when acquired, should be cherished.

PROPER CONDUCT

Proper social behavior is following the guidelines of proper conduct that have been recognized through experience in our culture. From generation to generation, people are encouraged to practice appropriate etiquette and manners.

Etiquette is a code of social behavior. It is often used synonymously with social behavior. The expected behavior changes over time as society changes. Following proper etiquette helps people get along and live in harmony. Each culture has its own system. Proper behavior in one culture may not be the same in another. A good example is where to put your hands at a meal. In the United States, the hands go on your lap; whereas, in France, the hands are placed on the edge of the table near your plate. Gaining a knowledge of correct social behavior is essential.

Being aware of social behavior encourages people to become more sensitive toward others. People are alerted to the impacts that their own conversation and behavior have on other people's feelings.

Knowing and understanding social behavior helps people get through awkward, unfamiliar, or unexpected situations. They also help people become more caring and considerate individuals. Remember that rude and inconsiderate manners turn people away.

Correct social behavior is not just important in "first impression" situations. It is essential and encouraged long after the first impression. Long-lasting friendships and secure relationships will develop through good and decent manners.

4-2. Looking your best is important!

BEHAVIOR VARIES

Social behavior is important. No matter what city, state, or country we find ourselves in, we need to learn the sociably acceptable codes of behavior. Etiquette and social behavior vary from one culture to another. Knowing the basic rules helps us to be comfortable with other people.

Learning social behaviors assists people with human relations, leadership, and communication. It increases a person's self-confidence level and creates a quicker link to making friends. Correct social behavior also improves business relationships by helping build a positive working atmosphere. Your social behavior will

4-3. Appropriate manners are best learned at a young age.

4-4. We learn social behavior by observing others. People notice our behaviors everywhere we go.

have an impact on your personal development, leadership skills, and success. Appropriate social behavior is required throughout life. Social behavior skills are needed at home, at school, at work, and at various social events. We cannot ignore social behavior and go about life in an acceptable way.

GUIDELINES FOR SOCIAL BEHAVIOR

Parents and other adults often say "mind your manners" to young people. When they do so, they are referring to having polite social behaviors. These are the basic manners that guide our everyday life. From day to day, we find ourselves in different situations and environments. There are several guidelines that should be remembered and followed in regards to social behavior.

CONVERSATIONS

What we say influences our relationships with other people. Our culture has important phrases that help people be polite and get along. Five basic conversational courtesies to use with sincerity are:

⇨ *Please*

⇨ *Thank You*

⇨ *May I*

⇨ *I'm Sorry*

⇨ *Excuse Me*

Undoubtedly, people have been taught these courtesies as soon as they were able to talk. However, do you ever catch yourself forgetting these simple but important words? It is sometimes easy to do in the fast-paced world in which we live. Turn your attention to your own manners. Think about the last time you used one of these courtesies. Remember to include them in your daily vocabulary and conversations.

In carrying on a conversation, know about the other person's interests and experiences. Select topics they will appreciate and understand. Avoid topics that are offensive or in which they have no interest. Knowing the other person helps in determining what to talk about.

Being well-informed helps in carrying on conversations. Keep up with current events and learn about areas that are interesting to other people. This will give you something to talk about that the other person enjoys.

Appropriate conversation is without slang or profanity. Your conversation will remain colorful without it. Profanity is not only inappropriate, but also relays that your vocabulary is lacking. Work on improving and increasing your own vocabulary with appropriate terms. Practice using good language all of the time and you will not have a problem with "special times."

Conversation is as much listening as speaking. We must listen to what is spoken. We watch for non-spoken cues, such as body movement. Actions sometimes communicate more than words!

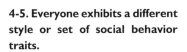

4-5. Everyone exhibits a different style or set of social behavior traits.

RESPECTING THE PROPERTY OF OTHERS

Having respect for the property of others is part of correct social behavior. Others' property includes that of family members and friends. It also relates to property owned by school, government, and businesses. Buildings, land, trees, animals, cars, clothing, and books are a few examples of property. Respecting other people's property allows you to earn even more respect from others.

Respecting the property of others includes being aware of the rights of property owners. Do not go onto posted land. Do not deface with paint, or in other ways, private or public property. Do not dispose of wastes or leave junk around that degrades property. Be careful not to destroy plants or other improvements on property.

EATING BEHAVIOR

Eating is a social event in our culture. Meals are times to visit with friends and share conversations about life. How you do it says much about you.

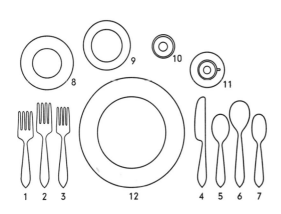

Using proper table manners is a part of every meal at home, school, or when "eating out." Learning involves practice at every meal. When table manners become routine, we will prevent embarrassing moments from happening to us. Being able to identify the various utensils in a table setting will remind an individual of what to eat first. Figure 4-6 shows a sample place setting at a table.

A good rule of thumb to follow is to use the table wear on the outside first. Table settings are always equipped with a napkin so be sure to use it. Place the napkin on your lap prior to eating. Do not begin eating until others at the table (or near you in case of a very large table) have been served.

1. Salad Fork
2. Dinner Fork
3. Dessert Fork
4. Dinner Knife
5. Coffee Spoon
6. Soup Spoon
7. Appetizer Spoon
8. Salad Plate
9. Bread Plate
10. Water Glass
11. Coffee Cup and Saucer
12. Dinner Plate

4-6. Sample place setting for one person.

Remember to eat quietly and neatly. Be sure to hold the tableware correctly. Chew your food with your mouth closed. Keep your elbows off the table and your hands on your lap. Use your napkin to remove any food around your mouth. Remain at the table until all have finished eating. (This varies among cultures. Be sure to learn about the expected behavior in a culture before you travel.)

FIRST IMPRESSIONS

Our actions and our attitudes are reflected in our social behavior. A *first impression* is what another sees the moment they first meet you. First impressions are part of the social behavior arena. People always want to look and act their best on first impressions. But that does not mean we stop looking and acting our best once we have been introduced. Looking and acting our best should be part of our daily routine. How do we look and act our best? People can start by being clean and free from offensive odors. Being neat is part of being well-groomed with a neat hair style and clean clothes. Use appropriate and good taste in clothing selection. If the occasion is casual, it is appropriate to dress casually. If a person plans to attend a formal dinner, it is wise to follow a formal dinner dress code.

4-7. Properly using a napkin at a meal becomes routine when one is used at each meal.

At one time or another, you may find yourself attending a formal or semi-formal event or other dress-up occasion. Looking your best is important. Selecting clothing and accessories is important to the message that we convey. When a tie is required for a young man, it is wise to know how to properly tie one. To the young woman, avoiding excessive jewelry helps make a positive impression. (Chapter 5 provides more information on proper dress.)

Social behavior includes guidelines in wearing a hat. Dinner tables are not appropriate places to wear a hat of any kind—western, baseball, or hardhat. It is also customary to remove the hat upon entering a public building.

4-8. Following proper dress codes reflects appropriate social behavior.

4-9. A handshake is part of exchanging a gavel at a meeting.

A GOOD HANDSHAKE

You have probably heard the saying "First impressions are lasting impressions." A handshake is part of that first impression. An appropriate handshake is described as firm and friendly. As you present your hand, it is appropriate to make eye contact with the other person. A friendly smile will improve your first impression as well. These same guidelines can be followed when you are greeting someone beyond the first impression.

Having a friendly and happy attitude creates a cheerful atmosphere. When you are visiting with another person, do not be the one to do all of the talking. Allow the other person to be part of the conversation.

MAKING INTRODUCTIONS

Introductions are a part of our daily routine. The first time you meet a person, extend a warm greeting. Look them in the eye, carefully pronounce your name, and extend a greeting, such as "hello" or "good morning."

■ Here is how you might introduce yourself to another person: "Hello, my name is ___ ___. It is nice to meet you." A handshake is usually a part of the introduction for both males and females, though it is more widely used by males.

■ Here is how you might introduce another person to an individual you know: "Mary, I would like to introduce my friend (or other relationship) John Smith. John, this is Mary O'Banion." (In making the introduction, the names of both individuals should be carefully pronounced.)

Other situations may require different approaches. Always use greetings and carefully pronounce names. Try to remember the names of others. People like their names and think that they are important!

Do you ever find yourself in a situation where you cannot remember someone's name? If someone greets you and you do not remember his/her name, offer a nice greeting such as "Nice to see you." Stimulate conversation until he/she offers a clue as to their identity. You may find yourself in a situation where you meet someone whom you have not seen for awhile. When this happens and they do not recall your name, offer the following: "Hi Mrs. Jones, I'm Jan Smith of Lake City." This provides a tactful way of re-introducing yourself.

TELEPHONE AND INTERNET TALK

Often times you may be required to speak on the telephone. There are also social behavior manners to remember when talking on the telephone. It is a key source of communication, so do your best at communicating properly. If your telephone call is for business, always indicate who you are, who you represent, and the purpose of your call. Be kind and courteous with your language.

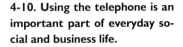

4-10. Using the telephone is an important part of everyday social and business life.

End a call properly. Do not talk too long. In ending a call, thank the person for calling or talking with you, clarify any facts, and say "Good-bye."

More people are using Internet and Email to communicate each day. Always be courteous and be careful with what you say. You never know who might have access to what you have said. Confidential information, such as a credit card number, should not be used—other individuals might gain access to it.

THE GUEST OF ANOTHER

If you are a guest at another person's home, be sure not to leave your manners at your home. Respect their property and offer to assist with daily tasks. It is also important to remember to thank your host/hostess. They will remember and appreciate their thoughtful, well-mannered guest.

In addition to an overall "thank you," it is a good idea to thank your host at different times. Thank them for the nice meal or dessert. Thank them for welcoming you into their home.

CONTROLLING THE LITTER BUG IN YOU

Our environment deserves your respectful behavior. This means that you should remember the "DO NOT LITTER" rule. When you set a good example, you remind others to do the same. Littering is distasteful and makes our environment unattractive, as well as polluted. Make respecting our environment part of your social behavior.

SOCIAL BEHAVIOR TRAITS

Social behavior relies on and is characterized by social traits within a person. *Traits* are those distinguishing characteristics about a person that make them unique. Everyone exhibits a different style or set of traits related to social behavior. Desirable social behavior traits will be reviewed.

As discussed in Chapter three, honesty is a most commendable social trait. Honesty is being truthful, trustworthy, and fair. It serves as a glue that helps build other desirable, social behavior traits.

COURTEOUS

Being *courteous* is a trait that relates to being polite and gracious. A person who is courteous displays good manners and is kind to others. *Being kind* is another trait that is closely linked to being courteous. When we are kind to others, we are benevolent, sympathetic, and gentle. Benevolent means that people want to do good and carry out acts of kindness.

CARING

Another desirable trait is *caring*. When an individual is caring, they accept responsibilities, especially the responsibility of helping provide for others. A person who is caring is concerned and interested about another's welfare (state of health). They pay close attention to other people's well-being.

CONSIDERATE

Being **considerate** is a trait not to be ignored. When a person is considerate, they have regard for other people. They also regard other people's feelings. A good way to approach being considerate is to think about how you would feel if you were the other person. Would you like to have done to you what you are doing?

RESPECT

Another admirable social behavior trait is that of respect. When you respect someone else you feel or show honor and esteem for another person. Youth are often considered respectful when they show respect for adults. Respect is a two-way street. When you give respect, you receive it.

4-11. Being patient (as in an airport) is a desirable social behavior.

WELL-MANNERED

Being **well-mannered** is carrying out the basics of common courtesy. Social courtesies are just as important today as they were yesterday. They help make a nicer world for all of us. Part of common courtesy is doing good deeds. Being well-mannered is simply being kind and respectful to others. Everyone needs to take the time to do a maintenance check on their own manners and social behavior.

EMPATHY—A LOVING PERSON

Empathy is trying to identify with the feelings of another person. By doing so, we can better understand their thoughts and emotions. Empathy allows us to be better communicators and have stronger relationships with people.

Being a *loving person* is a combination of all the desirable social behavior traits. Being a loving person motivates others to be the same way. A caring and loving society builds a happier, healthier, and safer environment for everyone.

4-12. There is a proper time and place for fun as a part of social behavior traits. This person is making an "angel-in-the-snow" on fresh blanket of snow.

LINKS WITH THE FUTURE

Social guidance is necessary to help people relate to each other more easily. We must remember that how we behave today has an impact on tomorrow. As people become older, social conditions change. At certain times, our proper social behaviors are challenged. With experience and knowledge, we can meet the challenge with increased confidence. With confidence, proper social behavior can be maintained. Maintaining proper behavior helps people avoid undesirable outcomes.

Social behavior traits are those traits that come from within a person. They are traits that come from the heart. When we are sincere in our behavior, others will recognize this. Sincere and caring behavior creates a brighter today and a rewarding tomorrow. Behavior directed by a spirited heart creates a confident tomorrow. Guidance in social behavior makes us more comfortable because we become more knowledgeable of our own

4-13. School events are social events. Taking time to have fun at a donkey basketball game promotes good social fun and laughs. (Courtesy, Crosby Donkey Basketball, Chippewa Falls, Wisconsin)

actions and attitudes. Everyone wants to be assured of acting on a solid foundation. A strong foundation is helpful, especially when social behavior is challenged. Proper social behavior helps build bridges instead of walls.

Social behavior characterized by negative actions and attitudes produces only negative results. A person's social behavior cannot afford an "I don't care" attitude. There are always repercussions of negative behavior.

Social behavior is observed by those of the same age and those who are younger and older. Our behavior has links with the future. People need to ask themselves such questions as: "What kind of example do I set through my social behavior?" "Am I setting a good example for my younger brother or sister?" "How do my parents/guardians view my actions and

4-14. Social behavior includes knowing how to relate to other people.

attitudes?" Hopefully, answers to these questions will reflect positive behavior. People also need to remember that there is always room for improvement. As proper social behavior is practiced, it will become polished.

It is always helpful to observe and talk with respected adults. Seek information from those who have experienced challenging situations. Situations may arise that tax proper social behavior. Remember that wisdom is gained from experience.

Practicing wise social behavior helps create positive links to the future. Proper social behavior is a necessary part of personal development and leadership skills.

REVIEWING

MAIN IDEAS

Social behavior is part of personal and leadership skill development. It is an expression of our actions and our attitudes. Social behavior is important for several reasons. It provides a person the advantage of being proper, courteous, and likable. Social behavior helps people get through awkward, unfamiliar, or unexpected situations. It secures friendships and relationships. People who work on improving social behavior improve their own skills related to human relations, leadership, and communication. It impacts personal development, leadership skills, and success.

Social behavior guidelines include being polite, tactful, and having respect for others' property. It also includes having proper table manners, dressing appropriately, and attention to grooming. People are encouraged to remember proper guidelines during introductions, speaking on the telephone, and while a guest. Our environment also requires respect and proper behavior.

Worthy social behavior traits include being honest, caring, considerate, respectful, well-mannered, courteous, and loving. People's social behavior impacts their future. Negative actions and attitudes often produce negative results. Practicing wise social behavior creates positive links to the future. It is a necessary part of personal development and leadership skills.

QUESTIONS

Answer the questions using correct spelling and complete sentences.

1. Why is social behavior important?

2. Provide a list of three social behavior guidelines.

3. List and describe five social behavior traits.

4. How does your social behavior impact your future?

5. Sketch and label an appropriate table setting.

6. How does the study of social behavior improve your leadership skills?

7. Why is it important to learn proper table manners.

EVALUATING

CHAPTER SELF-CHECK

Match the term with the correct definition. Write the letter by the term in the blank provided.

a. social behavior   d. etiquette   g. considerate
b. manners   e. trait   h. courteous
c. empathy   f. well-mannered

1. _____ having regard for other people's feelings.

2. _____ trying to identify with the feelings of another.

3. _____ carrying out the basics of common courtesy.

4. _____ having good manners or tactfulness.

5. _____ being polite and gracious.

6. _____ code of social behavior.

7. _____ way of behaving that is polite.

8. _____ distinguishing characteristic about a person that makes them unique.

EXPLORING

1. Demonstrate to the rest of your class the proper technique for setting a table. (This might be done prior to a school banquet or other important function.)

2. Help plan a field trip to a local dining restaurant. Experience social behavior by practicing good table manners. Create a list of do's and don'ts related to table manners after your dining experience.

3. Write an introduction of a person presenting information on leadership skills and personal development. Select a famous person you would like to learn more about. This will add interest to the assignment.

4. Assess your social behavior skills. Indicate strengths and areas where you want to improve. Develop a personal plan for improving the skills. This involves making a list of the skills, how you want to improve, and the steps you will take to improve. You may also want to set a deadline by which you will have accomplished your plan.

5. Practice introducing members of your class to each other. Follow proper procedures of eye contact and speaking names distinctly. This may be recorded on video tape and reviewed to help people develop their social skills.

5

DEVELOPING STANDARDS OF PERSONAL DRESS

> *You only have one chance to make a first impression.* **Anonymous**

Remember, when you were younger, how much fun it was to select a costume for Halloween? You probably put much thought and effort into picking out the perfect outfit to wear to parties and to go trick-or-treating.

Sometimes you picked a costume to make you look scary. Other times, you dressed up like a super hero or a famous person. No matter how you dressed, one of the primary reasons for your selection was how other people would react to you. Whether you wanted to look frightening or cool, the most important thing was to project the image effectively.

5-1. A clown wears a costume and makeup to give a desired image.

OBJECTIVES

This chapter is about proper dress and grooming. It has the following objectives:

1. Describe the importance of appropriate personal appearance
2. Explain the relationship between dress and image
3. Describe appropriate clothing
4. Explain personal grooming
5. Explain personal hygiene

TERMS

accessories
aerobic exercise
appropriate attire
blended fabric
draped
natural fiber
pattern
personal hygiene
synthetic fabric
texture

THE IMPORTANCE OF APPROPRIATE PERSONAL APPEARANCE

5-2. The Halloween costume is used to play the role of fire fighter.

It is important to recognize that what you wear on all occasions, not just Halloween, influences how other people notice and react to you. Clothing and personal grooming influence the way you feel about yourself. How you dress is an expression of who you are and how you feel.

Just as such costumes are appropriate for Halloween activities, there are certain clothes that are most appropriate for other events you take part in.

When an unfamiliar person walks into a room, people normally form a first impression about that person within 40 seconds. That is about the amount of time it takes to brush your teeth! Yet, many lasting ideas are formed in this short time.

VALUE OF A FIRST IMPRESSION

Most of the information used to make this impression is based upon how the person looks and how they are dressed. Based on this first impression, ideas are formed about things such as intelligence, wealth, confidence, and authority. Most important, the first impression decides if the newcomer will get a chance to make a second impression.

So many different factors influence how other people perceive you. Your posture, the way you walk, how you speak and shake hands, your voice, expressions, and your clothing are a few of these factors. These factors can encourage or discourage people to develop lasting friendships with you, work with you on projects, or even go out on a date with you.

5-3. FFA members value the importance of first impressions with their official dress.

There are things you can do to influence the first impression you leave with people you meet. Your appearance is one thing you can truly control. The clothes you select for various occasions, your grooming, and being conscious of personal hygiene are important as you develop a positive personal image.

MAKING YOUR FIRST IMPRESSION COUNT

How do you select the appropriate clothing for an occasion? An old saying states that it is better to overdress than to underdress for an event. What this expression means is that you would be better off dressing formally for a casual event than dressing casually for a formal event. Think about it. Would you rather stand out from a crowd because you look too nice or because you do not look nice enough?

Before going to an activity, it is always a good idea to find out what is considered appropriate attire for that occasion. *Appropriate attire* is the term used to describe the correct type of clothing to be worn to an activity. The best way to determine appropriate attire is to speak directly to the host of the activity. Find out their expectations of guests. The next best way to determine appropriate attire is to ask someone else who is attending the event.

It is especially important for young people to work hard to make a positive first impression. You never know if the next person you meet might have a job opportunity or influence on a scholarship committee. Extra effort to be dressed appropriately can leave a lasting impression that can affect your future.

THE RELATIONSHIP BETWEEN DRESS AND IMAGE

Take a minute and look at what you are wearing right now. Consider the clothes, jewelry, and shoes you have on. How did you decide what you would wear today? Why did you choose these items when you bought them? Some reasons for these decisions might be related to the weather or the activities of the day, but other reasons are much more complex. From an early age, even young children understand that clothes are a way to express an image or feeling.

WHAT YOUR CLOTHES SAY ABOUT YOU

Your clothes are a reflection of your tastes, your interests, and your beliefs. Just look at the T-shirts you own. Today, the imprints on T-shirts turn you into a walking billboard for different products, places, and philosophies.

5-4. T-shirts are popular with a wide range of words and logos.

When you wear a T-shirt from a restaurant, resort, or city, people assume you have been there. They might even ask you about the place. When you wear a shirt advertising a product, you are endorsing that product. You are saying that you use it and you like it. When you wear a shirt with a saying on it, people see what you think without you ever saying a word. Think about the messages you are sending with your clothes. Are those messages positive?

Other clothes have the same effect. Although they may be less obvious than a T-shirt, the type and condition of your clothes say a great deal about you. If this were not true, why do most people seek out particular brands and styles of clothes to wear to school?

Look around your class. Aren't people trying to project a certain image through what they wear? Even groups of people in your school are identified by what they wear. Some choose to wear boots and hats. Others wear the latest sports shoes and stylish shirts. Still other groups can be identified by their jewelry and the brand of jeans they wear.

Whether they are formal or casual, clothes are a kind of uniform that projects who a person is or at least who they want to look like. While clothes do not make the person, they do influence who people think the person is.

5-5. Dressing appropriately for riding the range

CLOTHING AND SELF-PERCEPTION

When comedian and movie actor Billy Crystal used to be on the TV show *Saturday Night Live*, he played a character named "Fernando." The Fernando character was famous for saying, "You look marvelous. And, when you look marvelous, you feel marvelous!" While this line was meant in fun, there is much truth to it. There are many reasons for trying to look your best, but perhaps the most important reason to dress appropriately is because of the way it makes **YOU** feel.

There is something special about wearing a new set of stylish clothes. Looking sharp can help build your confidence and self-esteem; and you feel like you are putting your best effort forward. When you are not dressed appropriately, your clothes can actually distract you and keep you from doing what you are capable of doing.

APPROPRIATE CLOTHING

Describing what to wear for every occasion is an impossible task. In fact, the issue of style is so subjective that a case could be made against most any recommendation. However, there are a few standards that provide a basic guide of appropriate dress for most occasions.

FIT

Generally speaking, most clothes should have a draped fit on your body. *Draped* is a term that describes clothes that do not conform to your body, yet look neat, and are comfortable to wear. This does not mean that clothes should be two sizes too large. However, tight clothes not only show every imperfection of your body, they are also not very comfortable. Here are a few guidelines for fit:

Shirts and Blouses

The cuffs of shirts and blouses should completely cover your wrist when your arm is by your side. They should not extend beyond where the outer edge of your thumb meets your hand.

Collars of shirts and blouses should fit tight enough that they do not gape open. They should be loose enough for you to comfortably put your finger between your neck and the collar.

5-6. Proper sleeve length for a suit jacket and dress shirt for a male.

5-7. Selecting a quality suit involves choosing a color, fabric, and style that are durable and stylish.

Collar styles vary a great deal. You can choose from several different types, based upon your taste and personal preference.

Jackets

Jackets should fit comfortably through your shoulders and conform more to your waist. You should be able to move your arms comfortably in all directions without straining yourself or the fabric. Currently, longer jackets are in style. Again, there are several different types of jackets and coats that can be selected to meet your preference.

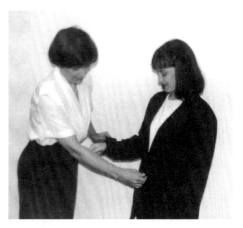

5-8. Good fit is important in selecting clothing.

Pants and Slacks

For men, cuffs of pants and slacks should be long enough to rest on the shoe when you are standing. The slacks should "break" above the ankle. For women, there is more variability among styles.

The waist should be loose enough that it does not conform to your seat and legs. The waist should not bunch up when you wear a belt. In slacks, you have the option of pleated or plain front.

5-9. Proper length of trouser leg for young men.

FABRICS

The type of fabric used to make clothing is an important factor for style and comfort. The material used to make the fabric influences the quality and the price of the clothing.

Types of Fibers

A good rule of thumb to keep in mind is to wear natural fiber fabrics when you can. *Natural fiber* fabrics are made of animal and plant products, such as cotton, wool, silk or linen, and are the highest quality. They usually last longer and look nicer than other fabrics. In fact, they are normally much more comfortable than blends or synthetic fabrics. *Synthetic fabrics* are nylon, polyester, and other manufactured products. *Blended fabrics* are a combination of two or more different types of fibers.

Textures and Patterns

Fabrics come in many different textures and patterns. *Texture* refers to the qualities of roughness or smoothness of fabrics. *Patterns* are composed of particular, distinctive weaves and printed shapes found in fabrics.

Textures and patterns can add a great deal to outfits. However, if they are not properly coordinated, they can detract from the look you are trying to project.

If you want a professional look, avoid shiny textures and "busy" patterns. They tend to look too "slick."

It is normally a good idea to have at least one textured or patterned article of clothing in an outfit. For instance, a striped shirt looks excellent with a solid colored jacket, or a plaid jacket goes nicely with solid slacks.

Generally speaking, two articles of clothing with distinct textures and patterns can be coordinated nicely as well. However, experts recommend that you do not try to put together three or more textures and patterns.

COLORS

Color is the most important factor in style, clothing selection, and excellence in dress. Color, even shades of the same color, sends powerful messages about you and your image. Certain colors suggest seriousness, elegance, and strength. Other colors suggest openness, casualness, and enthusiasm.

The Basics

For the most professional look, the best, basic colors to choose are blue, dark gray, and black. These colors are bold, impressive, and well liked by most people. When you choose one of these colors for a suit or jacket, it is easy to match a variety of skirts, slacks, shirts, and ties or scarves.

Light colors and most shades of brown are not generally recommended for professional looks. Not only are they less impressive than the dark colors listed above, they are also difficult to match with other clothes.

Another important factor to consider in choosing color is to determine what looks best with the color of your eyes,

5-10. Dark colors look professional and are liked by most people.

hair, and skin. If you have dark skin coloring, it is recommended that you pick clothes that contrast with your coloring. If you have light coloring, it is best to try to wear clothes that match your coloring.

Color Combinations

There is a huge variety of good looking, casual clothes in bright, bold colors that can be put together to give you a great look. When going for a professional or business look, there are some basic rules to keep in mind.

Begin with one of the dark-colored suits recommended above. You should select a shirt or blouse that is lighter than your suit. A white shirt will always work. It is distinctive and elegant. Light blue, yellow, pink, or ecru (a light tan or cream color) also go with many professional outfits.

A tie or scarf can really make an outfit. The tie or scarf should "tie" together the suit and the shirt. For the most professional look, your tie or scarf should be darker than the shirt. (More information on ties is included later.)

ACCESSORIES

In a professional outfit, the suit and blouse or shirt make up about 90 percent of the image you are trying to project. However, the things that make up the other 10 percent are very important. ***Accessories*** are clothing items, such as shoes, belts, ties, and jewelry, that complete an outfit. While each are relatively small items, they are very important to developing an appropriate image.

5-11. Selecting a tie is an important part of buying a new suit.

Ties and Scarves

For men, the tie is the best way to express personal style. Today, there are many different styles, colors, and patterns of ties to choose from. While not as important in ladies' fashion, scarves can add a distinct look to a professional outfit.

Ties and scarves do not have to be boring to be professional. Bright colors and bold patterns are very acceptable in business attire. The main rule to keep in mind is that the tie should bring together the other colors in the outfit. If you are wearing a navy blue suit, your tie or scarf should also have the same shade of blue in it.

Some ties are not recommended for professional attire. Ties that promote a product or company, though they may have the correct colors in them, normally do

Tying the four-in-hand knot

The four-in-hand is an elongated knot and is the most versatile and appropriate one to wear.

1. Start with wide end of the tie extending a foot longer than the narrow end.
2. Cross wide end over narrow end, and back underneath.
3. Continue around, passing wide end across front of narrow end once more.
4. Pass wide end up through loop.
5. Holding front of knot loosely with index finger, pass wide end down through loop in front.

5-12. How to tie a four-in-hand knot.

not complement a professional suit. Also, ties with cartoon characters or logos of sports teams lack the desired professional quality. However, such ties can work very well with more casual outfits.

The way a tie is tied is very important as well. Many men make the mistake of tying a tie too short. The rule of thumb is: the end of the tie should cover the belt buckle. Shorter ties detract from a professional look. Do not worry about the length of the back piece of the tie. No one sees that part anyway.

The size and style of the knot is also valuable to developing the proper effect with a tie. The four-in-hand knot will provide a small, well-shaped knot and the desired dimple in the tie below the knot. Figure 5-12 shows a diagram of how to tie the four-in-hand knot.

Shoes

Shoes are a very important part of your wardrobe. When you select your sports shoes, what do you look for? Most likely, things like style, color, and comfort are factors that influence your purchase. The same factors should be considered in choosing dress shoes.

Experts recommend that you buy the best shoes you can afford. Look for shoes that complement your professional outfits. The color and style should go with the rest of your clothes. It is also important that your shoes be comfortable. Often, when you are dressed up, you are at events that require you to stand. An uncomfortable pair of shoes can make such an event miserable.

Just like in sports shoes, there are many different styles of dress shoes. The colors of shoes that go with the greatest variety of outfits are black, dark brown, and cordovan (a dark, reddish-brown color). There are many appropriate options for lace up (oxford) and slip-on (loafer) shoes. Either type is acceptable in professional dress. It is best to get a smooth leather shoe, rather than suede leather. Be sure to keep them clean and shined!

Belts

The belt is another important accessory for professional dress. Even if it is not needed to hold up your pants, a belt is a necessary part to complete an outfit.

For men and women, the belt should match the shoes. Do not wear a brown belt with black shoes. Dress belts for men should be narrow and have a plain buckle. A much wider variety of acceptable styles can be worn by women.

Suspenders are also acceptable for professional dress. Cloth suspenders should go with the tie. Leather suspenders should match the shoes.

Never wear suspenders and a belt at the same time!

Socks and Stockings

Socks and stockings are usually not noticed unless there is a problem with them. When worn properly, they blend into the outfit perfectly; when they are wrong, they become very obvious.

The two basic rules for men's socks are: (1) they should be worn over the calf, and (2) they should be a dark color. There should never be any skin showing when you sit with your legs crossed. The color should be as dark or darker than your pants.

Professional dress for women includes stockings. Plain shades are recommended over bright colors. Care should also be taken to make sure there are no runs in the stockings.

5-13. Socks and stockings are not noticed unless there is a problem.

Jewelry

Proper jewelry can be the perfect finishing touch to a professional outfit. Overly bold jewelry can ruin the outfit. For a man, the only pieces of jewelry recommended are a watch and a ring (class ring or other signet ring). For women, a watch, rings, pins, bracelets, necklace, and earrings are acceptable if properly chosen and worn.

The most important thing to keep in mind concerning jewelry is that too much jewelry can detract from, or even cheapen, an outfit. Jewelry that is too bold overpowers all of the work you put into selecting and coordinating the other pieces of your attire.

Jewelry should be coordinated in color and style—gold with gold, silver with silver. Jewelry sets are recommended to ensure that the pieces go together well.

PERSONAL HYGIENE

Not even the highest quality of clothing, most perfectly coordinated colors, and best accessories can make up for poor personal grooming and hygiene. Maintenance and care of your body should be a normal part of your daily routine. Developing good personal hygiene takes only a few minutes every day, but it is critical to allow for interaction with other people.

Personal hygiene is the cleanliness and freedom of an individual from body odor. Regular baths and using deodorant are important in personal hygiene.

Our society places a high value upon personal cleanliness. Not only should clothes be neat and clean, our body, hair, and teeth should as well. Failure to take care of simple matters of personal hygiene can cause embarrassment for you and discomfort for those near you.

5-14. Shampoo, soap, deodorant, and toothpaste are important hygiene products.

CONDITION OF CLOTHING

A basic aspect of personal hygiene is the condition of your clothes. Even the best of clothes can send negative messages if they are not cared for properly.

For clothes to look impressive, they should be kept clean and free of wrinkles. Some simple steps can be taken to make sure your clothes always add to your positive image.

5-15. Clothing should be carefully washed to keep it clean and make it last a long time.

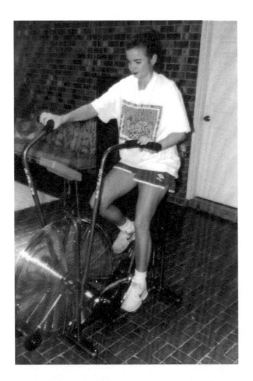

5-16. Regular exercise keeps a person healthy.

Most clothes are simple to care for at home, but others require special attention. Some have special instructions on a tag on the collar. Proper cleaning will assure that clothing holds its original color and texture.

Keeping clothes wrinkle-free is also simple. Many shirts and slacks can be pressed at home with an iron. Laundries provide services to starch and press clothes as well. Storing clothes neatly, by hanging them in your closet or folding them in a chest of drawers, will keep them ready for you to wear.

FITNESS

Personal fitness is not just a matter of looking good, it is also important to your health and well-being. Doctors and other health professionals recommend a daily routine of *aerobic exercise,* such as walking, running, or swimming. Aerobic exercises are physical activities that raise your heart rate for at least 20 minutes.

Another aspect of fitness is eating right. The habits you set now, while you are young, will benefit you for the rest of your life. Most nutrition experts recommend a balanced diet, low in fat content. It is also important that you do not start bad habits, like smoking, which can damage your quality of life.

Your clothes will not disguise a lack of body tone. If you are in good physical condition, your clothes fit better and your image is even more impressive.

HAIR

There are many different ways to wear your hair. Of all of the styles available, there are two important factors that should be considered when you make your choice. The first factor is the image you want to project. The second is the natural color and thickness of your hair. Most styles are very traditional and well accepted by men and women of all ages and backgrounds. There are some styles, such as extremely long hair in men and extremely short hair in women, which are not as well accepted or understood. It is important to know that people will look at your hairstyle, as they do your clothes, and form impressions of you.

Even more important than the hairstyle you choose is how well it is kept. Dirty, uncombed hair in any style is not professional and takes away from your appearance. You should make a habit of washing your hair often. For some people, it is necessary to condition hair to make it shiny and healthy.

It is a good idea to carry a comb or brush with you always. Check your hair frequently to see that it is as nice as it was when you left the house in the morning.

TEETH AND BREATH

One of the best things you can do for your personal appearance is smile! Therefore, it is important that your teeth be in excellent condition.

Dentists recommend that you brush your teeth after each meal. Not only will this practice help keep your teeth healthy

5-17. Grooming the hair is a part of looking good.

5-18. Brushing your teeth should be a regular, twice-a-day routine.

and cavity-free, it will also help your personal hygiene. Brushing your teeth helps make them white and clean. It also makes your breath fresh. In addition to brushing your teeth, breath mints and gum can help prevent bad breath. Of course, if you are concerned about bad breath, watch what you eat. Avoiding some foods prevents bad breath.

Regular dental appointments are also important in the care of your teeth. If you follow the advice you have received from your dentist, you will always have a pleasant smile.

BODY ODOR

The only place body odor is acceptable is in the locker room—and only then when the other people smell as bad as you! Several steps can be taken to make sure your body odor is not offensive.

The most basic step to preventing body odor is to bathe often. Young people and adults must bathe daily to clean themselves of naturally occurring odors. The use of deodorant soaps and drying off thoroughly also contributes to making you smell fresh.

There are many products you can apply to prevent body odors. You should always use some type of underarm deodorant or antiperspirant. Talcum powder and perfumes or colognes also help.

Do not wait for someone to tell you that you need to do something about your body odor. By the time they tell you, it is probably too late!

REVIEWING

MAIN IDEAS

Projecting an effective image is an important part of meeting and presenting yourself to people. When you make a good first impression, it is more likely that people will want to interact with you more in the future. Presenting yourself effectively also helps you feel good about yourself. It gives you confidence and allows you to put your best foot forward.

What you wear is an important factor in presenting your image. People associate dress with many characteristics and abilities. Clothes do not make you a different person, but they can enhance your best qualities.

There are some basic standards of appropriate dress, which should be observed to make the best impression. Clothes should have a draped fit, with sleeves, cuffs, and collars at the correct length and size for your body. The highest quality clothing is made of natural fibers. Such fabrics provide the best look and most comfort.

Textures, patterns, and colors can be mixed and matched to coordinate an outfit. While some variety is needed, too much can detract from a positive image. Likewise, accessories can add the perfect finishing touch to your image, but they can be overdone.

Personal hygiene is important for not only effective, social interaction, but also personal health. It is important to properly care for your body and your clothing. With proper care, both will last longer. Bathing and using personal hygiene products are essential if you expect people to work with you. Simple, daily routines can make all the difference as you project yourself as a leader.

QUESTIONS

Answer the questions using correct spelling and complete sentences.

1. Why is appropriate, personal appearance important?
2. What are some personal characteristics about which ideas are formed during a first impression?
3. What is the best way to determine the appropriate attire for an event?
4. What kind of messages are conveyed through the clothes you wear?
5. What are some of the standards for appropriate fit in professional attire?
6. Describe a complete, professional outfit.
7. How does fitness contribute to appropriate personal appearance?
8. What are some things that can be done to deal with body odor?

EVALUATING

CHAPTER SELF-CHECK

Match the term with the correct definition. Write the letter by the term in the blank provided.

a. accessories   d. blends   g. patterns
b. aerobic exercise   e. draped   h. synthetics
c. appropriate attire   f. natural fibers   i. textures

1. _____a combination of two or more different types of fibers.

2. _____physical activities that raise your heart rate for at least 20 minutes.

3. _____fabrics, like nylon, polyester, and other products, made from manmade products.

4. _____clothes that do not conform to your body, yet look neat and comfortable.

5. _____the qualities of roughness or smoothness of fabrics.

6. _____clothing items, such as shoes, belts, ties, and jewelry, which complete an outfit.

7. _____describes the correct type of clothing to be worn to an activity.

8. _____fabrics made of animal and plant products, such as cotton, wool, silk, or linen.

9. _____particular, distinctive weaves and printed shapes found in fabrics.

EXPLORING

1. List the desirable characteristics you would like people to see when you make your first impression. Discuss what clothing will help you best present these features. Write a short report of your findings.

2. Consult with a salesperson at a clothing store about a professional outfit. Pay attention to the way colors, textures, and patterns are mixed and matched. Submit the articles of clothing suggested and the cost for a professional dress outfit.

3. Look at each of the T-shirts that you own. Describe the messages that those articles of clothing convey. Decide if you believe they are positive representatives of your ideas and beliefs. Submit a short report.

4. Practice tying a four-in-hand knot in a necktie. Perform the task in front of the class.

5. Discuss with your parents, teacher, or other trusted person the quality of your personal hygiene habits. Do what you need to do to correct any problems.

6

DEVELOPING A SENSE OF VISION

> *If you don't know where you're going, any road will get you there.* **Anonymous**

Not knowing where you are going points out the importance of making a plan for your life. Many people appear lost as they travel through life. They wander around from one opportunity to another, never really using their talents and skills. These people need a "life road map," or better yet, a "life compass," to guide them through the opportunities and challenges they meet.

Another common saying is, "If you fail to plan, you plan to fail." A basic principle used by successful people and leaders of all types is life planning. Success does not happen by accident. Likewise, happiness does not come from good luck. To find happiness and success, you must have a plan, or a vision of what you want your life to become.

6-1. Project a positive self image through effective clothing selection—vision!

OBJECTIVES

This chapter is devoted to helping you develop personal vision for your life. It has the following objectives:

1. Describe the importance of visionary behavior
2. Contrast reactive and proactive behaviors
3. Clarify personal values
4. Develop a personal mission statement
5. Describe the importance of vision in achieving goals

IMPORTANCE OF VISION

When you think of the term "visionary," what comes to mind, maybe a person with magical powers who can predict the future? Perhaps someone who can see things in a crystal ball or who can read palms? Do you think of prophets or wizards? Actually, being a visionary is not mystical.

In the context of leadership, being a visionary, or having a vision, is simply having an overall picture of what you want your life to be. By definition, a *vision* is a well-developed, mental image of a possible and desirable future. Having a vision is an important tool to help you understand who you are and what you can become. A visionary person is one who has vision.

VISIONARY BEHAVIOR

Dan Marino of the Miami Dolphins is one of the greatest quarterbacks in professional football. He has set many records for passing the football. Experts say the reason he is such a great quarterback is because he can anticipate what is going to happen during a play before it occurs. Marino's ability is not mystical in any way. He has developed it from learning all he can about the game of football, working hard, and continually developing his skills.

Just as Marino sees what is going to happen on a football field, you can learn to anticipate and plan for what will happen in your life. This *visionary behavior* comes from understanding your capabilities, clarifying your values, and being proactive.

To develop visionary behavior, the first thing you must understand is that who you are is not determined by who other people think you are. No one else can judge your character, talents, interests, and needs better than you.

BENEFITS OF VISIONARY BEHAVIOR

Understanding your personal vision means you have the ability to shape what your life will become. **YOU** determine what you are going to do. **YOU** control your attitudes and feelings. **YOU** guide your relationships and actions. Situations do not control you; you control them!

The other side of this concept is that you cannot blame other people or circumstances for what you do. No one can make you act in a certain way unless you let them. The weather does not make you feel a certain way unless you allow it to. You are responsible for your successes and shortcomings.

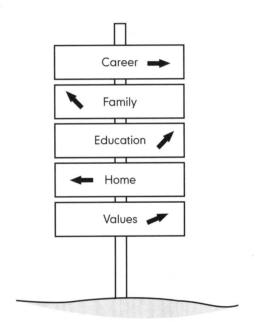

6-2. Selecting the best direction for our lives involves developing vision.

USES FOR YOUR PERSONAL VISION

Think of your personal vision as a compass to guide you through life. A *compass* is a device used for centuries by explorers and surveyors to determine direction. If you have ever hiked through wooded areas, you know how valuable a compass can be. Without a compass, it is almost impossible to make it through the trees and brush to your destination.

6-3. Foresters use a compass to find their way through thick woods.

When you have a reliable compass, and know how to use it, you can travel through even the thickest forest knowing you will reach your way.

Life can be much like a journey through a thick forest. There are many different pathways that represent good and bad opportunities. Trees and brush are like obstacles that get in your way and make it hard to see where you are going. However, a personal vision is like the compass that always points you toward your destination. Without it, you might end up walking around in circles. With it, you will always know where you are going!

REACTIVE AND PROACTIVE BEHAVIORS

To properly develop and use your personal vision, you need to know the difference between reactive and proactive behaviors. While the root word in these two words is the same, active, the similarity between them ends there.

6-4. A reactive behavior is when a given condition results in a specific response.

REACTIVE RESPONSES

In the 1920s, Russian psychologist Ivan Pavlov conducted experiments with dogs to better understand the relationship between conditions and responses. In his studies, just before he fed his dogs, he would ring a bell. He noticed that every time he rang the bell and fed the dogs, they would start to salivate. Later, he rang the bell, but did not present any food. The dogs still began to salivate when they heard the bell. He concluded the bell served as a condition that caused salivation—or a reaction. The term *reactive behavior* describes situations where a given condition results in a specific response. The behavior occurs after something has happened.

People can be reactive just like Pavlov's dogs. What does a person do if someone calls them a name? They come up with a name to yell back! That response is a reactive behavior. The condition of being called a name resulted in the reaction of more name calling.

If you think about it, when people use reactive behaviors, they are really lowering themselves to acting like dogs and other animals. When people are reactive, they let circumstances and conditions make them feel a certain way or do particular things. They then blame the condition for what they did and say they had no choice.

PROACTIVE RESPONSES

Because our brains are more developed and because we have the ability to reason, we have another option, proactive behavior. *Proactive behavior* is choosing our response to a given condition.

A proactive person carefully looks at conditions and uses their personal vision in developing a response. Being proactive means not blaming others for your problems. It means taking responsibility for whatever happens to you, good or bad, because of your choices.

The first step to developing and using a personal vision is to recognize the freedom and responsibility that go with being proactive. Once you realize your success is based upon your choices, you need to decide how you will make those choices.

6-5. Proactive behaviors help people anticipate what lies ahead.

6-6. Many people help shape our personal mission statement.

CLARIFYING PERSONAL VALUES

What is really important to you? What do you believe about human nature? Material possessions? The environment? Politics? Spirituality? Answers to questions like these are guided by our values. Values are a set of beliefs and standards that influence every aspect of our lives.

CRITERIA FOR VALUES

Think about the illustration of life being like a journey through a forest. Values determine where you are now. While you might not think about values a great deal, they do affect what you do.

In clarifying your personal values, keep in mind the three criteria for values.

- A value must be chosen freely—no one can choose what is of value to you.

- A value must be acted upon—it shows in everything that you do.

- A value must be publicly affirmed—you are willing to tell others what is really important to you.

If you cannot readily list your values, there are some things you can do to clarify them. Two of the best indicators of your values are how you spend your time and what you spend your money on. If you spend a significant amount of time doing homework and studying, you probably place value on learning and education. If you work out regularly or are active in sports, you value health and fitness.

Generally speaking, your values are those things that are at the center of your life. Clear values provide you the basis for determining your mission or purpose.

DEVELOPING A
PERSONAL MISSION STATEMENT

Would an architect build a skyscraper without a blueprint? Would a composer record a song without sheet music? Would a coach run a play in a game without first drawing the play on a chalkboard? Of course not! A written plan is essential to carrying out any successful venture. The transfer of a plan, or vision, to paper allows for ideas to be fine-tuned and clearly communicated.

ISSUES ADDRESSED BY MISSION STATEMENTS

Just as it is important for an architect, composer, or coach to have a written expression of their vision, you should have a written plan for your life. One of the best ways to illustrate your vision and values is to develop a mission statement. A **mission statement** is a document that expresses what you value and desire in life. It may be regularly reviewed and revised.

A useful mission statement should answer three key issues:

- What you want to be—character strengths you want to develop.

- What you want to do—things you want to accomplish or contribute.

- What you want to have—material and nonmaterial possessions you want to obtain.

As you think about these issues, you will probably find it easy to list the things you want to have. But, of the three, that issue is probably the least important. In fact, often, the possessions you desire come to you when you reach for the things you want to be and do.

CHARACTERISTICS OF MISSION STATEMENTS

Every person's mission statement will be different. It should include information about your special talents and interests. Your mission statement should have the following characteristics:

Brief

Keep it short and to the point. While your statement should cover every aspect of your life, it should also be short enough for you to remember.

Clear

Use words that are easy for you to understand and say what you really mean. You must understand your mission statement for it to be meaningful.

Stable

Since a mission statement is based upon your values, which do not change very much, it should be changeless, too. It should be solid and reliable in the best and worst of times.

6-7. A written plan is essential to be successful.

Future-oriented

It should focus upon long-term dreams and hopes. It should serve as a goal to strive toward, and it should direct how your time and talents are used.

Positive

Your mission should be worth working for. As you do the things within your mission statement, you should feel good about what you accomplish.

SAMPLE MISSION STATEMENTS

It might help to see what other people have developed as their mission statements.

Sample #1

⇨ *I am faithful*. I choose to live according to spiritual teachings and guidance.

⇨ *I am a son*. I am an important, helpful member of my family.

⇨ *I am a neighbor*. I will use my skills to help others.

⇨ *I am a student*. I will learn new and important things every day.

Sample #2

⇨ My mission is to live with integrity and to make a difference in the lives of others.

Sample #3

⇨ My mission is to be a good steward of my blessings through the investment of my gifts in the service of my family, friends, and co-workers. To reach my full capabilities, I dedicate myself to physical, mental, and social growth, as well as lifelong learning.

Sample #4

⇨ My mission is to give, for giving is what I do best and I can learn to do better.

⇨ I will seek to learn.

⇨ I will help other people and organizations develop and become better.

⇨ I will work to understand first, before working to be understood.

Note that each of these examples addresses the three key issues outlined previously. They also follow the common characteristics of mission statements previously discussed.

LINKING VISION TO GOALS

Your vision, as expressed in your mission statement, is an unchanging plan for your life. It is also an important guide to be used in setting your intermediate and short term goals.

Each time you set your personal goals, you should refer to your mission statement. The goals that are worth working toward will be the things that fit within your mission. If you are considering a goal that does not match your mission, perhaps you should reconsider it.

REVIEWING

MAIN IDEAS

The development of a clear, personal vision is important in your development as a leader. Before you can lead other people, you need to know where you are going. To develop a personal vision, you do not need any special, mystical skills. You just need to decide what is important to you.

The benefits of having a vision are great. It will serve as a constant guide for making personal choices. Your vision will help you stop reacting to conditions around you. Instead, you will be able to proactively control those conditions to your best interest.

To define your vision, you need to have a clear idea of your values. The best way to determine your values is to evaluate how you spend your time and your money. Values make up your life center.

A mission statement serves as a way to express your vision and values. A mission statement should be short, clear, future-oriented, and positive. It should address what you want to be, do, and have in life. It also is the most important reference to use as you set personal goals.

QUESTIONS

Answer the questions using correct spelling and complete sentences.

1. Why is it important to have a personal vision?
2. What are the differences between reactive and proactive behaviors?
3. What are the three criteria for something to be a value?
4. What are the three issues to be addressed by mission statements?
5. How does a personal vision help you achieve your goals?

EVALUATING

CHAPTER SELF-CHECK

Match the term with the correct definition. Write the letter by the term in the blank provided.

a. compass   c. visionary behavior   e. proactive
b. vision   d. reactive   f. mission statement

1. _____ a document that expresses what you value and what you desire in your life.
2. _____ anticipation of and planning for the future.
3. _____ situations where a given condition results in a specific response.
4. _____ using the ability to choose your response to a given condition.
5. _____ a device used for centuries by explorers and surveyors to determine direction.
6. _____ a well-developed, mental image of a possible and desirable future.

EXPLORING

1. Visualize what your life will be like twenty years from now. Projecting into the future, describe what you have done in your life, the things you have accomplished, and what you have.

2. List five things you can do to proactively take control of your life situations today. Think carefully about the things that cause you problems and how you can change those conditions to work better for you.

3. Collect vision or mission statements from local businesses and community organizations. Analyze the content of the statements to decide if they have the characteristics and criteria of good mission statements discussed in this chapter.

4. Develop your own mission statement. Evaluate your personal goals to determine if they fit within your personal mission.

5. Working with other class members, develop a mission statement for a school organization in which you are a member. Make sure it clearly describes what the group hopes to accomplish and contribute to its members, your school, and the community.

7

DEVELOPING SELF-DISCIPLINE AND GOALS

> By constant self-discipline and self-control you can develop greatness of character.
> Grenville Kleiser

Everyone has things they would like to achieve. These can be completing assignments in class, earning money, embarking on a career, or many others. The things we want to accomplish are goals. These goals can be small things we want to do immediately or larger things we would like to accomplish in the future.

Make a list of things you want to do. Distinguish those that will take much planning to accomplish from those that can be accomplished fairly easily or quickly.

If you are to achieve your goals, you must discipline yourself to establish the necessary work habits, do the required work, stay focused on your goals, and be persistent.

7-1. The goal of a cheerleader is to help a team do the best it can do.

OBJECTIVES

This chapter is about developing self-discipline in setting and achieving goals. The objectives are as follows:

1. Explain techniques for developing goals

2. Describe the importance of good work habits

3. Recognize the value of persistence and focus in attaining goals

4. Explain the importance of a positive attitude in goal accomplishment

TERMS

focused
goal
habit
intermediate goal
interpersonal goal
long-term goal
persistence
personal goal
prioritizing goals
procrastination
professional goal
Pygmalion effect
self-discipline
short-term goal

SELF-DISCIPLINE: THE PROCESS

Self-discipline is controlling yourself to achieve a goal. This means that self-discipline involves making choices that lead to goal accomplishment.

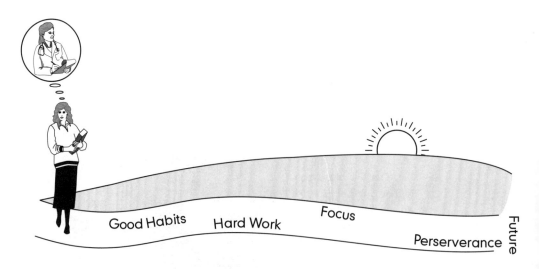

7-2. Vision begins with self-discipline.

Self-discipline is not the end result; rather, it can be seen as a process that you improve on throughout your life. The process starts with having a clear vision of your future. For instance, you may already have an idea of what career you would like to pursue.

GOALS: GET READY

To make your vision a reality, you have to set goals for yourself along the way. A **goal** is what you want to achieve. For example, if you have a vision of going to college and em-barking on a career, some of your goals might be to make at least a certain grade in each class you take in high school, to be active in a few leadership activities, or to become an expert in a field that interests you.

Goals can be long-term, short-term, or intermediate. A **long-term goal** is a goal that will take a long time (five years or more) to achieve and usually involves many steps. A **short-term goal** is one that can be achieved in a short period of time (no more than a year) in a few steps.

7-3. Passing a test could be a short-term goal.

Intermediate goals are between short-term and long-term goals. Most intermediate goals take one to five years to accomplish.

Long-term goals usually include short-term and intermediate goals along the way. If your long-term goal is to go to college, your short-term goals could include completing all of your assignments, passing tests, and making good grades in each class along the way.

SETTING GOALS

As you think about your personal vision of the future, you will naturally think about some of the goals you need to accomplish to make the vision a reality. Table 7-1 lists some of the advantages of setting goals.

There are other words that mean nearly the same thing as goal. They include objective, purpose, and intent. All refer to some accomplishment that is important to you.

```
┌─────────────────────────────────────────────────────┐
│                    Table 7-1.                         │
│              Advantages of Setting Goals              │
│  ┌─────────────────────────────────────────────────┐ │
│  │                                                   │ │
│  │  ▷ Establishes a clear direction for your efforts │ │
│  │                                                   │ │
│  │  ▷ Motivates by challenging                       │ │
│  │                                                   │ │
│  │  ▷ Reduces confusion                              │ │
│  │                                                   │ │
│  │  ▷ Makes you think through and set priorities     │ │
│  │                                                   │ │
│  └───────────────────────────────────────────────────┘ │
└─────────────────────────────────────────────────────┘
```

There are also different areas of your life in which goals can be important. You may want to set personal goals, professional goals, and interpersonal goals. **Personal goals** are goals that represent self-improvement, like learning or physical fitness. **Professional goals** are goals that represent success in your job or group activity, like becoming a supervisor or committee chairman. **Interpersonal goals** are goals that represent improving your relationships with other people.

When you begin setting goals for yourself, take time to consider some qualities that good goals should have. The following paragraphs describe some of the qualities of effective goals.

Clear

There should be no doubt in your mind about exactly what it is you intend to achieve. Sometimes writing your goals down can help. By seeing them on paper, they become more clear in your mind.

You should be able to form a mental picture, just as you do when you envision your future. If one of your long-term goals is to graduate from college, it should be easy to picture yourself accepting a diploma on the school auditorium stage.

Optimistic

All goals should have a desirable outcome. The outcome should be one that is both important to you and represents an improvement from present conditions. To merely reach the same outcome each time you do something removes the challenge from the activity and reduces motivation.

Challenging

A goal should give you something to strive for that requires some effort. To be challenging, goals should be high, but obtainable. When you work hard for something, you can be proud of your efforts when you finish. Obviously, you could set your goals so high that there is little or no hope of achieving them. You want to set challenging goals that will motivate you, not unrealistically high goals that will discourage you.

7-4. Goals should be desirable outcomes from your effort.

Prioritized

Prioritizing goals means that you decide which one is the most important, second most important, and so on. For instance, you may have goals to improve your performance in baseball and soccer. If the seasons run at the same time, you may well have to pick between the two. You will choose the one that is more important to you, that has the higher priority. This example may seem simplistic, but more difficult decisions will lie ahead. Prioritizing allows you to consider the relative importance of activities ahead of time.

Flexible

Things change as time goes by. If your goals are flexible, they can be readily adapted to changes around you. Our world is undergoing change, and it is doing so at a faster and faster pace. To see this fact in action, look at the fast pace of change in the computer industry where today's machine seems obsolete within a few months. People need to learn to cope with change.

Measurable

Being measurable does not mean that goals have to be reduced to numbers. What it means

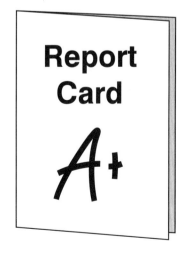

7-5. Goals should be measurable.

is that there should be no doubt about whether you met or did not meet your goal. For instance, rather than set a goal of "doing well in math this semester," make it measurable, as in "I will make an A in math." While the phrase "doing well" is ambiguous and open for interpretation, an actual grade is concrete and easy to interpret.

Include Ways and Means

Setting goals must include plans for achieving them. Many people like to list the steps required to attain a goal and the ways and means of

Guide for Goal Setting

Instructions: Write your goals below. Follow each goal with a list of the steps to accomplish it and the ways and means for accomplishing each step. Indicate a deadline date by which the ways and means are to be completed. Regularly evaluate how well you are doing in achieving your goals. Revise goals, steps, and ways and means as necessary.

Name _____   Date _____

Goal Number One: _____
_____

Steps to Achieve Goal	Ways and Means for Steps	Date
1. _____	a. _____	_____
	b. _____	_____
2. _____	a. _____	_____
	b. _____	_____
3. _____	a. _____	_____
	b. _____	_____

Goal Number Two: _____
_____

Steps to Achieve Goal	Ways and Means for Steps	Date
1. _____	a. _____	_____
	b. _____	_____
2. _____	a. _____	_____
	b. _____	_____
3. _____	a. _____	_____
	b. _____	_____

7-6. Simple written form for help in goal setting.

reaching each step. Deadline dates are needed. Having deadlines assures that we make progress towards our goals.

Some people like to use a simple form to help them set goals. This form helps organize goals and helps us specify how and when we want to achieve them. Organizing this information also helps us define our goals.

Writing our goals also helps to make adjustments in them. As people move toward goals, they often get new ideas or learn about new alternatives. This may result in modification to our goals.

HABITS: GET SET

Once goals have been set, you must establish the habits necessary to enable you to reach your goals. A *habit* is something you do a certain way so often that it becomes virtually automatic. Hopefully, you have already learned ways to study that produce good results. This might include having a specific place to study or using a certain technique, such as flashcards, to learn material.

Once you have developed your work and study habits, you must be ready to accomplish what, at times, might be very hard work. While in the midst of the hard work, remeber your vision. This will help you stay motivated.

Along the way, do not be surprised if you find that you have gotten off track. To avoid this becoming a frequent occurrence, it is important to stay focused on your goals and vision. You should be able to focus on your goals and vision just as you focus a camera lens for a photograph.

Hard work and persistence are characteristics of successful people who are able to attain their goals and live out their vision of the future. The going may get tough, but if you persevere, you will no doubt feel the pride of accomplishment when you reach your goals.

ESTABLISHING HABITS

To achieve your goals, you need to immediately establish the habits that will lead you to success. Just as starting a term paper on a clean sheet of paper is often difficult, starting good work habits can be a challenge. But once you do, repetition can lead directly to life-changing habits.

Many of the things you do everyday are done out of habit. Consider your morning routine. You probably get up at the same time each day during the week. After your shower, during which you wash your hair,

**Table 7-2.
Starting a New Habit**

Three Steps to Starting a New Habit

1. Begin the new behavior as strongly as possible

2. Look for the first opportunity to act on the new behavior

3. Never let an exception occur until the new behavior is firmly rooted

face, and body in the usual order, you brush your teeth, starting on the same side of your mouth each time. Clearly, we are at times operating on "automatic pilot."

Starting a new habit can be a challenging task. Often, we see the need to get in the habit of doing something new, but getting the new habit ingrained seems impossible. As they say, getting started is the hardest part.

The famous psychologist, William James, suggested three steps for starting a new habit. First, begin the new behavior as strongly as possible. Next, look for the first opportunity to act on the new behavior. And, finally, never let an exception occur until the new behavior is firmly rooted.

Suppose your grades in math have not been up to your expectations. You have not always been getting your homework completed because you usually leave it for after dinner and then find yourself in front of the television instead of a book. Your teacher suggests setting aside 30 minutes right after you get home for doing your homework.

Using the first step of James' approach, you might consider finding a room in your house with no distractions so you can work uninterrupted. For instance, the kitchen and family room would probably be high-traffic areas, neither lending themselves to peace and quiet. Your own room or a study may be a good choice. Try to start the new habit strongly by applying yourself fully to the new task.

The second step makes the point that it is best not to put things off. **Procrastination,** or putting tasks off until later, often leads to more procrastination. Having your first 30-minute study session the same day that this plan is suggested is the best way to avoid letting the opportunity slip away.

Finally, it is important to be persistent and keep up the study sessions without fail until it is part of your daily habit pattern. There is no set time, but the true test of a habit is whether it remains part of your daily routine for as long as the habit is useful.

PUTTING IT ALL TOGETHER: GO!

STAYING FOCUSED

Once you have established new habits, it is inevitable that distractions will occur. If they occur frequently enough, you may find yourself off track and no longer proceeding toward your goal. It is times like these when it is important to stay focused. Being *focused* means you have your attention on the things that are important to you.

Imagine watching a movie that is not focused. What would it be like? Confusing, frustrating, and boring are some words that probably come to mind. Likewise, if your vision or goals are unclear, these same feelings can result. Following are several techniques for staying focused.

Think About Your Vision

Remember the reason for your efforts. By focusing on your vision, you make it clear in your mind, just as you focus a camera lens to take a clear picture. If your goal is important to you, reminding yourself about it may provide the motivation you need to get back on track. The value of a clear and precise vision becomes apparent as you try to form a mental picture of it in your mind.

7-7. Effective study requires focus.

Remove the Distraction

If the distraction is something that can be easily avoided, do so. If the distraction is not easily avoided, consider alternatives or compromises. Sometimes, staying focused forces you to make choices between several things you would like to do when these activities conflict with each other.

Set Short-term Goals

Set a short-term goal as a stepping stone. Often, this sort of achievement along the way can serve as a source of motivation. Smaller and more quickly attained goals also give you a way to measure how you are doing in pursuit of your long-term goals.

Put Goals in Writing

If you have not already done so, write your goals down. Sometimes the act of putting things on paper makes them seem more real and reminds you of their importance. Put the written goals somewhere you will see them often and be reminded to stay focused.

7-8. Written goals help remind you of their importance.

PERSISTENCE

The bottom line in attaining goals is to work hard and be persistent. **Persistence** means continuing, even in the face of adversity. You have probably heard the phrase, "nobody said it was going to be easy." In life, real goals are usually achieved through real work, not by chance.

Salespersons sometimes seem to promise something for nothing. Further study usually reveals the "small print" with the catch. Hard work, on the other hand, not only helps us achieve our goals, but also provides a true sense of accomplishment as you get results for your efforts.

When some people hear "hard work," they think of back-breaking labor. While your goals may indeed require this type of physical exertion, it is more likely they will require much mental work.

THE POWER OF POSITIVE THINKING

Truly effective leaders in any organization share several traits, but possibly the most important is having a positive attitude. We all know people who are always up, always happy and motivated. They may be a relative, a teacher, a coach, or a friend. When you are around someone who is positive and happy, it is hard not to share the same enthusiasm. You find yourself feeling good, whether you want to or not.

This positive attitude is something that an aspiring leader needs to develop. The fol-

7-9. Effective leaders have the power of positive thinking.

lowing section discusses how a positive attitude can help you attain your goals.

THE PYGMALION EFFECT

In an ancient story told by Ovid in *Metamorphoses*, there was a sculptor named Pygmalion who was a prince of Cyprus. He created a sculpture of the ideal woman and named it Galatea. His creation was so beautiful that he fell hopelessly in love with it. In his desperation, he prayed passionately to the goddess Venus to bring his sculpture to life. Feeling pity for Pygmalion, Venus granted his request, and the couple lived happily ever after.

In more modern times, George Bernard Shaw wrote a play called *Pygmalion* in which Professor Henry Higgins proposes to take a poor flower girl and, with some intense training, pass her off as a duchess. His positive expectations are accompanied by plenty of work on his part, and when he succeeds, the result represents what is now commonly referred to as the Pygmalion effect. The **Pygmalion effect** is another phrase for a self-fulfilling prophesy. It means that when we expect something to happen, we change our behavior in such a way as to make the event more likely.

7-10. Positive expectations from a peer or superior can help motivate one toward success.

This effect takes place all around us every day, usually without our being aware of it. Imagine you have joined a basketball team and before practice the coach pulls you aside and says, "I've heard that you can really play some ball. I'm glad you are part of the team." You have always thought of yourself as just average. But as a result of these higher expectations, both you and your coach will put more effort into your basketball training. Odds are that your skills will improve much more under these circumstances than if the coach treated you as a "bench warmer."

When we have positive expectations about things in our future, we find ourselves motivated toward that eventuality, and the experience is usually a good one. But the Pygmalion effect also holds true for negative expectations. If you are at a party that you did not want to attend, chances are you will find lots of reasons why the party is not a good one, and you will not have a good time.

Understanding the effects of your attitudes and expectations is an important step in improving your future. When you are faced with a task that does not appeal to you, try to focus on the positive aspects and you may be surprised to find that the task was not so bad after all.

REVIEWING

MAIN IDEAS

Self-discipline is controlling yourself in order to achieve things that are important to you. These important things are called goals, and may be short-term or long-term. Your goals will flow from your personal vision of your future and should be clear in your mind.

To achieve goals, you need to establish solid work and study habits. Establishing good work habits requires your dedication in order to be successful.

Along the way to achieving your goals, you will need to work hard and stay focused on your goals and vision. Staying focused keeps you on track when distractions pull at your attention.

Persistence in the face of adversity and a positive attitude will go a long way in ensuring your success. Positive expectations foster an environment where goals can be achieved.

QUESTIONS

Answer the questions using correct spelling and complete sentences.

1. Why is it important to set goals?

2. Identify a short-term and a long-term goal you have set for yourself. What do you think will be required for you to achieve these goals?

3. Name four of the qualities goals should have and explain briefly why each quality is important.

4. Discuss three techniques for staying focused when distractions try to pull you away from goal accomplishment.

EVALUATING

CHAPTER SELF-CHECK

Match the term with the correct definition. Write the letter by the term in the blank provided.

a. goal
b. short-term goal
c. long-term goal
d. Pygmalion effect

e. self-discipline
f. persistence
g. procrastination
h. focus

i. habit
j. prioritizing

1. _____ something you do often and almost automatically.

2. _____ a goal that can be accomplished fairly quickly, with only a few steps.

3. _____putting things off until later.

4. _____determining an order of importance.

5. _____something you want to achieve.

6. _____using control over yourself to accomplish goals.

7. _____continuing even in the face of adversity.

8. _____staying on track in your pursuit of a goal.

9. _____a goal that takes a while to achieve and may involve numerous steps.

10. ____theory that positive expectations can have a positive affect on performance.

EXPLORING

1. Organizations set goals too. Pick an organization, like your school, a fast-food restaurant, or your parent's company, and find out what its goals are for the short-term and long-term. Talk to someone who works in the organization. Report your findings to the class.

2. Choose a career. Do research to determine what you would need to achieve to work in the career field. Make a list of short-term goals and long-term goals. For each, explain briefly how you would go about achieving the goal.

8

TAKING RISKS

> *If you play it safe in life, you've decided that you don't want to grow anymore.*
> **Shirley Hafstedler**

Have you any desire to try bungee jumping? Skydiving? White-water rafting? How about public speaking? If you said "yes" to any of these questions, you are a risk taker.

Not all risks are extreme, however. Make a list of things in your life that require you to take a risk. Did you include things like trying new foods, styling your hair a different way, meeting someone new? All of these things involve risk.

8-1. White-water rafting on Tennessee's Ocoe River is risky and fun.

OBJECTIVES

This chapter deals with taking risk and avoiding mistakes in doing so. It has the following objectives:

1. Explain the importance of risk taking for leaders

2. Describe ways to reduce risk to an acceptable level

3. Explain the importance of learning from mistakes

4. Describe several techniques for coping with stress

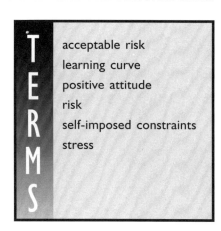

TERMS

acceptable risk
learning curve
positive attitude
risk
self-imposed constraints
stress

LEADERS TAKE RISKS

Effective leaders are usually the kind of people who like to experience new things. They enjoy the challenge and excitement. They are risk takers.

Risk is the possibility of failing, having a loss, or being injured. In sports, people run the risk of injury. In owning a business, people run the risk of losing the money they have invested. No one wants to take undue risk, but some risk is necessary.

Leaders are proactive. Being proactive, they take responsibility for their actions. A proactive person makes things happen, rather than letting them happen to him or her. A proactive person takes the initiative without being overbearing.

Being proactive and experiencing things for the first time involves risk, since very rarely do we do things perfectly the first time. When something has risk, there is a chance of failure. There are different kinds of risk, such as risk of embarrassment, risk of health, or risk of failure. But good leaders are willing to accept a certain amount of risk to broaden their horizons and learn.

DETERMINING ACCEPTABLE RISK

When investing money, it is often said that greater risk can lead to greater reward. What is equally true is that these same high risk investments can lead to great losses as well. As an investor, you must determine what level of risk is acceptable for you.

As you become a leader, you must also make decisions about how much risk you are willing to take in everyday situations. Unfortunately, there is no simple test for determining acceptable risk.

A cliff that might seem easy to a mountain climber would scare other people, while that same mountain climber might have a greater-than-average fear of public speaking. When a task is too easy, it probably will not motivate as well as a challenging task.

People are willing to take some risk, often known as acceptable risk. *Acceptable risk* is the risk that can lead to above average success without disastrous or unacceptable consequences for failure. Everything we do involves some risk, such as traveling in an automobile. We accept this risk every time we go some place.

8-2. Windsurfing involves acceptable risk to some people.

BE PREPARED

The most effective way to reduce the risk in any situation is through preparation. If you were going skydiving for the first time, it would not be too smart to jump out of the plane without getting plenty of instruction first. You would want to learn all you could about how the parachute works, what to do if something failed, how to land, etc.

By preparing and learning, you effectively make a risky situation less risky. Put another way, you make your own chances for success much higher. The knowledge not only adds to what you know, but also boosts your confidence.

8-3. Preparation helps overcome risk.

Let's say you are going white-water rafting. Your first trip should probably be with an expert, to keep the risk of injury from being too great. You might still be nervous, wondering what those rapids will be like.

Once you get your gear and learn how it works, your guide will probably explain the procedure in case someone falls into the rapids. This is not to scare anyone, although your stress level may rise. What this safety briefing actually does is reduce the level of risk by preparing you with knowledge.

If you are going to present a report to the class, you would want to practice beforehand. You might stand in front of a mirror or just repeat the words to yourself over and over. The more familiar you become with the information you are sharing, the more comfortable you will be when it is time to begin speaking.

THE WISE RISK TAKER

Someone who takes risks without preparation is destined for failure. However, the wise risk taker prepares and, in the process, actually reduces the risk of failure considerably. As a leader, there are several things you can do to weigh the odds in the favor of you and your followers.

Experiment First

When you have the time and ability, try out your plan first. This is similar to floating in calm waters and learning how to use the oars before setting out for the rapids. This is also what you are doing when you practice your speech in front of a mirror. There may be times when experimenting is not feasible, but it can be invaluable when it is possible.

Consider Any Ideas Proposed

Some of the best and most innovative ideas for achieving goals sound strange at first. But when an idea gets tossed around enough and everyone adds a little input here and there, problems get solved in effective and creative ways.

Model Risk Taking

Have you ever been in a group when it is time to start an activity and no one moves at first? Then someone steps forward and suddenly everyone follows the person with the initiative. When your followers see you taking risks and achieving high results, they will be encouraged to do the same.

Make the Environment as Informal as Possible

Research suggests that people are more creative in a relaxed and informal environment. Using formal titles and insisting on formal clothing tend to make people less able to think in innovative ways. They will be more self-conscious about their appearance or actions. Setting the tone for a relaxed atmosphere can get your group moving in the right direction toward greater creativity.

LEARNING FROM MISTAKES

When a leader or a group is taking risks and making things happen, mistakes are going to be made. Mistakes are a natural part of any problem solving process. The thing to remember is that successful people learn from their mistakes. In fact, they see mistakes as opportunities for learning. Seeing mistakes in a positive way is not easy, even for great people.

The great novelist Ernest Hemingway, in his first years of writing, lost a suitcase containing all of his manuscripts. In his depression, he talked to his friend Ezra Pound. Pound called his loss a stroke of luck. When asked what he meant, he told Hemingway that as he tried to recreate his stories, he would inevitably remember only the good parts. The end product would turn out better than the original. Pound helped Hemingway see the opportunity in what seemed to be misfortune, and Hemingway went on to become one of the greatest American writers of all time.

Seeing failure in a good light does not come naturally. It takes plenty of practice and constant refocusing on the "bigger picture" of your goals and vision. In other words, try to determine what can be learned from the failure. When the failure has tough consequences, it may be even harder to see the silver lining, but good leaders relentlessly search for the learning points.

Still, an effective leader must be willing to take risks and learn from the accompanying mistakes. Before being elected President of the United States, Abraham Lincoln was defeated six times in state and national elections. He never gave up and went on to become one of the greatest presidents in our nation's history.

There are many other, more down-to-earth, examples of people who took risks and failed repeatedly before finally attaining success. Taking risks gets the adrenaline flowing and provides the challenge that brings out the best in everyone.

We almost never do anything new perfectly the first time. It is by making mistakes and learning from them that we finally improve at the activity.

Effective leaders do not place blame on others for mistakes. Leaders, instead, look for what can be learned from the experience. They are already thinking about how next time will be different because of the additional knowledge they have gained.

CREATIVE PROBLEM SOLVING

Being an effective leader today requires finding solutions to organizational problems. These solutions often involve some level of risk. This does not mean that the leader must come up with a solution alone. In fact, it is generally other group members, people who are doing the day-to-day work within the group, who will most likely propose solutions.

8-4. Leaders must find solutions to problems that often involve some level of risk.

A leader provides an open atmosphere in which team members feel free to offer suggestions about how to best achieve group goals. An effort should be made to keep an open mind and not place too many constraints on the ideas proposed by the group. Often, a creative solution may come from a previously unrecognized area. A good leader can recognize an effective solution when it is presented.

The following exercise highlights the need to think creatively and with an open mind when confronted with a problem to solve. On a piece of paper, draw nine dots, as shown in figure 8-5. Now place your pen or pencil on one of the dots and, without lifting the pencil from the page, cover all nine dots with just four straight lines.

If you were unable to solve the puzzle, do not be discouraged. Many people have tried and come up with a solution that looks like the one in figure 8-6. For the actual solution, see the end of the chapter.

What probably strikes you immediately is that the solution does not follow one of the constraints that you placed on yourself—to not go outside the square made by the dots. A limit that you place on yourself is known as a ***self-imposed constraint***. When you looked at the dots the first time, you probably only thought of solutions that stayed in the imaginary box you created in your mind. Once you see beyond this self-imposed limit, the answer is easier to see.

Likewise, many times we place imaginary constraints on our problem solving abilities. To be good leaders, we must break free of these barriers to find the creative and best ways of achieving goals of solving problems.

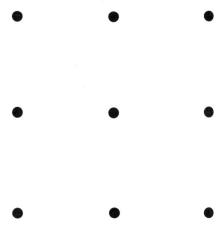

8-5. Can you solve this problem? (Connect all nine dots with four straight lines without lifting your pencil.)

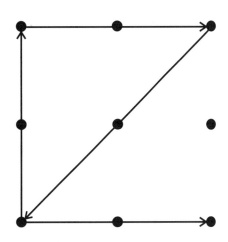

8-6. Limiting yourself often prevents problem solving.

8-7. A pitcher can be successful and not throw a strike every time!

FEAR OF FAILURE

No one wants to fail. Fear of failure makes some people very cautious and unwilling to attempt anything new. A fear of failure can cause people to avoid failure at all costs. The problem with this is that avoiding failure also causes us to avoid success, since success usually requires some risk. A better, more healthy attitude is to take acceptable risks and try to learn from mistakes and failures.

Because you are human, you will make mistakes. While you should always strive to keep from repeating past mistakes, you can try to see mistakes as an opportunity to learn. Thomas Edison went through numerous variations before inventing a working light bulb. Rather than get depressed about each of these failures and give up, he saw them as contributing in some small way to his eventual success.

Babe Ruth struck out over 1,300 times. In between these strikeouts, he hit 714 homeruns. Obviously, making mistakes does not make a person a failure.

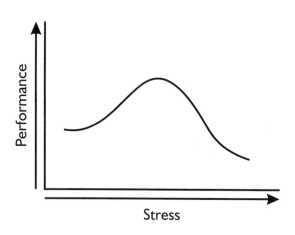

8-8. Stress improves performance up to a certain point.

STRESS

Fear of failure often leads to stress. **Stress** is being in a pressure situation or feeling nervous or frustrated. Interestingly, studies have shown that as stress increases, performance actually improves to a certain point. However, if stress gets too high, performance will get worse.

Research has shown that the stress of an upcoming exam helps students maximize their learning curves. A ***learning curve*** is a graphical representation of how quickly a person learns something new.

The stress of world class competition pushes athletes to world record performances. This does not mean stress is causing the good performance. Rather, it is how a person deals with stress that decides the outcome.

Coping With Stress

Unfortunately, if stress becomes too great, illness can result. Research has shown that big changes in your life can result in stress and make demands on your available energy. If you are using energy to combat stress, you have less of your total energy left for fighting illness. This is why stress can lead to illness.

8-9. Too much stress can leave you tired and lead to illness.

Researchers have found that the most effective way to deal with stress is to develop a positive attitude toward stressful situations. If you can see the experience as challenging, with an opportunity to learn something, chances are good that this ***positive attitude*** will reduce your stress level.

Many people talk about ways to eliminate stress, but this is clearly impossible. What is possible is reducing stress. There are many specific things you can do to reduce stress in your life. Here are some suggestions:

- Organize your day and ensure it includes some free time for relaxation.

- Break up your daily routine and have some variety.

- Establish long-term goals to keep from being brought down by day-to-day problems.

- Establish short-term goals to give yourself small victories along the way to achieving the long-term goals.

8-10. Having a sense of humor helps reduce stress.

- Exercise several times a week. Exercise is good for you, both physically and psychologically, as it makes you feel better about yourself.

- Eat well. Junk food cannot provide the energy needed for fighting stress or other illnesses.

- Get plenty of rest. You are more likely to handle stressful situations better when you are well rested.

- Have a sense of humor. Laugh with others and laugh at yourself.

- See the bright side. A positive attitude can work wonders in relieving stress.

REVIEWING

MAIN IDEAS

Effective leaders are willing to take risks. They are proactive, making things happen, and achieving personal and group goals.

Leaders are faced with the challenging task of determining acceptable risk. In general, risk can be reduced by preparation and knowledge. The leader should also foster an atmosphere in which risk taking is encouraged and people's creativity can come out.

To be successful, you must learn from your mistakes. Seeing failure as a learning opportunity is sometimes difficult, but always necessary.

To solve problems, leaders and groups often need to see beyond the imaginary boundaries they have created for themselves. Creative ideas often sound funny or strange at first, but can be effective when examined and implemented.

Fear of failure can lead to avoidance of success as well as failure. It also causes stress. While some stress can improve performance, too much stress can lead to illness. There are several techniques available for reducing stress to an appropriate level.

QUESTIONS

Answers the questions using correct spelling and complete sentences.

1. Why is it important for a leader to be proactive?

2. How can fear of failure reduce a leader's chances of success?

3. List five examples of ways to reduce stress and give an example for each.

4. What is the best way to reduce risk to an acceptable level?

EVALUATING

CHAPTER SELF-CHECK

Match the term with the correct definition. Write the letter by the term in the blank provided.

a. risk
b. stress
c. acceptable risk

d. self-imposed constraints
e. positive attitude

f. learning curve

1. _____ seeing the bright side, even of failure.

2. _____ a chance of failure.

3. _____ amount of risk yielding positive results without disastrous consequences for failure.

4. _____ imaginary boundaries to problem solving.

5. _____ being in a pressure situation.

6. _____ cumulative knowledge based on learning from mistakes.

EXPLORING

1. Consider an activity that you have wanted to do, but have not yet experienced. Some examples might be canoeing, skiing, or speaking in front of a group. Prepare to accomplish the activity by learning all you can about it. Try the activity and report your experiences to the class.

2. Visit a wellness center at a local hospital or health facility. Observe the various exercises, diets, and techniques for staying healthy and reducing stress. Report your findings to the class.

SOLUTION TO PUZZLE

The solution to the nine-dot puzzle involves going beyond the normal bounds.

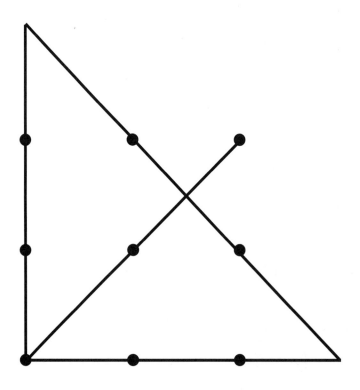

9

EFFECTIVE ONE-ON-ONE COMMUNICATION

> *The credibility of the sender affects how people perceive a message.* **Steve Fraze**

Have you ever heard or read something that you did not understand? Why did you not understand it? There are often several reasons why we fail to understand properly.

Communication involves people. Failures in communication may result from any number of factors. Being a good communicator involves overcoming the communication blocks and helping other people understand. A person who knows the communication process can use the process to effectively share information.

9-1. Communication involves expressing a wide range of ideas. What do you think the catcher is telling the pitcher?

OBJECTIVES

This chapter deals with the fundamentals of the communication process. It has the following objectives:

1. Explain communications
2. Discuss methods of effectively using feedback
3. Examine ways to reduce interference
4. Describe how to be a good listener
5. Explain the role of written communication
6. Write a business letter
7. Write a résumé

TERMS

channel
communication
communication model
decoding
encoding
feedback
filtering
hearing
interpret
listening
message
noise
perception
receiver
selective perception
semantics
source
total communication

COMMUNICATION IS A PROCESS

Communication is the process of exchanging information. If information is not accurately exchanged, the process has not worked well. Fortunately, people can take steps to assure improved communication.

The communication process involves each of us every day. It is central to all social behavior. Humans cannot socially interact unless they communicate through the sharing of symbols. We do this when we talk with family, friends, and business associates. We write letters, read letters, read the newspaper, and watch television to give and receive information.

Having good communication skills is one essential element of leadership. Without communication, there is no leadership. It is possible, however, to communicate without leading. In leadership roles, it is important that you communicate what you desire to communicate. Since people communicate daily, they mistakenly assume that they communicate clearly and

9-2. A map is used to show the route of each school bus.

effectively. This is not so. What is the communication process and how does it function? What is the goal of communication and the steps of achieving that goal?

THE COMMUNICATION MODEL

The ***communication model*** is a way of describing the communication process. The model has several parts that must function for the communication process to be successful. In addition, the model includes a method to decide how effectively the information was exchanged.

1.   ***Source***—Every effort in communication begins with a source. The source is the sender or initiator of the attempt to communicate.

2.   ***Message***—The message is the idea or information that is to be exchanged. The sender prepares it into a form for sending, known as ***encoding***. This involves using some kind of code system, such as written letters that form words, drawings, photographs, gestures, or movements. The sender must select a system of codes that have meaning for the intended receiver of the message.

3.   ***Channel***—The channel is the linkage between the sender and the individual(s) for whom the message is intended. The kind of channel selected depends, to some extent, on the coding system. Speaking to an individual involves using verbal communication that requires the sender to use language that the receiver can interpret.

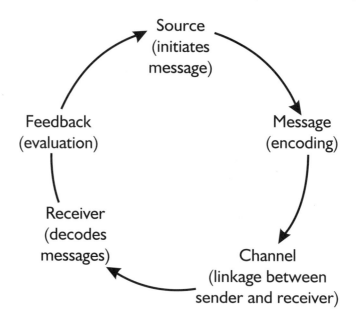

Communication Model

9-3. The communication model shows a circular process of communication.

4.   ***Receiver***—The receiver is the individual(s) for whom a message is intended. The encoded message is decoded. ***Decoding*** is drawing meaning from the symbols used by the sender of the message. Good communication results when the receiver gets the same meaning from the message as was intended by the sender. Blockages sometimes occur. Blockages are due to language, physical impairments, noise, or other factors that prevent the exchange of information.

5.   ***Feedback***—Feedback is the return channel from the receiver to the sender. It allows people to evaluate how well they have exchanged information. In speaking to another person, the individual might ask you to repeat your statement. In other cases, feedback could involve getting a wrong answer or no response at all. Following feedback, the sender encodes the message again and sends it or offers clarification.

   Feedback often occurs throughout the communication process. The sender and the receiver are simultaneously filtering the message. The communication process is incomplete until the sender and receiver agree on an understanding of that message.

Blockages

Blockages in the communication process are known as ***noise***. Noise includes sounds that interfere with oral communication and any other factors that cause the communication process to fail.

Any thing that distracts the receiver is noise. Sometimes, not knowing a language is a blockage. An example would be trying to order from a menu in a French restaurant without knowing the language.

Visual communication blockages are also noise. Loud clothing, excessive jewelry, pictures, animals, or any visual object that distracts the receiver is noise. This means that the sender should try to keep these away from a communication setting.

Perceptions

A ***perception*** is how people view or feel about something. It is based on what they have learned. Perceptions have powerful roles in how a message is encoded and decoded.

The sender selects codes and channels based on how they perceive the information and receiver. After receiving the message, the receiver uses experiences, values, and knowledge to decode the message. These experiences include an individual's culture, education, language, experiences, and many other factors.

ROLE OF THE SENDER

The sender must consider the characteristics of the receiver. Select appropriate codes and channels that the receiver can use to interpret the message.

The channel can be a spoken conversation, a written memo, a telephone call, a pantomime, or other means. It could take other forms, such as a pat on the back, a smile, or a frown. Still other channels of communication might take the form of a painting, sculpture, or music. These are means of expressing an idea or thought and must be appropriate for the receiver.

ROLE OF THE RECEIVER

The role of the receiver is to decode a message and draw meaning from it. The receiver can make the process easier by concentrating on decoding.

9-4. The National FFA Career Show uses a variety of media to communicate career information.

Carefully read, listen, or interpret what has been sent. Asking questions is an important part of clarifying the accuracy of information exchange.

If the receiver does not understand the message, the sender will need to re-send the message using different codes or channels or both. Sometimes, merely repeating the message is sufficient.

The receiver has the important role in the communications process of providing sufficient feedback to allow the sender to evaluate how well the information was exchanged. The sender can repeat the message or make any changes to assure comprehension.

THE GOAL OF COMMUNICATION

Total communication describes the exact duplication of what the sender intends to convey to the receiver with total understanding of the message. Total communication is the responsibility of both the sender and receiver. Without the cooperation of both parties, total communication will not exist.

Attempting to achieve total communication is important for everyone because communication is the key to human relations. The potential of human beings to understand and communicate varies due to the many internal and external filters through which messages travel.

FILTERING

Filtering is the group of perceptions that a message passes through when it is being exchanged. The result of filtering is that the receiver's perception of the message may not be as the sender intends. The potential for perception error applies to both the sender communicating with the receiver and the receiver responding to the sender.

Often, reception of a different message, part of the message, or none of the message occurs. Individuals ***interpret*** (draw meaning from) messages using their perceptions, including their values, needs, feelings, and experiences.

Filtration of the message may result in a loss of communication effectiveness. The senders and the receivers must understand the communication process and reduce the degree of filtering to achieve total communication, and, therefore, understanding.

USING FEEDBACK EFFECTIVELY

An important tool for maintaining and achieving total communication is the proper use of feedback. It is the sender's way of deciding the effectiveness of the message. During feedback, there is a reversal in the direction of the communication process. When providing feedback, the original receiver goes through the same process as the original source. The same factors influence them as influenced the source. The object of feedback is to report to the sender what the receiver sees, hears, and feels toward the transmission.

For feedback to be effective, the receiver must give it as soon as the transmission of the message takes place. Waiting decreases the impact that feedback will have on the communication. The passage of time may make the communication less accurate and contribute to communication errors. The sooner the sender receives feedback, the sooner they can adjust the message.

The receiver may use the same channel for feedback as the source used. This is usually the case in face-to-face conversation. However, the receiver can use a different channel. A leader may transmit a message to a group requesting specific action to a matter. The group's actions or lack of actions then become feedback.

Feedback is very important in the communication process. It is most effective in face-to-face conversation where feedback is instantaneous. The leader knows immediately that miscommunication has occurred. Feedback is the most effective method of checking the achievement of total communication. It leads to total understanding of the message or image sent.

BARRIERS TO COMMUNICATION

Communication is the transmission of common understanding with symbols. The sender transmits a message to the communicator through some type of medium. For effective communication to exist, all parts of the communication process must be in harmony. When there are barriers or interferences in the communication process, effective communication cannot exist. For example, you are listening to your favorite radio station and the telephone rings. After the telephone rings, you get called to do the dishes. These are barriers that hinder you from effectively listening to the radio station. As a leader, you must know the barriers that exist and try to reduce them.

There are several barriers to communication. The major ones are:

- Selective perception—**Selective perception** occurs when people block out information they do not want to hear. This is usually information that conflicts with their values, beliefs, or what they want to do. Selective perception can result in stereotyping or other problems. (Some people refer to selective perception as selective listening.)

  A person will have preconceived ideas about something and will therefore apply selective perception to confirm their ideas. For example, a health director might have trouble getting a community to support additional environmental controls on a local factory. This resistance could be because the community perceives that the idea might affect their jobs and the overall economy of the community. They hear what they want to hear.

- Poor listening skills—Poor listening skills can be caused by a number of different things. A person can have their mind on something else or have already thought about what they might say. Perhaps the receiver is just not interested in the subject or the receiver has a poor knowledge of the subject. Whatever the case, poor listening skills can reduce the effectiveness of the communication process. Help to overcome poor listening by concentrating on the message.

- Credibility of sender—The credibility of the sender affects how people receive a message. If the receiver perceives the sender as not living up to their word, communication barriers will exist. This can be caused by status differences between communicators, or, maybe, the receiver has negative feelings toward the sender. As a leader, you must build your credibility for people to trust and respect you.

■ Semantics—**Semantics** is when the same words mean entirely different things to different people. As a leader, you must make sure that the receivers understand what you say. A good example is the word "bad." To a teenager, bad might mean good, as in "Boy, that is a bad stereo system." To a parent, bad means undesirable. Another example would be the word "slowly." Slowly may be twice as fast to the learner as intended by the instructor.

■ Filtering—Filtering is the manipulating of information so it is perceived as the receiver desires. This occurs often with organizations that have several levels of management. Each level can filter what they do not want the next level to know or change the information to promote their ideas or feelings.

■ Avoiding details—The mind avoids detail and cannot remember many details in a short time. Consider these numbers: ten, twelve, six, eight, zero, sixty-three, four, sixteen. How many can you repeat in proper order?

REDUCING INTERFERENCE

Interference is anything that is or could be a blockage in the communication process. There are three major ways to improve communication.

■ Improve perception—As a leader, you can improve your perception by first putting yourself in the other person's position and assuming their emotions. This means that you should know your audience or the people with whom you are communicating. Individuals have different backgrounds and experiences, and, as a result, they look at things differently. It does not mean that you are right and they are wrong. It means that people place different emphasis on some of the evidence than you might.

Another way to improve perception is to separate facts from opinions. Opinions contain emotions. Facts reflect available evidence. One should cultivate looking objectively at an issue and realize that changes are necessary when new evidence becomes available.

■ Improve physical processes of communication—When improving this area, look at providing feedback, improving listening and speaking skills, and simplifying language. These can be barriers if they do not receive attention. For example, the sender might not make eye contact with the audience when speaking. Another example would be the speaker who uses language that is too complex. A person can practice these physical processes and use them to simplify communication.

■ Improve relationships—This is a very important area that, if improved, can really help the communication process. As a leader, you should build a relationship of trust and confidence. If the receiver of a message knows you keep your word, they are more likely to listen to what you say. Another important factor in improving relationships is to focus on a person's strengths. Look for the good in everyone and show a sincere interest in their well-being.

Removing barriers to communication takes more than knowing how to speak well. As a leader, you must build trust and respect into your relationships. Be empathetic—put yourself in the receiver's shoes and ask yourself: What are their needs? Why do they feel that way? Ask questions that produce actions. Recognize individual differences and judge people accurately. In any situation, trust and respect are the foundation of many relationships, and relationships affect communication.

LISTENING

Listening is just one part of communication; however, it is the basis for successful communication. If one does not listen closely to the person

9-5. Attentive listening and responding are obvious by these two individuals.

communicating, part of the message may be lost. This will result in mix-up or confusion.

The listener has the responsibility to make every effort to understand the message being sent. This is not as simple as it may seem. You listen to people speaking many times every day, but are you listening effectively? Are you able to understand and remember? What makes listening difficult and how can you improve your listening skills?

LISTENING PROBLEMS

There are three types of barriers that interfere with the listening process:

■ External factors—External factors are those that distract the listener, such as noise or people walking in and out of the room. Simply closing the door to block out the noise or moving to a more private area often removes these distractions. Sometimes, removing distractions is physically impossible. In these instances, you must concentrate on the speaker. In other words, tune out the distractions.

■ Poor listening habits—Poor listening habits prevent you from receiving the entire message. These habits include:

➪ *Interrupting the Speaker*

➪ *Completing the Speaker's Sentences*

➪ *Not Having Eye Contact*

➪ *Doing Other Things While the Speaker is Talking*

■ Bias—Some destructive elements are created by the listener. One major element is prejudice. If you do not like what the person is saying, the natural tendency is to stop listening or to argue. Avoid jumping to conclusions. It is better to continue listening with an open mind. If you receive the entire message, you can respond more effectively.

Another destructive element is self-importance. You might not think you have time to listen. In this case, be honest about your time limits instead of becoming uptight. Sometimes, you are only waiting for a chance to talk. Wait for the other person to complete the message. Also, if you lack interest in the subject, your mind starts to wander. A person can listen three times faster than the other person can speak. The listener needs to use this extra time to evaluate the message and think ahead to what the speaker might say next. Prejudice, conceit, and lack of interest are all barriers to effective listening because you are not paying attention to the other person.

THE DIFFERENCE BETWEEN LISTENING AND HEARING

Listening and hearing are not the same. Of course, individuals cannot decode sounds that they cannot hear.

Hearing is the physical process of detecting sound. Hearing is the first step of listening. It is the physical condition of the auditory organs of a person to detect sounds. Sometimes, people have impairments that keep them from hearing. Fortunately, most people have normal hearing.

In general, the listener hears only 70 percent of the message and remembers only 50 percent or less. "It goes in one ear and out the other." This is a popular phrase used to describe a person as hearing the words, but not listening to the meaning.

Listening is an active process requiring hearing, concentration, assimilation, understanding, and remembering. Here are some pointers on improving the listening process:

- Receive—Receiving information begins with paying attention to the speaker. Concentrate on what is being said. Consciously focus on hearing the message.

- Interpret—Put the message into a form you can understand in your own words. What did the speaker really say? Try to avoid bias and always consider the speaker's background. The codes are selected based on the education, experiences, and culture of the speaker.

- Evaluate—In your own mind, carefully consider the message. Do you feel that you understand what the speaker is saying? Fortunately, you can respond to the speaker with questions or statements that show your understanding of the message.

- Respond—Provide feedback to let the speaker know you are listening and understanding. This is a chance to ask questions and clarify the message.

You can only be an effective listener if you can understand and remember the message. Your goal is to receive, interpret, evaluate, and respond to the complete message.

LISTENING SKILLS

Good listening habits take time to develop. Listening is a major part of everyone's daily life. It should not be a difficult skill to learn. However, it is a good idea to evaluate your listening skills. Determine how many of the following listening tips you put into practice.

Develop a habit of listening:

- Get ready to listen
  - ⇨ Stop talking (You cannot listen if you are talking.)
  - ⇨ Remove distractions

- Listen to understand
  - ⇨ Do not worry about what you are going to say next
  - ⇨ Ask questions
  - ⇨ Pay attention to nonverbal communication
  - ⇨ Repeat the message

- Control emotions
  - ⇨ Be patient
  - ⇨ Hold your temper
  - ⇨ Avoid argument and criticism

- Be mentally flexible
  - ⇨ Think ahead of the speaker
  - ⇨ Weigh the evidence
  - ⇨ Interpret
  - ⇨ Relate the message to similar experiences

9-6. Listening is a major part of daily life.

Asking the right questions helps to clarify points further. Repeating the message is a way of asking the speaker if you understood the message as they intended. Listening to nonverbal communication is important because people speak with the body and the mouth. Body language can tell you if the person is angry, confused, confident, lying, etc.

Controlling emotions prevents confusion. If you become angry with the speaker, you may interpret a different meaning. Be patient, allow the speaker to complete the message and then respond. Releasing your emotions could put the speaker on the defensive and result in communication breakdown.

WRITTEN COMMUNICATION

Writing is an important type of communication. We write for many reasons. It may be on a test, to show that we understand what has been taught. It could be a letter of application to get a job or continue education after high school. Of course, there are many reasons that we write! Written communication serves a primary purpose—to inform.

PLANNING AND ORGANIZING A DOCUMENT

Several kinds of written documents are used. Reports, letters, articles, and forms are frequently used.

Two types of letters are used: business and personal. A business letter may ask about a job, send or request information, or have another purpose. A personal letter is one that we write to a friend or family member.

Whatever we choose to write, it will need planning. Planning involves having a purpose and preparing an outline. In planning, the writer decides what style of writing fits the occasion. In addition, the writer makes decisions on the length and purpose of the correspondence and who will receive it.

Good writing requires an outline of the points you want to present. This will reduce the chance of repeating yourself. Writing should be natural and reflect your personality, regardless of the form. Good reference materials will be needed for technical reports. Never copy the work of another from a book or pamphlet.

9-7. Good writing begins by planning and outlining before starting to write.

DEVELOPING WRITING SKILLS

You can be a good writer! More than anything, a commitment to developing writing skills will be needed. Here are some helpful hints to becoming a more effective writer:

- Keep it simple—Simplicity is the key to communicating with writing.

- Write from an outline—An outline organizes the information.

- Keep the reader in mind—People write to exchange information.

- Be precise—Say exactly what you mean.

- Be concise—Use as few words as possible to convey the information.

- Be informal—Use writing that is to the point.

- Be brief—Get to the point of the information quickly.

- Omit jargon—Avoid slang and "shop talk" that does not communicate well.

- Avoid cliches—Overused and slang phrases detract from writing.

- Reduce redundancies—Avoid using words in a sentence that have the same meaning (example: We combined two departments *into one.*).

- Use simple, short, familiar words—Long words result in writing with a higher reading level.

- Use as few words as possible—Select words that are to the point.

- Avoid exaggeration—Tell the truth in what you write.

- The closing is almost as important as the opening—Have a strong closing in what you write. Make sure to meet all of your objectives.

- Make your writing visually interesting—Limited use of asterisks(*), *italics*, <u>underlining</u>, dashes(—), HEADINGS, SUBHEADINGS, and **bold type.** The use of these should clarify organization and enhance the exchange of information.

- Be your own editor—Quietly criticize your writing to improve it by rewriting and editing.

These hints are for any type of writing. A point to remember is that correct language is critical to effective writing.

WRITING A BUSINESS LETTER AND RÉSUMÉ

Writing letters and résumés takes on many forms and styles. However, all must follow basic guidelines. Some tips on writing letters are: (Refer to Appendix B for résumé information.)

- Use good grammar.
- Use correct spelling (use a dictionary or spellcheck).
- Do not use slang.
- Be brief, but cover the subject.
- Stick to the point of the letter.
- Make the letter readable—written or typed.
- Proofread before sending the letter.
- Ask for help, if needed.

Business letters should efficiently exchange information. Here are a few pointers:

⇨ Keep the letter brief—discuss the purpose of the letter.

⇨ Strive for neatness—it portrays your personality.

⇨ Always include a title of respect (Dr., Mr., Ms., etc.).

⇨ Be sure to include a return address and zip code.

Effective letters should perform two basic communication functions:

⇨ Carry a message.

⇨ Project the desired image of the writer or business.

Business letters can differ in style. There are two standard styles:

⇨ Block style—Every line in a block-style letter starts on the left margin. There are no indentations in this style.

⇨ Modified block style—The modified block style uses indentations. Each new paragraph is indented. The writer's address and the date begin in the middle of the page and go across. The closing and signature start in the middle as well.

Any business letter should contain some basic points:

▷ The writer's address and the date the letter was written. (This is often known as a heading.)

▷ The name and address of the person to whom the letter is being sent.

▷ The salutation, usually "Dear_____."

▷ The body of the letter.

▷ Complimentary close and signature.

▷ Other parts, sometimes used, include reference initials, enclosure notation, copy (name of another person who is getting a copy of the letter), and postscript.

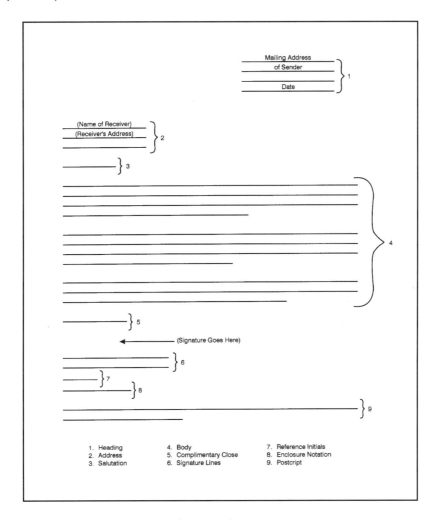

9-8. Parts of a letter.

Writing letters is one of our oldest forms of communication. It allows us to present our ideas, thoughts, and information. Writing serves as a primary recording system for preserving our thoughts for the future. Developing good writing skills is essential to effective communication in all of our lives.

P. O. Box 393
Raymond, MS 39154
February 15, 1998

Mr. James W. Smith
Personnel Manager
Carson-Scott Packing Company
15 Windham Road
Columbus, MS 39701

Dear Mr. Smith:

Please accept this as a letter of application for the position of assistant cattle buyer with Carson-Scott Packing Company. Ms. Pamela Jenkins, agrimarketing instructor at Hinds Community College, indicated that your company would be filling the position later this spring. I feel that I have the education and experience for the position.

In May of this year, I will complete the Agrimarketing Technology Program at Hinds Community College. I have considerable emphasis in livestock marketing and management. As you may know, my college has a beef cattle performance testing program for producers in the area. Students gain practical experience in their classes by using the facilities for teaching. My grade point average is currently 3.4 out of a possible 4.0.

In addition to my education, I have worked part-time for a local cattle company after school hours and during the summer while in college and high school. More information about my qualifications is presented on the enclosed personal data sheet.

My education, experience, and sincere interest in working as an assistant cattle buyer are reasons I believe I have the necessary qualifications for the position at Carson-Scott Packing Company.

I would be pleased to meet with you at your convenience to discuss my qualifications in more detail. I can be reached at 800-555-6103 during the evening hours.

Sincerely,

Susan Ann Sloan

9-9. Sample letter of application for a job.

REVIEWING

MAIN IDEAS

Communication is the process of exchanging information. It involves a sender, a message, a channel, and a receiver. Feedback is used to evaluate the effectiveness of the communication process. Noise sometimes interferes with communication.

The sender must select codes that the intended receiver can decode. If not, the communication process will not effectively occur.

Receivers have a responsibility to decode the message. They need to concentrate on the decoding if the communication process is to be effective. Listening is a key element in oral communication.

Letters, reports, and other written documents are important in our culture. Good communication skills are needed to prepare written documents. People can develop good writing skills if they dedicate themselves to doing so.

QUESTIONS

Answer the questions using complete sentences and correct spelling.

1. Describe the communication process.

2. Why is effective communication difficult to achieve?

3. How does a leader achieve total communication?

4. What is required for feedback to be effective?

5. What are three barriers to communication and how would you overcome them?

6. What are three poor listening habits that prevent you from receiving the entire message?

7. What are the four main tips to develop a habit of good listening?

EVALUATING

CHAPTER SELF-CHECK

Match the term with the correct definition. Write the letter by the term in the blank provided.

a. communication   d. message   g. source
b. semantics   e. hearing   h. feedback
c. channel   f. receiver

1. ____ return channel from receiver to sender that allows the evaluation of communication.
2. ____ initiator of message.
3. ____ codes or symbols used to convey information.
4. ____ interpreter of message.
5. ____ the process of exchanging information.
6. ____ linkage between the sender and receiver.
7. ____ concept of the same words having different meanings.
8. ____ physical process of detecting sound.

EXPLORING

1. Assess your communication skills. List your strengths and weaknesses. Develop a plan to improve areas of weakness.

2. Write a sample business letter to a fictional employer about a job in an area that interests you. Select a job title before you begin to write. Stress your qualifications for the job. Use either the block or modified-block form. Have your teacher critique your letter and rewrite it to improve your chances of getting the job should it actually exist.

3. Explain a difficult process to a friend or family member. Have them repeat the process back to you. Assess how well you communicated.

4. Organize a small group discussion on litter in the local community. Develop a plan of action to prevent litter and clean up areas that have been littered. Write a brief summary of how you feel your group communicated.

5. Role play answering the telephone in class. Critique the role play and make a conscious effort to improve your answering techniques.

6. Prepare a résumé following the example shown in Appendix B. Get suggestions for improvement from your teacher.

10

NON-VERBAL COMMUNICATION

> *Your actions speak louder than your words.*
> **Anonymous**

Animals communicate in various ways. Dogs wag their tails, growl, and bark; cats purr, meow, and hiss. What about humans? They communicate through both verbal and non-verbal means.

Did you know that as you are reading this you are communicating? How are you sitting? What are you wearing? We are constantly sending messages to others around us, even though we may not do so intentionally.

Look at people around you. Note the different expressions on their faces and the different postures. You will see much non-verbal communication.

10-1. Body posture and facial expressions non-verbally communicate. (Courtesy, Mississippi Governor's School)

OBJECTIVES

This chapter is about the ways we communicate non-verbally. It has the following objectives:

1. Describe non-verbal communication

2. Explain the various types of non-verbal communication

3. Describe the powerful effects of non-verbal communication

4. Demonstrate positive modes of non-verbal communication

TERMS

action language

context

gesture

non-verbal communication

non-verbal cues

object language

paralanguage

personal comfort bubble

sign language

IT'S WHAT YOU DIDN'T SAY

We are all aware of the power of words in the communication process. The last chapter focused on the importance of the written and spoken word. Sometimes, however, what we do not say sends an even stronger message.

Non-verbal communication is exchanging information without the use of words. As with other types of communication, non-verbal communication requires a sender, a receiver, a message, and a medium. Unlike other forms of communication, however, with non-verbal communication, the sender may not be aware that a message is being sent.

Have you ever had someone ask you, "What's wrong?" without your ever having said a word. Chances are, you were sending information about your emotional state through non-verbal cues.

Non-verbal cues are the signals we use to tell others about our emotional state, our attitudes, and information about ourselves. We also use them to provide others with feedback. When someone tells you a joke and you laugh, you are providing that person with feedback. Through the non-verbal cue of laughter, you are letting the joke teller know your attitude about the joke.

Non-verbal cues can be used in other ways, too. In the performing arts, they are used to add meaning to a story. Mimes use non-verbal cues exclusively to tell a story. They never speak a word, but those who watch a mime's performance have little trouble understanding the meaning they are trying to convey.

TYPES OF NON-VERBAL CUES

There are four major forms of non-verbal cues: sign language, action language, object language, and paralanguage. Within these forms are many types of cues. Let's first look at the major forms.

Sign language includes those forms of communication that take the place of spoken words. This includes things such as head movements, shoulder shrugs, and salutes. Nodding your head to show agreement or shaking your head to show disagreement is an example of sign language.

10-2. Performers often rely on non-verbal cues to tell a story.

Actions or body movements that transmit meaning, even if they are not specifically intended to do so, are known as *action language*. Walking rapidly down the hallway can say, "I'm late and in a big hurry!" Staring into space can signal a lack of attention.

Paralanguage is the vocal sound that influences the expression of spoken words. Volume, tone, and pitch are elements of paralanguage.

10-3. This animal trainer communicates non-verbally with a seal at the Honolulu Aquarium.

Finally, **object language** includes the physical items that convey messages. Furniture, clothes, jewelry, and other possessions are elements of object language. Designer labels on jeans, shirts, and shoes are examples of object language.

INTERPRETING NON-VERBAL CUES

Non-verbal cues can send many different messages. There are cultural and contextual factors in both the messages we send and the messages we receive.

We should be aware of the non-verbal cues we send because problems in communication are often the result of differences in how non-verbal signals are used. This can lead to misunderstandings. Education and training on the use of non-verbal communication in your own culture, as well as that of other ethnic and cultural groups, are important in avoiding misunderstandings. Also, if you are traveling to a foreign country, it is a good idea to read a book on that country's customs. This could make you aware of any gestures that might be offensive and help you avoid unnecessary embarrassment.

10-4. Can you identify the messages in these facial expressions?

Cultural Variations

There is a great deal of research on cultural differences and similarities in the meaning of non-verbal cues. For example, there is a great deal of similarity in the meaning of facial expressions across cultures. However, the degree of facial expression varies. Japanese culture is more restrained. Therefore, the degree of facial expression by an individual from that culture is less than that of an American. Figure 10-4 shows some common facial expressions.

Gestures are more complex than facial expressions. For example, cues, such as shoulder shrugs, clapping, pointing, and waving the hand, share a similar meaning across many cultures. Conversely, there are gestures that are similar, but whose meanings are different. Sticking out the tongue can mean many different things, most of them unrelated.

There are also gestures used in some cultures that have no meaning in others. For instance, some cultures use gestures in conjunction with speech to communicate. In Italy, a number of hand signals are used that have no meaning to most of us in the United States.

Context

The message of non-verbal cues also varies in relation to timing and other contextual signals. **Context** refers to all of the things in the environment that help determine the meaning of a cue. Social setting, familiarity between those involved, and timing are some examples.

10-5. This couple walking on the beach is non-verbally showing their affection.

Consider the following example. A kiss on the cheek can have many different meanings. Accurate interpretation depends on who it is you are kissing, where the kiss takes place, and the time at which it takes place. Kissing your parent on the cheek as you are leaving home to go to school is a way of saying, "Goodbye." Kissing your girlfriend or boyfriend on the cheek is a sign of affection. Both of these are acceptable uses of the same gesture. However, it is unacceptable to stop total strangers as you pass on the street and kiss them on the cheek. Without the contextual cues, accurate interpretation would be impossible.

SPECIFIC CUES

The following are some of the more commonly analyzed non-verbal cues and their general interpretations. Remember, however, that cultural differences may exist. Table 10-1 provides information on the cultural variation in non-verbal communication.

Table 10-1.
Cultural Differences in Non-Verbal Cues

EYE CONTACT

European American	generally prefer direct eye contact; seen as a sign of confidence and respect
African American	adults usually use a direct gaze; children may not out of respect for the adult; often interpreted as a desire to ask a question; looking away is seen as a "thinking" response, not one of disinterest
Native American	direct eye contact is seen as intrusive and often not made out of respect for the party with whom they are speaking; maintaining direct eye contact may be seen as rude or even hostile
Asian American	inappropriate, or even shameful, especially in formal settings and between individuals who do not know each other well; gaze is often cast downward, especially by children, as a sign of respect
Hispanic American	contact is acceptable for most; however, prolonged contact may be disrespectful; interrupted gaze is very common

DISTANCE

European American	personal space distance is usually about 20 to 36 inches; closer if conversation is intimate; distance is a sign of respect and, possibly, power
African American	often sends contradictory message; on one hand, prefer closeness to transmit emotions, on the other hand, need more space because of tendency to use body movements when speaking; acceptable personal space is usually about 6 to 12 inches
Native American	do not need to be face-to-face when conversing; often do so side by side; personal space of 2 to 3 feet; individual wishing to speak may just enter a person's line of vision and wait to be recognized
Asian American	prefer a more formal distance; personal space greater than that of European Americans; closeness of family members at home is acceptable
Hispanic American	conversation distance 6 to 8 inches less than that of European Americans, closer distances reserved for family or others of the culture; conversation commonly takes place side-by-side instead of face-to-face

(Continued)

Table 10-1 (Continued)

TOUCH

European American	handshake is acceptable formal form of touching; familiarity may be shown as a hug, maybe a kiss on the cheek, among women; hugs between men becoming more acceptable, more often a slap on the back is the greeting; older children and adults do not touch unless they are family or close friends
African American	reciprocity is the key; if one touches another, it then becomes okay for the touch to be returned; touching of the hair, or other subservient-type touches, are unacceptable; touching on the shoulder, back, arms, and hands usually reserved for adult, intimate relationships; however, among school-aged children it is also accepted
Native American	public displays of affection are rare; handshakes are done by gently clasping hands; more intense handshakes may be seen as disrespectful; children are encouraged by gentle hugs and touches
Asian American	prefer not to shake hands; touching of strangers is inappropriate; friends of the same sex can hold hands, but men and women do not in public; a slight bow or clasping of hands in front of the chest is an appropriate greeting; pats on the head are very offensive as the head is considered sacred by many
Hispanic American	embracing and kissing on the cheek is a common greeting, especially among those within the culture; usually touch friends and relatives with whom they are talking

Note: These are general non-verbal differences that tend to be present.

Eye Contact

Eye contact is useful for letting someone know you are paying attention to them. If you look at a person when they are speaking to you, it lets them know you are interested in what they are saying. Looking down or away can be viewed as a sign of disinterest, boredom, or shyness.

Eye contact can also be used by the person sending a message. When speakers make eye contact with listeners, they are demonstrating their self-confidence and honesty. They are also conveying that they are knowledgeable and interested in what they have to say. When the President delivers a speech on television, notice how he looks directly into the camera. That is because he knows viewers are looking directly at him on their television sets. He wants the people watching to believe in what he is saying.

Other aspects of eye contact, such as the amount of eye opening and pupil expansion, have also been identified as non-verbal cues. Research has found that when a person meets another person they are attracted to, the pupils dilate or expand. Unlike other forms of eye contact, these physiological responses are beyond the control of the sender.

10-6. Important eye contact is obviously occurring here.

Facial Expressions

The mouth, eyebrows, skin, and facial muscles work together to create non-verbal cues. Smiles and relaxed facial muscles send an entirely different message from the one sent by raised eyebrows, a wrinkled forehead, and a frown. Who would you rather approach—a clerk in a store who is smiling, or one who is frowning and whose forehead is wrinkled? Even though we do not know either of them, most of us would rather approach the smiling clerk. Why? Probably because the messages we are receiving are much more pleasant and welcoming than those being sent by the other clerk.

We make countless facial expressions every day. When you sense an unpleasant odor, your nose probably wrinkles. If someone is telling you something you do not believe to be true, you might roll your eyes. All day, every day, your facial expressions are providing others with information about you.

Distance

The distance between senders and receivers is another way we communicate non-verbally. There are acceptable distances between the speaker and listener, depending on the social situation.

Research has determined a comfortable distance for personal conversation to be 2 to 4 feet. This is sometimes referred to as a ***personal comfort bubble***. Think of it as an invisible bubble surrounding your body. When someone stands closer to you than this, thus violating your bubble, you will likely notice it and feel uncomfortable.

As the level of intimacy decreases, the acceptable distance increases. The less familiar you are with a person, or the less personal the situation, the greater the acceptable distance. For formal meetings, the acceptable distance is 4 to 8 feet, and for public speaking events, 12 or more feet is best.

During the course of your day, test these distances. When you are speaking with a friend, notice how far apart the two of you are. How far away does the teacher stand from the students on the front row in the classroom? During assembly, how far is the podium from the first row of the audience?

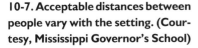

10-7. Acceptable distances between people vary with the setting. (Courtesy, Mississippi Governor's School)

Tone of Voice

Can you remember a time when you were trying to tell someone about something and you were really excited? You probably talked faster and louder, and the pitch of your voice was probably higher than normal. This, too, is a way of communicating non-verbally.

Tone of voice is an especially effective non-verbal cue for relaying emotion. When you are watching your favorite television show, close your eyes and listen to the performers. You should be able to distinguish between various emotions just by the actors' tones of voice.

Appearance

In an earlier chapter, the importance of personal appearance was discussed. Hair, clothing, and personal hygiene are powerful non-verbal cues. They are the first elements of communication in any face-to-face encounter.

When overdone to the point of being meticulous, these things can signal obsessiveness. A casual observer might describe someone like this as stiff, stuffy, and vain. The other extreme can signal depression. Messy hair, torn or stained clothing, and poor hygiene communicate a lack of concern for one's own self.

Other appearance-related cues include clothes that are inappropriate for one's age, outdated, or outrageous or attention-getting. These can be clues about a person's self-image.

10-8. Posture is another form of non-verbal communication.

Body Movements

There are many body movements, or **gestures,** used to communicate non-verbally. Finger pointing, head nodding or shaking, posture, clapping, and hand waving are just a few. How many others can you think of?

Gestures can be used to add emphasis to verbal communication. A teacher might point to a location on the map or to a word on the board while delivering a lesson. These gestures are used to emphasize the information that was also being delivered orally. Too many gestures, however, can be annoying and distracting.

Twisting your hair around your finger, biting your finger nails, strumming your fingers on the table, and slouching in your chair are negative cues. They can indicate nervousness or boredom. However, an erect posture, open arms, and feet on the floor are indicators of interest and comfort. When you are in class, what messages do you send through body movements?

Other Non-verbal Cues

Laughing, coughing, and yawning are non-verbal cues that do not fit well into any of the above categories. The meanings of these cues are dependent upon other cues present in the environment. For example, yawning can show both boredom and tiredness. The meaning depends on where you are and what you are doing.

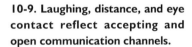
10-9. Laughing, distance, and eye contact reflect accepting and open communication channels.

AVOID GENERALIZATIONS

When dealing with people, there are no absolutes. Remember, every person is an individual, so there will be exceptions. Non-verbal cues should be seen as tools to use when interacting with others. Alone, they can be misinterpreted. Always remember to consider the other factors mentioned in this chapter.

Table 10-2.
Common Non-Verbal Cues and Their Meanings

CUES	MEANING
open hands, unbuttoned jacket	openness
arms crossed at chest, crossed legs, fist-like gestures, pointing index finger	defensiveness
hands to face, tilted head, chin stroking, peering over glasses, playing with glasses, cleaning glasses, hand to nose	evaluating
crossed arms, sideways glance, touching/rubbing nose, rubbing eyes, buttoned jacket, pulling away	suspicion
flesh pinching, pen chewing, thumb over thumb, nail biting, hands in pockets	insecurity
open hands, leaning forward, sitting on edge of chair, hands to face gestures, unbuttoning jacket	cooperation
hands behind back, steepled hands, stiffened back, hands on jacket lapels, hands in jacket pockets with thumbs out	confidence
throat clearing, "whewing," whistling, flesh pinching, fidgeting, hand over mouth, money or key jiggling, ear pulling, hand wringing	nervousness
short breathing, "tsking," clenching hands tightly, hand wringing, fist-like gestures, pointing with index finger, rubbing hands through hair, rubbing back of neck	frustration
uneven voice intonation, hand wringing, poor body posture, failure to make eye contact	depression/stress warning signal
reduction in gestures, sitting sideways in a chair, monotone voice or reduction in inflection, reduction in eye contact, widening of the eyes, slight hint of a smile	dishonesty

Source: The Book of Secrets (1991)

REVIEWING

MAIN IDEAS

Non-verbal cues are a powerful part of communication. We use them to provide others with feedback and also to make others aware of our emotional state, our attitudes, and information about ourselves.

Eye contact, facial expressions, distance, tone of voice, appearance, and body movements are all forms of non-verbal cues. Accurate interpretation of these cues relies on cultural information and other contextual cues. Education helps us become aware of non-verbal cues and their messages. It can also help us avoid misunderstandings.

QUESTIONS

Answer the questions using correct spelling and complete sentences.

1. Define non-verbal cues. List three types and give an example of each.

2. What is the relationship between intimacy and distance?

3. In what way does culture affect non-verbal cues?

4. What is context? What is the relationship between context and non-verbal cues?

5. Explain how **you** would use each of the major types of non-verbal cues in a job interview.

EVALUATING

CHAPTER SELF-CHECK

Match the term with the correct definition. Write the letter by the term in the blank provided.

a. context
b. gesture

c. non-verbal communication
d. non-verbal cues

e. personal comfort bubble

1. _____ signals we use to tell others about ourselves.

2. _____ body movements used to communicate with others.

3. _____ imaginary space around the body that defines the acceptable distance for conversation.

4. _____ all of the things in the environment we use in understanding non-verbal cues.

5. _____ giving or exchanging information without the use of words.

EXPLORING

1. Videotape yourself having a conversation with someone. When you play it back, make a note of the non-verbal cues you use. Are your messages positive? Do you use any annoying gestures?

2. Research the customs of another country or another culture in this country. Note the similarities and differences between it and your culture. Share your findings with the class and compare them with those of your classmates.

3. With the sound turned off, watch 30 minutes of a movie video you have never seen. Pay attention to non-verbal cues. Make notes about what information you think the actors are trying to convey? Play the video again, with sound. How accurate were you?

11

DEVELOPING PEOPLE SKILLS

> *Look at things from the other person's perspective. Give honest and sincere appreciation. Become genuinely interested in the other side.* **Dale Carnegie**

Our world has people with many differences. These differences are placed to good use by a capable leader. This is the main reason that developing "people skills" is important.

Having people skills is not just the responsibility of a leader. It is the responsibility of everyone. Part of developing people skills is learning to work with others. Daily living and work routines often, unfortunately, have conflict. Some conflict is too often a part of human life!

How do you identify your own abilities related to people skills? People skills have a major role in leadership and personal development. A definite need exists for developing people skills.

11-1. Many different "people skills" are found in large crowds.

OBJECTIVES

This chapter deals with identifying and developing important traits to relate to other people successfully. It has the following objectives:

1. Describe the importance of developing people skills
2. Recognize personality styles in people
3. Identify positive characteristics to uphold when working with people
4. Explain how to deal with personal conflict

TERMS

compromiser
contributor
cooperation
distractor
dominator
elaborator
encourager
information-giver
information-seeker
integrator
manipulator
no-show
opinion-giver
opinion-seeker
people skills
personality
personal conflict
protestor
recognition-seeker

IMPORTANCE OF PEOPLE SKILLS

People skills are important abilities to get along with other people and help them work together. Having these skills helps people in being leaders. It earns them respect from other people.

Important traits that show people skills are:

⇨ respecting other people

⇨ being courteous to other people

⇨ using common greetings, such as "thank you," "excuse me," and "good morning"

⇨ commending other people when they have done well

⇨ seeking the advice of other people

⇨ recognizing different personality types

⇨ communicating effectively

⇨ criticizing carefully

⇨ helping people feel good about themselves

⇨ allowing other people to help make decisions

⇨ considering the situations and needs of others—empathy

⇨ using good nonverbal communication toward other people

PEOPLE SKILLS IN LEADERSHIP ROLES

People skills, when used properly, will help in developing realistic and inspiring leadership roles. Developing people skills will help in bringing forth cooperation, dedication, and commitment from others.

People skills are helpful in organizations, especially when an individual assumes a leadership role. Practicing appropriate people skills helps unite members in an organization. When members are united with a common binding thread, they work better together. Members in an organization will then select a worthy cause to work toward.

People skills help everyone communicate better. Communication gives us basic tools necessary for leadership. People skills help us connect actions and ideas with others to achieve day-to-day goals.

Increasing our people skills will help us reach out to others. Positive interaction between people is very important. A leader of an organization

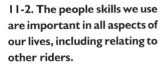
11-2. The people skills we use are important in all aspects of our lives, including relating to other riders.

needs the assistance of others. This is how organizations make a difference. For a leader to get assistance, people skills are needed. Respect for the leader is a necessary ingredient as well.

People are often faced with challenges and changes. It is at this time that people skills are most critical. Through people skills, positive decisions can be made. People skills also allow for active growth within individuals and organizations. Through active growth, positive contributions can be made to society.

People skills help everyone direct their energy and enthusiasm in a positive direction. An identified work project usually has an identified direction. People working together, with people skills, can produce outstanding results. People skills help us to share the work load and lead to greater success. You may have heard the saying, "No one can do everything, but everyone can do something." Properly applied, people skills can help others recognize this fact. Once this is recognized, everyone can work together more easily.

People skills must be used properly. Using them to manipulate other people is the wrong use. A big difference exists between being a leader and being a manipulator (managing for one's own purpose). Being a leader is the positive position to carry in people management. It is through the leadership role where the goal is to motivate people for the common good. A leader recognizes each individual for their contributions, skills, and abilities. A leader works to create an atmosphere of respect, kindness, and willingness to "do your best." A ***manipulator*** is one that uses people for their own selfish reasons. This is definitely an avenue to avoid as it would lead to unhappiness and failure.

People skills help build productive results. Productive results are built up best through a process of small wins.

11-3. Developing people skills requires effort.

PEOPLE SKILLS REQUIRE TIME AND EFFORT

Developing people skills does not happen instantly. It is a molding process that develops through time. Time is needed to practice skills, work with people, and get education and training. Job experiences and assignments are great ways to develop and mold people skills.

Broadening your own people skills helps build a solid foundation. A solid foundation is necessary for leadership position assignments.

Developing people skills requires commitment. A person must practice people skills. If we practice them enough, they become routine to us. We then use people skills without any thought or effort. They are automatic.

PERSONALITY STYLES

Personality can be defined as a collection of a person's distinctive, individual qualities. Personality is the way a person thinks, functions, and relates to others. Everyone has traits that make up his or her personality.

Some people are cautious, while others are carefree. Some people can be described as spontaneous and daring.

Each personality style has distinctive characteristics. In any given group of people you may find one or all of the following types of personalities.

- Dominator—A **dominator** is one who dominates the group. This type of person likes to control the group and set the rules.

- Compromiser—A **compromiser** tries to see all sides of an issue. Each side usually has merit. A compromising person likes to have both parties meet half way in a dispute.

- Follower—A follower is one who watches and listens and usually goes along with the rest of the group. All leaders need followers. Without followers, there is no leader. Roles may reverse in different groups. In some situations, leaders are followers, while followers become leaders in other situations.

- Protestor—A **protestor** is one who protests. This type of person speaks out strongly against an issue. Protesting may be done out of habit or for logical reasons.

- Encourager—Most groups have an **encourager**. In practice, groups benefit by having an encourager. Encouragers are people who give courage, hope, confidence, and support to the rest of the members of the group.

- Integrator—Some groups may have an *integrator* among them. An integrator is a person who removes barriers. They try to bring separate ideas together to help form a major goal or plan.

- Contributor—An organization may include a *contributor*. A contributor likes to share information and initiate projects. They contribute whenever they can.

- Opinion-seeker—*Opinion-seekers* are also found in organizations. They often seek opinions of others. They like to get other people's opinions. Sometimes, they may even seek the opinion of an expert.

- Opinion-giver—*Opinion-givers* are the opposite of opinion-seekers. Opinion-givers are constantly providing their own opinion on every matter or issue that arises.

- Information-seeker—There are also those people whose personality represents that of an *information-seeker*. They seek out facts and information. They want to make informed decisions.

- Information-giver—*Information-givers* are those who always have answers to questions. They have information that can help solve problems in groups. Their information should always be assessed for accuracy.

- Elaborator—Groups can have *elaborators*. An elaborator is one who wants to see every project plan in complete detail. This type of person may also elaborate on every issue with the smallest of details.

- Recognition-seeker—A *recognition-seeker* is an individual who always seeks recognition. They want to be recognized for any and all contributions made or goals achieved. They want to be recognized for any contribution, no matter how large or small.

- Distractor—There are those who may be described as a *distractor*. They want attention, so they sometimes do silly or foolish things to attract attention.

- No-show—Unfortunately, some individuals may be described as *no-shows*. They do not show up for any events or activities of the group or organization. They may prefer to be left alone.

Leadership is a people-oriented task. Wide variation exists in the way people act. A leader works with others to seek a common goal or purpose.

When a leader interacts and uses positive people skills, positive results will be produced.

A true leader makes everyone feel like they belong to a group. Everyone has positive contributions to provide to an organization. A leader needs to strive to bring out the positive, distinctive qualities from all members. A good leader works with people. A leader recognizes everyone for who they are and what they contribute. Gaining people skills allows a group to be people-focused and have a positive outcome.

POSITIVE CHARACTERISTICS

Working with people successfully requires positive characteristics. Identifying traits or qualities helps improve people skills. Leaders practice a variety of positive characteristics when working with people.

BEING COOPERATIVE

Being cooperative is an essential characteristic. **Cooperation** means recognizing that everyone contributes to the success of a project. Being cooperative means working and helping others to be successful in their work.

RESPECTING AUTHORITY

Recognizing and respecting authority is an important characteristic. Those in authority need to be recognized for their experience and knowledge. People in authority have earned their position through their own merits. Relationships with those in authority are healthier when respect is the basis.

11-4. Cooperation is needed to get jobs done, such as carrying a package.

Respect for authority also extends to older people with experience. Older people have valuable insight that can help younger people succeed.

HANDLING CRITICISM

The ability to handle criticism is another positive characteristic. Use the suggestions of other people to help improve and develop personal skills. Look at criticism as a helpful form of review. There is always room for improvement. Constructive criticism may help point out those areas that need improvement. Workers improve their performance when criticized constructively.

Be careful when you criticize people. They may not appreciate what you have to say. Carefully select how the criticism is offered. Criticism is best provided in private. Remember, "praise in public and criticize in private." (Constructive criticism is covered in Chapter 14.)

DOING QUALITY WORK

Doing a job well is important when working with others. When people work with others, good job habits are easy to see. Often, people observe others and decide to improve their own work skills. We may not always realize those times when we are setting an example for others to follow.

11-5. Doing a job right is important. Planting a tree so it lives requires following the proper procedures.

BEING ENTHUSIASTIC

Being enthusiastic and having a sense of humor are helpful characteristics. People's attitudes impact the working environment. Help build a cheerful and pleasant environment by maintaining these characteristics.

BEING FLEXIBLE

Being flexible, within limits, is a beneficial characteristic. People need to be open to change. Extra hours or resources are often needed to get the job done. Being flexible may very well help meet the goal. People want to avoid getting "set in their ways."

OFFERING COMPLIMENTS

Remember to be complimentary toward others. Being complimentary makes you a more enjoyable person with whom to work. It also helps build a positive working environment. It is always in order to commend people on their work. A simple "I'm proud of you" goes a long way.

ASSESSING YOURSELF

People need to carefully examine their own characteristics. When people uphold positive characteristics while working with others, success will follow. Self-assessment helps identify our strengths and weaknesses. It helps us know the areas where we need to improve.

11-6. Complimenting another person is an important part of people skills.

PERSONAL CONFLICT

People are different. No two people are alike. These differences sometimes result in conflict.

Personal conflict is a difference between people that disrupts and impairs the achievement of goals. Personal conflict is often based on a difference of opinion that interferes with people working together.

Knowing how to deal with personal conflict is an important trait of a leader and a follower. Preventing conflict before it happens is best.

Poor communication is often the source of conflict. When people fail to communicate clearly, a common understanding does not exist. Work on communication skills and sharing your own feelings. Remember to communicate through an informative conversation to prevent and clear up conflicts.

Low self-esteem can also be a cause of conflict. If people are ignored, when they should be recognized, low self-esteem arises and conflict develops. Reinforce other people's self-esteem with compliments to help reduce conflicts. If conflict does arise from lack of recognition, create a new form of recognition for that person. Continue to recognize them even when they are not expecting it. Doing this will help create a wholesome self-image, which is a healthy self-image.

11-7. Personal conflicts may involve emotion that is out of control.

Personal conflicts can also arise from stress and stressful environments. Learn to recognize symptoms of stress and stressful environments. Recognizing these will help you select appropriate actions that may help in reducing conflicting situations. If conflicts arise because of stress, allow the other person time to "cool off." Then discuss the conflict and work out an appropriate solution.

Making poor choices can create conflict. This is why decision-making is a helpful tool throughout life. No one likes to make a poor choice, but, when it happens, handle the situation with care. Conflict is not always the result of another person's actions or attitudes; it may result from a poor company choice. Recognize the primary cause of conflict.

Conflicts also stem from holding grudges. Holding a grudge is neither wise nor healthy for a person. Holding resentment toward another person does not solve the problem or the conflict. It will only create more conflict. Pardon the person or situation and concentrate on working together to create a workable solution.

People need to work on being part of solutions, not a prevention to solutions. Conflicts are not avoidable, but they can be manageable. Be thoughtful and considerate as you work with others to prevent and to heal conflicts. When working through conflicts, think of past resolved conflicts and what helped resolve the conflict. Everyone can work on preventing conflicts and resolving those conflicts that do arise. Resolve conflicts in a calm and reasonable manner.

REVIEWING

MAIN IDEAS

Our world is full of diverse types of people. This makes having good people skills essential. People skills are learning to work with others and recognizing different personalities. People skills are based on communicating effectively, criticizing carefully, and reinforcing reverently.

People skills are important for several reasons. Developing these skills yields realistic and inspiring leaders. People skills help organizations by encouraging teamwork and achieving tasks. People skills direct energy and enthusiasm in a positive direction to create productive results.

Personality can be described as the way a person functions and relates to others. When a group of people is working together, you can probably recognize the following personality types: dominator, compromiser, follower, protestor, encourager, integrator, contributor, opinion-seeker, opinion-giver, information-seeker, information-giver, elaborator, recognition-seeker, distractor, and no-show. A leader strives to bring out the positive, distinctive qualities from all members.

Positive characteristics to uphold when working with people are: being cooperative, respecting authority, handling criticism, doing quality work, being enthusiastic, having a good sense of humor, being flexible, being complimentary of others, and assessing ourselves.

When interacting with others, conflicts may arise. People need to try to prevent conflicts before they happen. Personal conflicts can be resolved by communicating effectively.

QUESTIONS

Answer the questions using correct spelling and complete sentences.

1. Define "people skills."
2. List three reasons why people skills are important.
3. How do organizations benefit from those who know and understand people skills?
4. List and describe five different personality styles that may be found in a group or organization.
5. What seven positive characteristics should be upheld when working with others?

6. Describe one personal conflict and how it might be resolved.

7. List and describe three methods used to help reduce personal conflict.

EVALUATING

CHAPTER SELF-CHECK

Match the term with the correct definition. Write the letter by the term in the blank provided.

a. personality   d. encourager   g. integrator
b. people skills   e. manipulator   h. compromiser
c. personal conflict   f. dominator

1. _____ likes to control group and set rules.
2. _____ help people get along well together.
3. _____ encourages both parties to meet half way.
4. _____ a disagreement.
5. _____ collection of distinctive individual qualities.
6. _____ uses people for selfish reasons.
7. _____ provides hope and confidence to others.
8. _____ one who works to remove barriers.

EXPLORING

1. Research five former individuals who served as President of the United States. Describe their personalities and how it impacted their presidency.

2. Search your library and create a list of philosophies and quotations related to the topic of "people skills." Write your new found information on a poster board and post it in class to share with others.

3. Write a play that would include roles of the personality styles presented in this chapter. Upon approval of your instructor, act out the play in class. This will provide a better understanding of personality styles and people skills.

4. Use a standardized instrument to help you understand your personality. The Myers-Briggs Type Inventory (MBTI) personality instrument is a good example. Your teacher or counselor can help you with this.

12

KEEPING COMMITMENTS

When you make and keep a commitment, others will notice what you have done. **Sharon Hunter**

Think of an adult whom you admire, whether they are a parent, a teacher, or a famous person. Chances are, you can think of several organizations or activities with which they are involved. Perhaps they coach a ball team, teach a class, raise a child, or are active in a club. They have many commitments.

Over the course of your life, you will make more commitments as you gain additional responsibilities. The process starts when you are young and is a stepping-stone approach. You are gradually given more responsibility as you show you can handle it. You show this by keeping the commitments you make.

12-1. Parents make strong commitments to properly care for their children.

OBJECTIVES

This chapter deals with making and keeping commitments. It has the following objectives:

1. Explain the importance of keeping commitments
2. Describe the process of choosing and prioritizing activities
3. Describe the role of time management in scheduling commitments and some available time management tools

T E R M S

commitment
daily planner
involvement
responsible
time management
to-do checklists
weekly planner

MAKING AND KEEPING COMMITMENTS

As you get older and gain more responsibility, you will make many commitments. Once made, you should strive to always keep your commitments. A commitment should not be made without thought. When you make a **commitment**, you are making a promise to give your time and effort to a group, an activity, or a cause. When you keep a commitment, you are being **responsible**. You are fulfilling your obligations.

When you make and keep a commitment, others will notice what you have done. You will be showing that you are responsible, and you will likely be offered further opportunities for commitment.

Keeping commitments is also an important part of your growth as an individual. Your self-esteem grows each time you accomplish what you set out to do. This, in turn, gives you the confidence necessary to make and keep further, more important commitments.

GETTING INVOLVED

One way to gain experience in leadership is to get involved early in various activities. **Involvement** is being an active participant in an activity or group. Since an important part of being a good leader is knowing how to follow, do not always insist on being at the top.

Being involved, as either a leader or a follower, is valuable experience for future leadership roles. It helps for a leader to know how the details of an organization are carried out, and personal experience is one way to learn these details.

Choosing Activities

Choosing among numerous activities is often difficult. There might be more groups you would like to join than you can realistically expect to have time for. The proverb "Don't bite off more than you can chew" suggests that there are problems associated with trying to do too much. People are not impressed by the member who promises and does not deliver. For instance, trying to perform in the school play and make the track team, when the practices are at the same time, would be "biting off" too much.

Prioritizing

12-2. Setting priorities may involve deciding between going to school or going surfing.

To help you choose, make a list of the activities you are interested in and prioritize them from most important to least important. Next, develop a weekly schedule that shows when each activity takes place. When there is overlap, choose the activity with the highest priority and be willing to say no to the conflicting activity, at least for now.

These activities and the priorities you assign should also tie into your personal goals and vision discussed in earlier chapters. Often a clear vision can bring some order to the task of choosing among activities.

Committing for the Right Reasons

When you voluntarily join a group, you are more likely to sincerely commit if the group's activity is something you are interested in or care about. Joining for the wrong reasons, like trying to impress others or become more popular, often leads to a declining sense of commitment.

A Promise to Others and Yourself

Making a commitment applies to both a promise you make to others and the goals you set for yourself. Both require your integrity to see them through and keep your commitments.

Having integrity means you are honest and do what you say you will do. When you do follow through on your promises and goals, you gain the respect of others and achieve personal satisfaction. You also gain the confidence to take on more responsibility.

Start Small

As a young person making commitments, start small. By making and keeping small commitments, you will build the character and confidence necessary for larger commitments. People will learn that they can count on you when you give your word. They will be willing to offer you greater responsibility in the future.

You might be mowing lawns in the summer, babysitting, or volunteering at the local hospital, but whatever activities you choose, always do your best. Often, you will find that the best jobs are reserved for those who have done some of the "not-so-good" jobs well in the past. People will notice a job done well.

12-3. Look for opportunities to contribute to a group. (Courtesy, Mississippi Governor's School)

BEING AN ACTIVE PARTICIPANT

When you make a commitment to a group or activity, you are promising to be actively involved. If you join a group and never show up for meetings, other group members will gradually lose respect for you.

Being involved means more than being present. Some people go to group meetings and never say a word. They watch the clock, or daydream, and leave when the meeting is over, without having made a contribution of any kind. This is not true, meaningful involvement.

When you are a leader or member of a group, you should be looking for an opportunity to contribute something to the group. Whether it is a new idea about how to accomplish a group objective or volunteering your time to help in a smaller matter, everyone appreciates a member who is involved.

TIME MANAGEMENT

As you choose among activities and consider where to make commitments, time management becomes a useful tool. ***Time management*** is getting productivity out of your time. It includes scheduling your activities so you get them done. Without a way to see how all your activities fit into the day or week, it is more difficult to know beforehand the effects of an additional commitment.

All people have the same amount of time. We all have 60 minutes in an hour, 24 hours in a day, and seven days in a week. It is what we do in the time that makes a difference. Some people know how to get more done.

Today's time management tools emphasize making room on your weekly schedule for things that are important to you. They assist you in prioritizing activities around your personal goals and vision. They center on a weekly schedule instead of a daily one to lend a broader perspective.

12-4. Part of keeping commitments is scheduling your activities so you can get them done.

TO-DO CHECKLISTS AND DAILY PLANNERS

Older, more basic time management tools included to-do checklists and daily planners. **To-do checklists** are simply a list of things you need to accomplish for the day with a place to check them off when completed. Checklists are still popular with many people, as they can provide a sense of accomplishment as activities are checked off.

However, to-do lists are missing an important ingredient. They do not reflect any effort to prioritize tasks to ensure you are accomplishing things important to you and your personal vision. Rather, items are generally an unorganized collection of tasks that have your attention for the moment.

Daily planners add the advantage of seeing all the events for the day and where they fit in time. This feature can at least keep you from scheduling more activities than you have time for.

There are some drawbacks to the daily planner. It provides less perspective than a weekly planner since it reflects only one day's activities.

To Do Checklist

☐ _____
☐ _____
☐ _____
☐ _____
☐ _____
☐ _____
☐ _____
☐ _____
☐ _____
☐ _____
☐ _____
☐ _____

12-5. To-do checklists are designed to help people identify tasks.

Daily Planner for Monday

8:00　am _____

9:00　am _____

10:00　am _____

11:00　am _____

12:00　pm _____

1:00　pm _____

2:00　pm _____

3:00　pm _____

4:00　pm _____

5:00　pm _____

12-6. Daily planners let you see the schedule of events for a day.

Also, people who focus on one day often try to fit as many things as possible efficiently into the day.

The focus on efficiency can often lead to scheduling trivial activities and losing touch with really important matters. A problem with trying to so efficiently use your time is you become a slave to your schedule. When something unexpected gets you off-track, you can be thrown into a frenzy to get back on schedule.

WEEKLY PLANNERS

Weekly planners show a week at a time and usually have a place to show your priorities for the week. By expanding your planning to a weekly basis, you have a much broader overview of your upcoming time. By setting priorities first, you can make sure that the tasks that are important to you get scheduled.

When scheduling the important matters throughout the week, you will probably be surprised at how much time remains unfilled. This extra time adds flexibility to your schedule, because it is nearly certain that unexpected events will occur that may force you to shift items on your schedule or set new priorities.

Experts identify four key activities you should accomplish when organizing your weekly planner. They are:

- Identify areas of your life.

- Set goals for the week.

- Schedule your activities.

- Leave some flexibility daily.

Identify Areas of Your Life

You fulfill several roles in your daily life. For example, you may be a son or daughter at home, a student at school, and a member of a club in your spare time. Each of these areas offers an opportunity for personal growth and development. Within each area, you should have hopes and aspirations and a vision of where you want to be in the future. From this vision you set goals.

Set Goals for the Week

For each area that you identified, think of some results you would like to achieve in the coming week. For example, at school you might have a history test on Thursday, so your short-term goal for the week could be to make an "A" on the test. This should fit into your long-term goals, among which could be making an "A" in history for the semester.

Perhaps you identified your personal fitness as an area of your life to improve. Suppose running is part of your personal fitness program and you have gotten your time for running a mile down to 8:10 during the past month. For your weekly plan, your short-term goal could be to beat 8 minutes in your mile run.

Whatever short-term goals you come up with, they should fit into your larger plan and be prioritized so the most important activities get the most attention. If you prioritize in writing and work these priorities into your schedule, it becomes easier to keep them in mind when unexpected crises pop up.

To begin your weekly planning, determine a few results you would like to achieve in each area of your life during the coming week. Remember, start small so the accomplishment can add to your confidence for setting higher goals the next week.

Scheduling Activities

Once you have set some short-term goals and prioritized, decide what you must do to reach your goals and then schedule these activities.

Try to avoid the tendency to over-schedule. When first using a weekly schedule, some people go too far and try to schedule everything they do, no matter how trivial. This takes away your flexibility and makes it more likely that time conflicts will arise when your hectic schedule gets interrupted. Such interruptions can be discouraging, so start scheduling only relatively important matters for a while.

Leave Daily Flexibility

You will probably end up with lots of unscheduled time. This is good, as it gives you flexibility. You will have time to do things that come up

	Sunday	Monday	Tuesday	Wednesday	Thursday	Friday	Saturday
8:00							
:30							
9:00							
:30							
10:00							
:30							
11:00							
:30							
12:00							
:30							
1:00							
:30							
2:00							
:30							
3:00							
:30							
4:00							
:30							

12-7. Weekly planners let you set priorities for a week.

on the spur of the moment. You will have time to do things you forgot to schedule. You will have time to relax.

Putting It Together

If you follow these scheduling tips, you may find that it becomes possible for you to do more. This is because a weekly planner organizes things for you. There are also other organizing tools you can use to help you accomplish your goals. Some of these are computer organizing programs, notebook organizers, and a diary.

Whatever works best for you is fine. Give several of them a try. For instance, you may find a daily diary helps to remind you of what your goals are by writing down your thoughts every day, or a notebook may help you keep track of many of the details of your daily life. Whichever you choose, make sure that it reflects what is important to you.

12-8. Good planning may allow time for a game of softball in the snow with your friends.

REVIEWING

MAIN IDEAS

A good leader learns to make commitments after giving some thought to the matter. Once committed, a leader is actively involved and always follows through on promises made.

The best way to gain experience is to get involved in new activities. Commit yourself to groups or activities that are important to you. Start with just a few small commitments, and as you succeed with these, you will be offered more opportunities.

Leaders effectively manage their time. Older time management tools emphasized efficient use of daily time, but they often got bogged down in the details. Today's time management tools emphasize setting priorities and using a weekly planner that gives you more perspective.

When organizing on a weekly planner, there are four key activities to accomplish. Identify the roles you assume in your life, set goals for the week in each area you identified, schedule your activities, and leave some daily flexibility for the unexpected.

QUESTIONS

Answer the questions using correct spelling and complete sentences.

1. What are some of the rewards for keeping your commitments? What are some of the consequences for not keeping commitments?

2. What are the benefits of being involved in a team effort as a leader? As a follower?

3. What are the advantages and disadvantages of using to-do lists and daily planners?

4. What advantages does a weekly planner hold over to-do lists and daily planners?

EVALUATING

CHAPTER SELF-CHECK

Match the term with the correct definition. Write the letter by the term in the blank provided.

a. commitment   d. time management   g. weekly planner
b. involvement   e. to-do checklists
c. responsible   f. daily planner

1. _____schedules one day on a page.

2. _____being an active member of a group.

3. _____mastering the scheduling of your activities.

4. _____a promise you make to others or to yourself.

5. _____schedules a week on a page.

6. _____list of things you would like to accomplish.

7. _____keeping your commitments.

EXPLORING

1. Research two or three popular time management computer software programs and choose one to begin using. Many are available free from the Internet or computer user groups. Prepare a report on your findings. Describe the program's features, along with its advantages and disadvantages.

2. Create a weekly planner for your week and schedule all of your activities. Pick at least three areas of your life and set two goals for each during the week. In which areas do you spend the most time? Does your scheduling reflect your personal goals?

3. Interview two adults and ask for their techniques for time management. Compare the two and report your findings to the class.

13

LOYALTY AND OPENNESS

> *You cannot buy loyalty . . . you cannot buy devotion of hearts, minds, and souls. You must earn these.* **Charles Frances**

Loyalty and openness are two characteristics of effective leaders and groups. Both are traits that must be shared within a group for the group to be as effective as possible.

What makes a basketball team a winner? The players share a mutual goal. The team members are loyal and open with each other. They practice and work to learn their plays. They share suggestions with each other on how to work together to win.

Loyalty and openness are important in our personal as well as career life. Developing loyalty and openness is essential for leaders and followers to efficiently reach their goals.

13-1. Loyalty and openness are important in successful groups.

OBJECTIVES

This chapter introduces the importance of loyalty and openness in leadership roles. It has the following objectives:

1. Explain the importance of loyalty and openness

2. Explain why loyalty must go both ways in a leader-follower relationship

3. Describe ways to enhance loyalty and openness within a group

4. Explain the importance of feedback to achieving openness

LOYALTY: A TWO-WAY STREET

Loyalty between leaders and followers is built on mutual trust and respect. It is a two-way street where leaders and group members must trust and respect each other. It is not automatic, and it usually takes time to build.

As a leader, you can provide an atmosphere of trust and loyalty in two important ways. First, you can show others that you trust them and will support them. Second, you must show them that they can trust you.

Loyalty is usually referred to in the sense of being loyal to the leader. However, it is just as important, or more so, for leaders to show that same loyalty to their followers. If leaders stand up for their people when they are challenged, the followers are more likely do the same for the leader when the time comes.

Openness refers to having good communication between members of a group. Many bosses have what they call an **open door policy**, meaning that subordinates can feel free to come see that boss any time. But, openness also means that group members share information with each other to solve tasks as efficiently as possible.

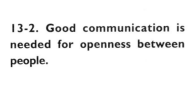

13-2. Good communication is needed for openness between people.

SHOW OTHERS YOU TRUST THEM

There are several ways you can show others you trust them. Probably the most important way is to support and stand behind their decisions and actions whenever possible. You can also delegate responsibility, showing that you trust them with important tasks. Finally, avoid second guessing. Once you have given followers the results you expect, allow them the freedom to make choices about how to accomplish those results.

Support Them

Sometimes, people from outside the group may challenge the actions of one of your members. When possible, you should support your group members. At the very least, you should withhold your judgment until you have heard all sides of the issue. This gives people confidence that you trust them and will treat them fairly.

Delegate

You should delegate tasks that can be accomplished by someone other than yourself. This gives your members a feeling of being valuable to the group.

Delegation is sharing responsibilities with other people. When you delegate, try, as much as possible, to give the member full power to accomplish the task without dictating how the task should be performed.

13-3. Delegation is an important way of encouraging loyalty.

Don't Second Guess

Avoid the tendency to use hindsight to second guess others. If mistakes were made, they should be acknowledged and learned from. But placing blame often leads to group members being afraid to try anything that is the slightest bit risky. Look forward and be positive, and your group members will do the same.

SHOW OTHERS THEY CAN TRUST YOU

There are several ways you can show your followers that they can trust you. First, you must have *integrity*. If you say you will do something, do it. Integrity further implies doing what is right according to your set of values. Next, and closely linked to integrity, is honesty. If you always tell the truth, even when the truth might not help you, people will recognize this and trust you. Finally, you must be responsible. A good leader takes the blame when things go wrong and praises his followers when things go right.

Above all, a leader's personal example will create loyalty or destroy it. Fol-

13-4. Dr. Martin Luther King, Jr., is known as an individual who inspired loyalty among followers.

lowers look to their leader for an example, which they often try to emulate. Make sure they have a positive example to follow.

One example of a leader who inspired loyalty in his followers was Dr. Martin Luther King, Jr. His followers helped him bring about sweeping changes in our country's civil rights laws. He led by example and gave his followers a role model to emulate. Today, we have a national holiday every year on his birthday.

CONFLICTING LOYALTIES

There are also other types of loyalty. You may be loyal to an organization, to a cause, or to a set of values. At times, these other loyalties may conflict with your loyalty to a leader or a group. When *conflicting loyalties* occur, you may be forced to choose among them.

If a leader you felt loyal to asked you to lie, you would have to choose between loyalty to that leader and loyalty to your own value of honesty.

People in the military are loyal to the country in such a way that they are willing to risk their lives to defend it. Workers in a company often feel a loyalty to the company or the people in it. Can you think of several different loyalties you have?

OPENNESS

Openness within a group means that the group and its leader communicate and share information effectively. If people feel comfortable in a group, they will be more likely to be open. In an atmosphere of fear or distrust, people are not as likely to be open with one another.

CREATE AN OPEN ATMOSPHERE

A good leader ensures that the group atmosphere is one that encourages communication between group members and between the group and the leader. Following are several ways you can create this kind of open environment.

Be Informal

The more formal the environment, the more likely people will feel uncomfortable and not risk being open. There are several things that can be done to make the environment more informal. Using first names and allowing casual dress are two examples. Be creative and think of ways you can make your group less formal and promote openness.

Start the Discussion

Sometimes, the hardest thing for the group to do is get the discussion started. Everyone is afraid to be the first one to say something, for fear of saying the wrong thing. As a leader, take the initiative and speak out. Ask questions to get people talking.

To keep people talking, you need to show an active interest in what they are saying. Harsh or sarcastic answers can cause everyone to keep their mouths shut, and communication will come to a standstill. Let others know you are willing to listen.

Ask for Feedback

A good leader always asks for feedback. Feedback allows you to gauge how well the organization is running, how effective your leadership is, and where improvement could be made. Sometimes, asking for it is the only way to get feedback. Followers may feel embarrassed or unsure of what is expected of them and may be reluctant to give you feedback unless you ask for it.

13-5. A good leader asks for feedback.

When you get feedback, do something about it. If group members feel that their remarks are being ignored, they will probably not continue to provide feedback. This does not mean to just verbally thank members for their help, but also to incorporate their suggestions when possible.

American businesses are beginning to rely more than ever on the actual front-line, blue-collar workers for ways to improve processes within their companies. In the past, higher paid, white-collar management employees made decisions, and their subordinates carried them out without input into the design of the process. But today, companies realize these workers are a great, untapped resource. By listening to workers' feedback, companies can expect organizational improvement in the future.

This management style of emphasizing process improvement through front-line employees is part of **Total Quality Management** (TQM). Feedback is a very important part of this management style, both from employees and customers. To get this feedback, companies use numerous techniques, such as questionnaires, suggestion forms, and interviews.

For feedback to be effective, there must be a foundation of trust between leaders and group members and also between members of a group. Only when there is this trust, will all members feel comfortable enough to share feedback with one another.

When you have asked for and received feedback, listen to it carefully. We all have "blind spots" that keep us from seeing certain things about ourselves the way others might. Feedback can help you widen your perspective and see things from a different angle.

Give Constructive Feedback

Criticism can be a good thing, but it is often misused. It can lead to hurt feelings and barriers to effective communication within a group. When giving constructive criticism, or constructive feedback, the emphasis is not on the negative aspects of a person's behavior. Rather, it is a positive way to point out preferable behavior, along with the reasons for the preferred behavior.

Since feedback is necessary to ensure openness in a group environment, the leader must try to ensure that feedback given to the group is always constructive. For more suggestions on how to provide constructive criticism, see chapter 14.

BE RECEPTIVE TO CHANGE

Openness can also refer to having an attitude of being receptive to change, new ideas, and differing opinions. Change is all around us, and a leader must recognize this and be willing to adapt. Continuing to do something that does not seem smart just because "that's the way we've always done it" can lead to an organization's decline. A leader must look at changes and decide what course of action will lead to organizational success in the future.

13-6. A good leader should have an attitude of being receptive to new ideas and differing opinions.

As a leader, you should realize that when people are used to doing things a certain way, they will resist change. Change often makes people feel as if they are being put down for the way they have been performing. It can be a negative experience unless the leader can convince the group members that the change will lead to success. This is known as selling an idea.

As our world changes, innovative people will always come up with new ideas for how to do things better. A good leader must be willing to recognize a good new idea when it is presented. When a group member makes a proposal, listen attentively and give the idea sincere consideration. When group members realize you are receptive to new ideas, they will be more willing to propose them.

Just as change is certain, so is the fact that people will disagree. Good leaders listen to opposing opinions and are willing to change their minds when convinced of a better option. A leader who stifles differing opinions is deprived of potentially valuable information from other group members.

REVIEWING

MAIN IDEAS

Loyalty is a two-way street. Leaders must be loyal to other group members, and the members must be loyal to the leader.

Leaders can do two important things to inspire loyalty. They can show trust for others, and they can show others they can be trusted.

People have other loyalties besides loyalty to a leader. Sometimes these loyalties conflict with one another, and a choice must be made.

An open environment, which reflects the group's ability to communicate, is crucial to success. A leader encourages an open environment by making it as informal as possible and asking for feedback. The leader also provides feedback to the group.

Openness also refers to a willingness to consider change, new ideas, and differing opinions. By being attentive and receptive to differing views, a leader fosters good communication within the group.

QUESTIONS

Answer the questions using correct spelling and complete sentences.

1. How can a leader inspire loyalty in other group members?
2. What things can a leader do to create an environment in which group members will be open?
3. Why is it important that feedback be constructive?

EVALUATING

CHAPTER SELF-CHECK

Match the term with the correct definition. Write the letter by the term in the blank provided.

a. conflicting loyalties   c. integrity   e. openness
b. delegation   d. open door policy f. Total Quality Management

1. _____ an environment of effective communication.
2. _____ a current management philosophy stressing feedback from employees and customers.
3. _____ sharing responsibilities with others.
4. _____ subordinates can see their leader at any time.
5. _____ a situation where one is forced to choose among loyalties.
6. _____ being honest and following through on commitments.

EXPLORING

1. Pick a historical leader whom you admire. In what ways did this leader inspire loyalty in his followers? In what ways did the leader show loyalty to followers? Prepare a short report on your research.

2. Visit a local business and talk to at least one employee. How do the leaders in the organization encourage openness? What kind of feedback are the workers given? Are they asked for their feedback? Report your findings to the class.

3. Assume your school has asked for feedback on how to improve some activity, such as scheduling of lunch periods, grading policies, or a recreation program. In small groups of three or four, pick a school activity and come up with at least three suggestions for improvement. Make sure that your suggestions are constructive.

14

ENCOURAGING OTHERS

> *A leader is best when people . . . after the work is done . . . say we did it ourselves.* **Lao-Tse**

We all like to be around people who are positive. We do not like to be around a person who is always complaining. It is pleasant to talk with a person who is happy and upbeat. Likewise, members of a group or team like to be around a leader or other team member who is positive.

Think about some of the qualities a favorite teacher or fellow teammate possesses. What are they? Do they include things like, "They compliment others" or "They always have something nice to say"? What things do you do that serve as encouragement for others?

14-1. Leaders encourage others in ideals and goals.

183

OBJECTIVES

This chapter focuses on the importance of providing encouragement to others. It has the following objectives:

1. Explain the effects of positive motivation

2. Describe techniques for encouraging others

3. Explain techniques of constructive criticism

TERMS

constructive feedback
competent
extrinsic motivation
intrinsic motivation
motive
personal effectiveness
positive reinforcement
reinforcement
self-determination

POSITIVE MOTIVATION: PROVIDING ENCOURAGEMENT FOR OTHERS

Have you ever wondered why people do the things they do? Why do you study for tests or practice your instrument or sport? *Motives* are what cause people to behave in certain ways. They are the internal forces that direct our conscious behaviors toward satisfying our needs or achieving our goals. They include not only the choice of activity, but also the intensity and persistence at which the activity is pursued.

REINFORCEMENT

Reinforcement is strengthening the responses people give. It is used to cause a person to give the same response in the future or to change their response. Reinforcement is by giving something (reward) or by taking something away (punishment).

Reward is the kind of reinforcement that gives thanks, recognition, or praise when a person does something the way it should be done. It is used to help people feel good about what they have done so they will repeat the behavior in the future. Reward is a type of *positive reinforcement*.

Punishment is used to get people to change their behavior by associating what they do with unpleasant events. Shock from touching an electric fence is punishment that trains animals not to touch the fence. Likewise, people may be punished for not having a desired behavior. Punishment is sometimes said to be negative reinforcement.

MOTIVATION

Motivation is what a leader does to encourage a person or group to work to achieve the organization's objectives while also working to achieve their personal objectives. There are three primary purposes of leadership motivation:

⇨ to encourage potential members to join the group or team.

⇨ to stimulate production or performance by present members.

⇨ to encourage present group or team members to remain.

These purposes are based on two very basic assumptions: First, human behavior is caused; and, second, this behavior is goal directed. Motivation can be extrinsic or intrinsic in nature.

14-2. Receiving a plaque is a form of extrinsic motivation.

Extrinsic Motivation

Extrinsic motivation is motivation that results from the desire to obtain an external reward. These rewards might be tangible in nature, such as money or awards. However, they could also be something intangible, such as praise.

Though tangible rewards have their place and are sometimes useful, care should be exercised when using them. Research has shown that improper use of extrinsic rewards may actually decrease motivation.

Intrinsic Motivation

Intrinsic motivation stems from the inherent desire one has to feel competent and self-fulfilled. It is the development of intrinsic or self-motivation that is the goal.

There are some basic principles of intrinsic motivation of which every leader should be aware. First, everyone has the need to succeed and to develop a positive self-concept. Leaders should use practices that will increase the self-confidence of others and provide them with a sense of personal effectiveness and self-determination.

Personal effectiveness means feeling as if you have a positive impact on the outcome of things you do. If you feel effective, you believe you are capable.

Self-determination means feeling as if you have control over what happens to you. Personal effectiveness is a direct result of self-determination.

A second principle is that everyone has a desire to be competent and to have control over their environment. Outstanding leaders are those who make others feel strong by enabling them to take ownership of, and responsibility for, their successes. When people do things because they want to, not because they are told to, they perform at their best. People who feel weak, unappreciated, and incompetent will not only be less productive, they usually will not stay in that organization or job. They will search for a more positive environment.

No one specific thing motivates every person all of the time. However, as a leader, there are five basic ways you can encourage and strengthen

14-3. People who fly in airplanes must believe in the inspector of the aircraft.

others: believe in them, show sensitivity, provide them with choices, develop their competence, and offer them visible support.

Believe in Others. Successful leaders are those who know that little can be accomplished by people who do not feel strong and capable. As a leader, if you share your power with others, you are demonstrating trust in their abilities and respect for their decisions. If you remain open to others' influence and listen to their suggestions, you will not only be effective, you will be respected.

Show Sensitivity. One of the most significant differences between successful and unsuccessful leaders is the ability to understand and be sympathetic to the views of others. To do this, a leader must be able to understand the factors behind another's actions. This requires being familiar with the person's role in the organization, their personality, and their strengths and weaknesses. Being arrogant, betraying another's trust, failing to delegate, and failing to contribute to the building of the team are insensitive and counterproductive.

A good leader understands that people's needs and desires are different. You should be familiar enough with those you lead to know what motivates them. This will help you understand why they do certain things or behave a certain way.

14-4. **A good leader understands other people's needs and desires.**

Provide Choice. Providing others with choices is a highly effective way to encourage others, enhance their sense of well-being, and increase their effectiveness. Good leaders constantly look for ways to increase choices and provide others with greater decision-making authority. By doing this, they are increasing others' senses of responsibility.

When people are involved in situations where they feel highly dependent on someone else to get things done, they tend to feel frustrated and helpless. After a while, people in this type of situation stop taking the initiative.

As a leader, if you want others to be less dependent and perform at higher levels, you must be proactive. Being proactive means you create opportunities for others to make choices. You let them be creative, make decisions, and exercise judgment. Good leaders are proactive.

Develop Competence. Feeling *competent* means believing that you are capable and have the ability to do something. As a leader you can encourage others by helping them develop their sense of competence. You can do this by providing them with opportunities to use their various skills. If you always make the decisions, others on the team may begin to feel they are incapable of making good decisions and develop a sense of incompetence.

Another way to encourage competence is to be capable yourself. By demonstrating a willingness and ability to contribute to the group's goals, you are providing them with a successful model.

Provide Visible Support. As a leader, if you want to encourage others, one of the best ways is to ensure that individual and group efforts get noticed by others. Giving credit to those who performed and contributed to an accomplishment shows everyone their efforts are valued and appreciated. This makes them feel good and provides motivation for future efforts.

This recognition might take place in a formal setting, such as an organized meeting. Deserving members might be awarded certificates or

14-5. Providing feedback on work i important in helping people reac their goals. This shows discussion o plans for a building.

another tangible reward. Other times, and probably most often, you might provide recognition informally. This could be in the form of praise while others are present.

FEEDBACK

Your expectations of others affect your behavior toward them. When your expectations are high, your behavior reflects this. You act favorably toward them. This, in turn, increases their performance because your actions have increased their motivation. As a result, you will tend to offer them more feedback.

When you provide feedback, you are returning part of the information you received. You are letting someone know your perceptions of their behavior, how a situation appeared to you.

Constructive Criticism

One of the most difficult things for a leader to do is to offer ***constructive feedback***—feedback that is evaluative or critical in such a way as to not discourage the receiver. For this type of feedback to be constructive, it must be given in ways that do not elicit a defensive response. The following are some suggestions that may prove helpful in keeping feedback constructive.

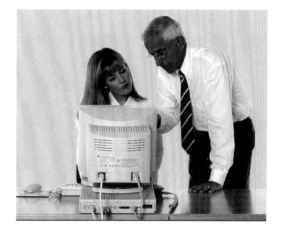

14-6. A leader should give constructive feedback in a way that does not elicit a defensive response.

- Timing is everything—As with rewards, feedback is most useful when it closely follows the behavior. The individual must be able to make the connection between the behavior and the feedback.

- Be informative—Rather than give advice, make sure you provide the receiver with information they can use. Be specific and focus on the behavior, not the person. However, it must be a behavior the person can control. You do not want to attack a behavior a person cannot change, such as a speech difficulty.

■ Be descriptive—Describe your reactions to the behavior. Use "I" messages. Begin by saying "I felt . . . ," "I thought . . . ," or something similar. Never begin with "You." The receiver is immediately put on the defensive.

Consider this scenario: There is a member of your group, Bill, who tends to monopolize discussions. He has been doing this at most meetings for some time, but no one has said anything to him. One day the two of you are having lunch, and you decide to tell Bill. You say to him, "In our meetings, you always take too much time to present your viewpoint. No one else gets a chance to express their views." This is not constructive. It will be difficult for him to connect his actions and the feedback since it was not offered in a timely way. This feedback is also not descriptive. By saying "you" instead of "I" there is a risk of making Bill defensive.

An alternative to this scenario might be: Immediately after a meeting you say, "You offered some very interesting points in the meeting. However, it appeared to me that you took a great deal of time presenting your viewpoint. I feel that others did not have the same opportunity." The feedback and action are closely related in time, are informative, and are descriptive.

■ Confirm understanding—To do this, you might ask the person to repeat what they heard. Our perceptions are colored by our emotions, and often, criticism or feedback causes a person to feel threatened no matter how it is handled. If a person is feeling threatened, their perception of what is being said might be distorted to some degree. This will make anything you say less constructive.

REVIEWING

MAIN IDEAS

Outstanding leaders are those who use their abilities to increase the self-confidence of others by enabling them to take ownership of, and responsibility for, their success. They do this by believing in them, showing sensitivity, providing choices, developing their competence, and providing them with visible support.

Feedback is used to help others develop. Through feedback, you relay your perceptions and expectations.

Constructive criticism is a form of feedback. It must be used properly to avoid eliciting a defensive response and becoming ineffective.

QUESTIONS

Answer the questions using correct spelling and complete sentences.

1. List and explain the ways leaders can encourage others.
2. Define motive. Contrast the two types of motivation.
3. How can you ensure feedback is constructive?

EVALUATING

CHAPTER SELF-CHECK

Match the term with the correct definition. Write the letter by the term in the blank provided.

a. constructive feedback   d. reinforcement   g. personal effectiveness
b. competent   e. intrinsic motivation   h. self-determination
c. extrinsic motivation   f. motives

1. ____ having control over what happens to you.
2. ____ motivation that stems from the desire to obtain external rewards.
3. ____ strengthening desired responses from others.
4. ____ having a positive impact on events in your life.
5. ____ motivation that stems from the desire to feel self-fulfilled.
6. ____ having the ability to accomplish a task.
7. ____ evaluative or critical feedback that does not elicit a defensive response.
8. ____ cause people to act in certain ways.

EXPLORING

1. Contact a local business. Ask how they provide employees with feedback about job performance.

2. With several other classmates, role play techniques of constructive criticism with the following scenario:

There is an individual in your group who refuses to accept suggestions offered by other team members. No matter what, this team member sees their way as the only way to do things. You are the leader of the group and have to talk to this member because the other team members are becoming discouraged.

3. Develop a reward system for an organization that you are a part of. Report on its successes and challenges.

15

CONFLICT RESOLUTION

> *The greatest honor history can bestow is that of peace maker.* **Richard M. Nixon**

Dealing with people is sometimes like a balancing act. Many different personalities must be dealt with effectively. Keeping conflicts to a minimum is a challenging role for a leader.

When a conflict arises, leaders carefully select strategies to follow in a calm and appropriate manner. When this is done, everyone feels that the conflict has been controlled.

Conflicts can be productive. A conflict can be seen as a natural and positive way to bring ideas together to create workable and powerful solutions. Have you found yourself in a conflict with another individual? How have you resolved conflicts in the past? Conflict is a natural part of life.

15-1. Resolving conflicts requires good communication.

OBJECTIVES

This chapter introduces conflict resolution. It has the following objectives:

1. Explain conflict resolution
2. List and describe ways in which conflicts can be resolved
3. Describe how decision-making relates to conflict resolution
4. Explain the importance of learning from mistakes

T
E
R
M
S

conflict
conflict resolution
cultural diversity
emotion
gossip
harassment
informed decision
jealousy
reflective listening
violence

UNDERSTANDING CONFLICT RESOLUTION

Conflict resolution is using techniques that allow people to quietly resolve problems that arise between them. Everyone needs to learn to get along. It will help create a safer environment and a more peaceful world for all of us.

Conflict resolution is often mistaken for crisis management. Crisis management requires quick and hasty decisions, which can often lead to poor results. To avoid a crisis, we need to know conflict resolution.

Conflict resolution is a necessary skill for leaders and serves as a helpful skill to everyone. Leaders, in some situations, may be called upon to be the "peacemaker" to help resolve conflicts.

Violence may result if problems are not solved peacefully. Violence is using physical force against others to resolve conflicts. It is not a good way to settle differences. Guns, knives, and physical attack have no place in an orderly society.

All too often we read headlines in the newspapers that relate negative actions of people. Violent acts stem from conflicts. Conflict resolution provides us with techniques that reduce conflicting situations. Reducing conflicts will reduce violent acts. Conflict resolution is a process that will help prevent violence. Ending a conflict violently through physical force

15-2. **Even among close friends, conflicts sometimes arise.**

is not the answer. People can diffuse a conflict through conflict resolution. This often produces a more peaceful solution to problems and conflicts.

Conflict resolution allows people to reconcile. Reconciliation is the act of reestablishing friendships after conflicts. Practicing conflict resolution techniques will help people now and in the future. It helps us become quality citizens and leaders!

RESOLVING CONFLICTS

When resolving conflict, it is important for us to first understand how a conflict arises. A *conflict* is a difference of opinion between two or more people. The two forces compete with each other. Mental struggles may develop. In some cases, hostility and violence may result.

Conflicts often surface from arguments and disagreements that have escalated out of control. A conflict is disruptive and destructive to a group and its leader.

Conflicts also arise from jealousy, gossip, dirty looks, invasion of privacy, harassment, and diversity in culture and beliefs.

Jealousy describes the behavior of a person who is envious or resentful of someone else. An individual may be jealous of another person over grades they got at school or an honor they have received from an organization.

Gossip is lying about another individual behind their back. Participating in gossip often results in the original information becoming even more harmful. Often, people add to the story, making it more untruthful than it was before.

15-3. Relationships flourish when people respect each other and work to resolve conflicts.

Dirty looks are unkind looks or stares from another person. It is important for us to realize that sometimes these happen because the person had a bad day. These looks may have no meaning behind them at all. Careful interpretation is important.

People do not appreciate the actions of others when their privacy is invaded. Examples of this might include opening someone else's mail or looking at someone else's test score. People need to respect the privacy of others. When we lose that respect, conflicts arise.

Harassment is doing something that disturbs another person. It includes many different actions. These actions may be name calling, unkind gestures, threats, or insults. A person who harasses others can be described as a "bully." Sexual harassment includes unwanted touching or comments of an inappropriate or sexual nature.

Diversity of cultures and beliefs allows an avenue for conflicts to arise. This is especially true when people are not accustomed to dealing with diversity.

Avoiding these type of behaviors and being open-minded to diversity will help avoid conflicts. Avoiding conflicts is wise. It will prevent people from becoming involved in conflicting situations.

PROBLEM-SOLVING SKILLS

Conflict resolution requires problem-solving and decision-making skills. There are basic steps to problem solving that you may have already been introduced to. These basic steps are:

⇨ *Identify the problem*

⇨ *Evaluate the problem*

⇨ *Gather information about the problem*

⤷ *Generate alternatives*

⤷ *Decide on an appropriate plan of action*

⤷ *Select and plan a course of action*

⤷ *Carry out the plan of action*

⤷ *Evaluate the results of action taken.*

When applied to a conflicting situation, problem-solving can assist us in helping people get along better with others. We need to be creative with our problem-solving skills.

There are several basic parts to conflict resolution that people need to understand. Gaining an understanding will help an individual apply conflict resolution techniques. This will help in keeping problems from escalating.

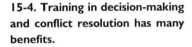
15-4. Training in decision-making and conflict resolution has many benefits.

REFLECTIVE LISTENING

Reflective listening is used to help gain understanding of the situation that has caused the conflict. It is listening in such a way that the listener demonstrates understanding and acceptance. This may require that the listener restate what is being said. Reflective listening involves the use of eye contact, voice, and gestures to relate to the other person that you are indeed listening. Using these conveys to the other person that you are listening and understand the message that he or she is sending. You need to act like a receiver using language such as "I see," "uh-huh," and "really." These reinforce the person trying to communicate with you.

15-5. Being an empathetic person helps resolve conflicts.

Being an empathetic person will help us in resolving conflicts. Empathy requires a person to be extremely understanding of the feelings, thoughts, and actions of the other person. By putting ourselves in the other person's shoes, we better understand their point of view.

Maintaining good self-discipline is another positive characteristic that reduces conflict. Self-discipline requires people to take control of their actions and attitudes. Viewing situations in a positive perspective will help eliminate escalation of conflicts.

Understanding the consequences of negative behavior is important. By knowing and understanding consequences, people can be encouraged to make the right decision. Making the decision to avoid negative behavior will reduce the number of conflicting situations.

Everyone needs to gain an appreciation of **cultural diversity**. Cultural diversity includes cultural beliefs and ethnic groups. Having an open-mind to differences in cultures will help. As people increase their understanding of cultural diversity, cultural tensions will lessen. Hopefully, this will assist in reducing cultural conflicts. Work on identifying those things that you have in common with people who are culturally different.

There will always be conflicts that arise in a person's life. Knowing how to deal with conflicts through conflict resolution will help. Hopefully you can diffuse conflicts through conflict resolution.

DECISION-MAKING

Conflicts require decision-making. These decisions are sometimes difficult. People need to make decisions that are fair and just. When faced with decisions, there are certain questions that need to be asked and steps that need to be taken. These usually occur in this order:

⇨ *What is the decision that needs to be made?*

▷ *What are the possible choices or alternatives?*

▷ *What are the consequences for each of these choices or alternatives?*

▷ *Is the decision based on accurate information?*

▷ *How successful was my decision?*

Decision-making is a skill that is a challenge throughout life. Every day we are required to make decisions. Some decisions that we make, we do not even think about. Other decisions require us to apply the questions and follow the process.

It seems that teenage years are especially difficult for decision-making. People want to make the right decisions and still keep their friends. When people become adults, they need to make sure that informed decisions are made. Even adults want to make decisions that are not overly-influenced by their peers.

INFORMED DECISIONS

A key word in decision-making as it relates to conflict resolution is *informed*. **Informed decisions** are based on the best available information. We need to gather accurate information in order to be properly informed before a decision is made. Therefore, it is important that the resources from which we gain our information are accurate.

Often, conflicts arise in organizations when everyone does not agree. It is then that people can apply their leadership skills and constructively disagree. When this is done, make sure factual information is presented. You may or may not have an influence on the rest of the members in your organization. They may or may not agree. But, you have shared your opinion in an appropriate manner, thus reducing the chance for conflicts to escalate. After controlled discussion of a conflicting issue, an organization may be able to arrive at a consensus (agreement).

IDENTIFY PROS AND CONS

Another technique that will help organizations with decision-making is that of recording the pros and cons. Use a chalkboard or large piece of paper that is visible for everyone. Record the pros and cons of the decision being presented. This makes it clear for everyone involved. It will help reduce conflict and assist the group in arriving at an agreed upon decision.

Selecting a Solution to a Conflict	
Pro	Con
1.	1.
2.	2.
3.	3.
4.	4.
5.	5.

15-6. Using a "pro and con" sheet can help in making decisions.

When a decision is made, make an effort to understand the basis of the decision. Knowing the basis of the decision made will provide clearer direction. Clear direction needs to be understood by leaders and by members of an organization.

Emotions sometimes interfere with problem solving. An **emotion** is a deep feeling a person may have about an issue. In solving conflicts, the emotions must be handled first. Intense emotions make decision-making difficult. In some cases, people feel much better after they have stated how they feel and done what is called "emptying their bucket."

CHANGE AS A SOURCE OF CONFLICT

It is important for any organization or business to stay on top of new technology or information. Often times, new information requires changes. Many people do not feel comfortable with changes. Change can cause uneasy feelings. Changes often require decision-making on the part of a leader or an organization. Appropriate decision-making skills can reduce potential for conflicts in these situations.

Training in decision-making can help everyone. Careful and considerate decision-making can reduce conflict. Controlled discussion, as in parliamentary procedure, may help in the process, but research has not proven this to always be the case. There are many leadership skills that tie together and help build good leaders. When offered training in decision-making skills and leadership skills, do take part. It is valuable training that will always benefit people throughout life.

A peaceful and safe environment can only be accomplished through the cooperation of everyone. Gain training to reduce conflicts. Decision-making and conflict resolution are important parts of that training.

Table 15-1
Suggestions for Preventing and Controlling Conflict

Avoid Roadblocks	Go about leadership by using language and actions that do not create conditions for conflict. Do not threaten, order, or unfairly judge another person.
Control Issues	Follow procedures that control issues before they become conflicts. Be alert and avoid areas that may create conflict.
Increase Tolerance	Become more accepting of differences of opinion. Increased tolerance especially applies to potential conflicts based on cultural diversity.
Increase Emotional Support	Empathy by a leader helps prevent conflicts from becoming major problems. Develop a personal understanding of people and adjust to their needs as appropriate.
Allow People to Talk	Provide an opportunity for people to express their feelings without threat. A process known as "bucket dumping" may be used, which lets people express themselves in a safe environment. Once a person talks about problems, they usually feel better.
Be Part of the Solution	Leaders should not get involved in emotional conflicts between followers or other leaders. They should use approaches that make them a part of the solution and not a part of the problem.

LEARNING FROM OUR MISTAKES

Everyone makes mistakes. Mistakes are a natural part of life. However, no one likes to make mistakes. Mistakes can cause conflicts. Learning from our mistakes will help us with future conflicts. We need to reflect on our mistakes to learn from them.

Football games are often filmed or taped. Why? For the players to see their performance and learn from their mistakes! After a football game, teams will often gather to view the tape. What do teams specifically learn from doing this? They are able to identify not only their mistakes, but what they did well. They also discuss what parts of the game they can improve on to avoid further mistakes. There is always room for improvement. That's how we learn and grow.

A person who makes a mistake should take the time to talk it over with others. Think about those people who influence you the most. Think about those who have the most positive influence on your life. Those with the most positive influence are the people that will be easy to talk to. Often those people are parents, an older brother or sister, a trusted relative, a neighbor, a coach, a teacher, or a counselor. Discussing the mistake with others will help. It will help identify what you have learned from the mistake that was made. It will help you sort out your own feelings about the mistake and decide how to deal with them. It is important to put the mistake behind and carry the lesson forward. Carrying the lesson forward will help in preventing future mistakes.

Take some time for history. Take time to read some biographies of those leaders in history. Identify the mistakes and challenges previous leaders have made. What were the mistakes? How did those leaders handle the challenges? What were the lessons learned? We do not have to make a mistake to learn a new lesson. We can learn from others to prevent ourselves from making the same mistakes.

We are allowed to make mistakes, isn't that why pencils have erasers? As leaders, we should not fear trying something new because we are afraid of making too many mistakes. By trying something new, we broaden our horizons. It helps us move forward and learn, even though trial and error may be part of the learning process. By trying something new, such as a leadership role, we learn about ourselves and about life. People can learn valuable lessons that will contribute to leadership skills.

REVIEWING

MAIN IDEAS

Conflict resolution is using techniques that allow people to resolve problems peacefully. Identifying the source of conflict is an important part of conflict resolution.

Conflicts come from several behaviors, including jealousy, gossip, dirty looks, invasion of privacy, harassment, and diversity in cultures and beliefs. Recognizing the source of conflicts will help in eliminating conflicting situations.

Conflict resolution requires several skills on the part of each person. Problem-solving and decision-making skills are helpful skills. Being an active listener with empathy will assist in reducing conflict. Maintaining good self-discipline, understanding consequences, and gaining an appreciation for cultural diversity will also help.

Conflict resolution requires decision-making skills. When we ask ourselves the right questions, we will make better decisions. Hasty decisions are not always wise and can lead to unnecessary conflict.

Learning from our mistakes is also a part of conflict resolution. We grow by learning from mistakes. When we recall the details of our mistakes and the outcome, we learn. Hopefully, we will not make the same mistake again. We become wiser by learning from the mistakes that we have made.

QUESTIONS

Answer the questions using correct spelling and complete sentences.

1. What is conflict resolution?
2. List five examples of conflict.
3. List five conflict resolution techniques that could have been applied to the examples you recorded in question number two.
4. Identify the eight steps to problem-solving.
5. Why is decision-making an important part of conflict resolution?
6. Define cultural diversity and explain how it can be a source of conflict.
7. Record three advantages of conflict resolution.

EVALUATING

CHAPTER SELF-CHECK

Match the term with the correct definition. Write the letter by the term in the blank provided.

a. cultural diversity   d. emotion   g. violence
b. reflective listening   e. informed decision   h. conflict
c. gossip   f. conflict resolution

1. _____ decisions based on the best available information.
2. _____ using physical force to resolve a conflict.
3. _____ lying about another person.
4. _____ difference based on cultural background.
5. _____ a disagreement.
6. _____ using voice, eye contact, and gestures to relate understanding.
7. _____ techniques that allow people to resolve problems peacefully.
8. _____ deep personal feelings that may damage judgment.

EXPLORING

1. Interview a leader in your school or community. Ask questions concerning conflict-resolution, decision-making, problem solving, and learning from mistakes. Ask for advice that would help future leaders and existing organizations. Share your information with the rest of the class.

2. Identify common conflicting situations that may arise during school or on the job. List ways in which conflict resolution can assist in dealing with the situations identified. Construct a chart and record the information and post it in the classroom. Discuss these situations with your instructor and classmates. You will find that the chart will bring about much discussion concerning conflict resolution.

3. Select a leader found in historical resources. Research and record information about that leader. Record challenges and conflicting situations faced by the leader. Recognize ways in which these situations were handled by the leader. Relate the reactions to conflict resolution strategies. Report your findings to the rest of the class.

16

SERVICE TO OTHERS

> *Service above self . . . He/she profits most who serves best.* **Rotary Club Motto**

Service to others is a heartwarming experience. When people are of service to others, they carry a spirit of volunteerism and cooperation. It is an American spirit!

People can share their talents through a spirit of service. Many needy people and communities can benefit from what we can do. What are your talents? How can you volunteer your time for the benefit of others? What opportunities exist in your community for volunteering? How can your community benefit from volunteer work?

16-1. These students are providing a service in their community: building and installing bluebird houses. This will attract bluebirds to the parks and other areas near their homes.

OBJECTIVES

This chapter focuses on being of service to others. It has the following objectives:

1. Describe the meaning and importance of service

2. List and identify community service organizations

3. Describe how to recognize personal talents

4. Develop a personal plan of service

TERMS

citizen
civic club
community service
community service campaign
plan of service
service
volunteer
volunteerism

THE NATURE OF SERVICE

16-2. The Statute of Liberty is a symbol of life in the United States that includes volunteerism.

Service is helping others. It is providing for other people through helpful acts. Sometimes, it is for individuals who may have special needs. Other times, it is for the overall benefit of the communities where we live. Examples of service include raking the lawn for your neighbor, visiting an elderly person, or participating in a community fund-raiser.

Winston Churchill once said, "We make a living by what we get, but we make a life by what we give." Service projects help others and make people feel good about themselves.

Service projects can vary in size. A large community service campaign can last days. A *community service campaign* is an organized and intense effort to carry out an activity. These are used for larger activities. Many people may volunteer to help with a community service campaign. Picking up trash along the road in front of your school may only take an hour. Picking up trash on streets and roads throughout the community will require a campaign.

Service projects may include charitable activities, community improvements, or fund raising. These types of projects often require service of others and volunteer work.

Some group service projects require more organization than others. This depends on the number of people involved and the nature or objective of the project.

COMMUNITY SERVICE

Many youth already serve their community through various projects. *Community service* is performing activities that improve the quality of life in our communities. These service projects are important for the individuals who benefit from them, as well as for the individual who does them. It is important for us to think about the benefits. By doing this, we will increase our respect and appreciation for service.

Benefits

Providing service gives people a new perspective on life. People discover the joy in giving. When the project requires the efforts of several people, you soon learn to work with others.

Service projects can be a learning experience that extends the boundaries of the classroom. Each of us should appreciate our opportunities to help others in relation to school projects.

Community service projects pull communities together. Community projects may include cleaning up a local park. Other projects include cleaning up roadside litter, or holding a campaign for charity. A community grows closer through these types of projects. People also feel like they belong to their community when they become involved with these projects.

16-3. Painting equipment in a park makes a worthy service contribution to a community.

People can learn from service projects and programs. If the project involves building a fishing dock for people with disabilities, a person would learn much about construction. If the project is centered around a charitable fund-raising campaign, you would learn much about money management. No matter what the service project or program, those involved will also learn valuable teamwork and communication skills.

Volunteerism

Volunteerism is giving one's time and talents without monetary benefits. Many benefits may come from the work. Volunteerism makes our communities better places to live and helps people feel better about themselves.

A *volunteer* is an individual who willingly performs a service without pay. Every person has a responsibility to volunteer as best they can. Each person has a skill or ability that will be useful in improving our communities or helping other people. Our schools and communities have given much to us and we can show our appreciation by being a volunteer.

Leadership does begin with volunteerism. A true sense of accomplishment can be gained by working through a volunteer service project. Often, a community project, such as landscaping a town park, will be the visible accomplishment. It is these visible projects that encourage others to become involved.

When you work on service projects, you will find yourself having fun. This is a benefit that comes from this type of work. When we are of service to others, we find a new definition behind fun.

The work of volunteers helps reduce the cost of government and reduces taxes. This is true in many ways. When citizens, for example, voluntarily

16-4. Many communities rely on volunteers to fight fires.

clean trash from a roadway, there is a savings to the responsible government agency.

Many times, people volunteer to work on charitable campaigns. These campaigns might involve a local community or an entire state. Being actively involved in fund-raising helps accomplish things that otherwise might not have happened.

CITIZENSHIP DEVELOPMENT

Service projects provide opportunities for people to be actively involved. When people help with a project, they feel like they are making a positive difference through a worthy cause. Contributing food items to a local food pantry for those less fortunate allows individuals to be actively involved.

Decision-making skills can be strengthened by being of service to others. Decisions have to be made in the planning stages and when those plans are put into action.

Participating in service projects produces responsible citizens. A *citizen* is a person who lives in a certain location. You are a citizen in many ways. You may be a citizen of a rural community or large city. You are also likely a citizen of a county or parish and a state. Responsible citizenship is an important asset that will always be valuable—valued by others who also are responsible and respectable citizens working to make a positive difference in the world.

There are also those difficult times that people are called to be of service to others. These times are often during periods of disaster. Areas affected

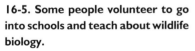

16-5. Some people volunteer to go into schools and teach about wildlife biology.

by hurricanes, floods, earthquakes, or drought often require extra assistance. People unselfishly provide their assistance in many ways.

People also learn and apply problem-solving skills through service projects. Problem-solving skills are lifetime skills that will always be beneficial. Problem-solving skills contribute to the success of a service project.

TEAMWORK

Service projects usually require teamwork. Teamwork is an important concept to learn—people working and sharing together. Service projects teach people to work together for a common cause.

Being involved in service projects gives a person a variety of experiences. Volunteers can evaluate their own skills and abilities and how they like to work with other people. They can reflect upon the success of a project upon its completion. It also allows people to evaluate their own outlook on life and how they can be of better service to others.

16-6. Youth often work as teams to perform useful services.

MATCHING INTERESTS TO SERVICE PROJECTS

Many kinds of service projects are available. Some are indoors; others are outdoors. Some require special skills; others need only our time and willingness to work.

Service projects can take people outdoors and provide a worthy release from stress of school and work. With outdoor projects, people can work with others and have projects visible to everyone. Outdoor projects can bring people closer to nature. Outdoor service projects can give people that "down-to-earth" feeling. Outdoor projects can add to the fun and adventure of being of service to others. Examples of outdoor projects include installing a new landscaping project in town, renovating a park, removing debris from a small stream, and restoring wildlife habitat.

Service is important and does take time. People can usually find the time to do things that are a high priority to them. How much time do you spend being of service to others? When we carry out the spirit of volunteerism, we take time to help others. It is up to each of us to decide when and how we can be of service to others. This is where making a positive difference starts. People greatly appreciate volunteer efforts.

When people actively support service projects, they soon find themselves asking others to help. This is how support is built.

16-7. Removing trash from a small stream is an excellent service project to improve our communities.

Solid values are gained by helping others. It boosts are self-confidence while promoting positive team development. Volunteerism, in the spirit of service, strengthens us emotionally, physically, and spiritually. It helps build healthy people, environments, and communities. Today's youth can prepare themselves for a successful future by learning volunteerism.

COMMUNITY SERVICE ORGANIZATIONS

Each community has service organizations. Community service organizations can make a big difference in a community. Each organization has purposes, goals, and objectives. These can range from very basic ideas to very complex plans. Meeting times vary according to each organization.

Service projects may be carried out annually by each organization or several times throughout the year. It depends on what the board of directors decides is necessary to accomplish the projects and the wishes of the members of each organization. Service organizations are designed to make a positive difference in the lives of others.

Most service organizations select activities to inspire people to volunteer and become involved. Perhaps there were service projects in your own area that inspired you to become involved. There is always room for more volunteers in each organization. Membership, in most cases, is unlimited.

Community service organizations are organized to be of service to others. Some national organizations reach out and serve more than one community, state, or nation. Examples of these include the American Red Cross, American Cancer Society, the Salvation Army, the Christian Children's Fund, and March of Dimes. These organizations are all built on volunteerism. These organizations also hold fund-raising activities and many solicit donations.

CIVIC CLUBS

A *civic club* is a group formed to improve life in the local community. The nature of these organizations varies greatly. Civic clubs carry out activities to promote volunteerism among their members. The work of civic clubs is financed by the dues of members and projects that raise funds, such as an auction or broom sale.

Every local community has one or more civic clubs. The members are typically business and career leaders, as well as people who want to make contributions to their communities. Examples of civic clubs include the Lions Club, Kiwanis, Rotary Club, and Optimist Clubs. Some organizations with specific career or educational interests also volunteer for civic activi-

16-8. The local Rotary Club in White Horse, Yukon Territory, has established a park for all citizens of the community.

ties. These include the Business and Professional Women (BPW) and American Association of University Women (AAUW).

RELIGION-BASED ORGANIZATIONS

Communities in the United States typically have a wide range of religions or faiths. These churches and synagogues provide benefits to their members, as well as all citizens of the community. Both youth and adults are a part of these organizations.

YOUTH ORGANIZATIONS

Most communities have organizations that focus specifically on youth. These organizations work to foster volunteerism and improve communities. Examples of programs predominantly for youth include 4-H, Girl Scouts of America, Campfire Boys & Girls, and Boy Scouts of America.

STUDENT ORGANIZATIONS

Schools have a wide range of organizations to serve the needs and interests of students. Student organization work often includes community service. Youth can learn the importance of volunteerism and develop important leadership skills.

Examples of student organizations that provide community service include the National FFA Organization, Future Homemakers of America (FHA-HERO), Future Business Leaders of America (FBLA), Vocational Industrial Clubs of America (VICA), National Honor Society (NHS), Distributive Education Clubs of America (DECA), and Junior High National Honor Society (JRNHS).

What organizations do you belong to? What community service organizations would you like to belong to? These are questions that need answers. Service opportunities are easy to find. You have a responsibility to explore and decide when and where you can help make a positive difference.

RECOGNIZING YOUR PERSONAL TALENTS

Throughout your life you will continue to recognize your personal talents. By discovering and recognizing your talents, you can then share them with others. This is one special way to be of service to others. Sharing your talents allows you to let others know you care. Being of service to others helps bring balance into a person's life.

How do you continue to discover your new talents? You can start by trying something new. Paint a picture, learn a new dance, or sing a new song. Discovering and recognizing personal talents is important.

Agree to help someone else help others. You will be amazed at what you can learn and discover by doing this. Even if the project does not require much time on your part, it still offers you an opportunity to discover.

Listen to others. People compliment you because of your talents. Listening to those compliments will help you discover your strengths. Listening can also direct us to other opportunities where we can discover our hidden talents. Recognizing our personal talents is a journey of discovery.

This journey of discovery can help meet our own needs of being useful and helpful to the community. Meeting our needs is important. Recognizing our talents is a way of taking care of ourselves.

It is important for a person to take time out of their schedule for improving their own talents. List all of your talents you have already discovered. Then create a list of those talents you would like to acquire. Search your school and community for avenues in which you can perfect your talents. Often times, people provide lessons related to talents, such as horseback riding, painting, piano playing, dancing, and singing. These are opportunities to recognize or improve personal talents. This will result in an increase of self-confidence and self-esteem.

Everyone's talents are different because everyone is different. It is not just by chance or luck that we have talents. Personal talents are gifts. When we pursue our abilities and talents, we become well-rounded individuals. Every talent a person has needs to be valued. It gains value when shared with others through service.

There are many ways to recognize our own talents. Our families, friends, schools, churches, and communities all help us discover our talents. Take time to reflect and appreciate your own talents. Have fun on your journey as you continue to discover your talents.

DEVELOP A PLAN OF SERVICE

Service activities may be carried out by individuals or groups. Large projects often require the resources of groups. Groups are made of dedicated individuals who must plan in order to have time for volunteering.

Format of Personal Plan of Service

Name: _____

Address: _____

_____

School: _____

Your Talents: _____

_____

_____

_____

School service-oriented organizations to which I belong:

_____

_____

_____

_____

Community service-oriented organizations in my community:

_____

_____

_____

_____

Ways in which I can be of service to others:

_____

_____

_____

_____

Dates and times I can provide service to others (refer to my personal planning calendar):

_____

_____

_____

_____

Successful service project(s) that I have been a part of:

_____

_____

_____

_____

16-9. Form for developing a plan of service.

16-10. These team members must work together to win the "bed race" for their local service projects fund raiser.

A *plan of service* should be prepared. It is a written statement of a person's talents and skills and ways of providing service. A plan of service helps schedule activities to assure completion.

You need to plan to use time for service work. Personal calendars are helpful for keeping up with times when you will help with service activities, recording birthdays, scheduled tests, family gatherings, holidays, and other events. Calendars help people carry out their personal plan of service.

Volunteers need to have a good attitude about service. They need an attitude of caring and sincerity. Positive attitudes create positive results. Once you make a commitment to service, do not back down. Your reputation is on the line. You will want to do a quality job with your assignment.

"Plan your work and work your plan" is a phrase commonly used by leaders. Good planning is essential for community service. If you plan, for example, on participating in a local walk-a-thon for the American Cancer Society, plan ahead and write down the date in your calendar, collect your pledges, get in shape, and then walk!

Many service activities require teamwork. Being a part of a service team is a privilege. Teamwork creates energy and enthusiasm. While working as a team member, keep an open mind to the ideas of other people.

Keep informed about the service projects of your organization. A good understanding helps you fulfill your duties. Carry out your activities with the same high energy and enthusiasm as the rest of your group. Now and then you may need to encourage members along.

Being part of a service project has rewards. Hard work pays off. Being of service to others is truly a rewarding experience.

REVIEWING

MAIN IDEAS

Service and volunteerism are essential in being a leader. Service is a way to help others, as well as those involved, feel good about themselves. It gives people a new perspective on life, and, at the same time, pulls communities together. Service projects are places where we can learn, see our accomplishments, and have fun. By participating in service, people become actively involved in decision-making, problem-solving, and teamwork. Providing service to others develops good citizenship skills.

Volunteers need to recognize their personal talents. This is by trying something new and listening to others. Discovering our talents helps people meet their own basic needs. Recognizing our talents is a journey of discovery. When people find their talents, they can share them with others through service.

Everyone needs to take the time to develop their own plan of service. It starts with acquiring the right attitude toward service. People need to plan and participate. Service projects allow people to work in teams and stay informed. Service to others benefits everyone.

QUESTIONS

Answer the questions using correct spelling and complete sentences.

1. In what ways can you become involved in service-oriented activities in your school?

2. List reasons why service is important.

3. Identify examples of difficult times when people are called to be of service to others.

4. How can service projects improve the problem-solving skills of people?

5. List three ways in which you can discover your own talents.

6. Why is a personal plan of service important?

7. How can you become involved in a service-oriented project in your community?

EVALUATING

CHAPTER SELF-CHECK

Match the term with the correct definition. Write the letter by the term in the blank provided.

a. service   d. volunteerism   g. civic club
b. volunteer   e. plan of service
c. community service campaign   f. citizen

1. _____ performing activities that improve the quality of life in a community.
2. _____ helping others.
3. _____ giving time and talent without monetary benefit.
4. _____ individual who performs a service without pay.
5. _____ person who lives in a certain locale.
6. _____ group formed to improve life in a local community.
7. _____ written statement of a person's abilities and activities in community service.

EXPLORING

1. Identify a need within your school and community. Initiate a class project by planning a service project. Remember to involve local school representatives and administrators. Record the progress of your service project and write a news release on your success.

2. Survey students in your school to find out their views on service to others and service projects. Report your findings in a local school newsletter or newspaper.

3. Interview someone who has been involved in a school or community service project. Report your findings to the rest of the class.

17

LEADING IN CONSTANTLY CHANGING TIMES

> *Keep your mind open to change at all times.*
> **Dale Carnegie**

Times change. Situations become different. People respond in different ways and to different things.

Leaders must be able to adapt to change. Different groups respond to different leadership approaches. Successful leaders study the groups they are preparing to lead and use approaches that will work best. A leader who does not adapt will be replaced by one who does.

Today, a leader must be sensitive to the needs and interests of followers. Being open and involving followers is essential for a successful leader.

17-1. Careful thought may be needed to determine how to adapt to the situations in which leadership is provided. (Courtesy, Texas Tech University)

219

OBJECTIVES

This chapter is about how leaders adapt to changes in the individuals they are leading, and how to select the best leadership style. It has the following objectives:

1. Explain leadership roles

2. Describe situational leadership and identify the factors that determine the best leadership style

3. Assess how leaders emerge from a group

4. Discuss the approaches to improving leadership

TERMS

goal-oriented leader
leadership role
member-oriented leader
relationship leadership role
selection
self-oriented leader
situational leadership
situation engineering
task leadership role
training

LEADERSHIP ROLES

Leadership roles are the roles that leaders assume in providing leadership. These roles vary based on the followers.

Effective leaders have two roles to achieve in providing leadership for their groups. The two roles are task and relationship. As you study the two roles, decide which type of leader you would tend to be.

TASK LEADERSHIP ROLE

The *task leadership role* deals with getting tasks done. It involves providing direction to the group in working toward accomplishing the group's goals. Leaders keep the group moving toward its objectives and help the group be productive and efficient. Getting the job done is the key concern in fulfilling the task role.

Task leadership roles are based on groups having worthy, achievable goals. Many groups set programs of work, which describe the activities to be carried out. Task leadership roles involve organizing the group so the program of work is achieved. The focus is on getting activities done.

RELATIONSHIP LEADERSHIP ROLE

The ***relationship leadership role*** has a "people" focus. It involves building, enhancing, and maintaining positive relations within the group. Members within groups need to get along and be able to work together if their group is to remain productive over time.

With the relationship leadership role, leaders build cooperation among members and develop the group into a team working together for a common cause. Having good relationships is as important as achieving goals.

COMBINING THE ROLES

Effective leaders concern themselves with both task and relationship activities. Groups must be productive, and members must work together if their groups are to remain viable.

The long-term welfare of a group is based on leadership that combines task and relationship roles. Successful leaders are able to accomplish both in the groups they lead.

17-2. Preparation to be a leader can begin early in life by participating in group activities. (Courtesy, Texas Tech University)

LEADERSHIP BEHAVIOR

Leadership is an interaction between a leader and followers. The nature of the interaction varies with both the people and the situation. Different styles of leadership are needed. (Leadership styles were introduced in Chapter 1.)

A widely used model that allows flexibility in leadership style is situational leadership. This model was developed by Paul Hersey and Ken Blanchard. It is popular today. (Complete details on the model are available from the Center for Leadership Studies in Escondido, California. Good references include *Management of Organizational Behavior*, *The Situational Leader*, and *Classics of Organizational Behavior*.)

Situational leadership is a leadership model based on determining the demands of the situation. The readiness of the followers is determined. A leadership style is selected based on the situation as related to readiness of the followers. With the same group, leaders need to be more directive in some situations than in others.

Hersey and Blanchard's model has four categories of style. Each represents a range of similar styles. The four categories of style and their descriptions are:

Style 1. Telling

- Leader tells the group what to do.
- Decisions are made largely by leader.
- Leader places emphasis on completing tasks.

Style 2. Selling

- Leader sells decisions to group.
- Decisions are made by leader with some group input.
- Leader places high emphasis on building relationships and completing tasks.

Style 3. Participating

- Leader works with the group in making decisions.
- Decisions are made jointly by group and leader.
- Leader places high emphasis on building relationships.

Style 4. Delegating

- Leader delegates decision-making to the group.
- Leader provides a description of task.
- Group works independently.

THE BEST STYLE

A common myth related to leadership style is that one style is superior to the other styles. Any of the four styles listed above is appropriate, depending on the situation.

Leaders need to answer three basic questions before selecting a leadership style:

■ Is there an obvious solution to the task?

■ Is it important for the leader to make the decision?

■ Is there inadequate time to involve others in the decision?

If the leader answers "yes" to any of these questions, the leader should make the decision. Some input from members might be helpful, but the leader should be directive. If the answer to these questions is "no," the leader assesses the situation and selects a style. Leaders can assess the situation by determining the members' ability and willingness to complete the activity.

Leaders need to evaluate the individuals involved for each activity or task. An individual might be able and willing to perform Task A, but unable to perform Task B. In these situations, the leader selects two different leadership styles to use with the same individual.

Table 17-1
Assessing the Leadership Style to Use on the Basis of Group Members' Ability and Willingness to Make Decisions

Assessment of Members	Style	Who Makes Decision
Not able, not willing	Telling	Leader
Willing, not able	Selling	Leader; Consults Group
Able, not willing	Participating	Jointly—Leader and Group
Able and willing	Delegating	Group

There are several ways to detect the members' willingness and ability. Leaders who know their members are better equipped to assess the members' willingness and ability.

Indicators of Willingness — The individual . . .

1. Has an interest in the activity.
2. Volunteers for the activity.
3. Discusses the activity with others.
4. Displays a positive attitude toward the group.
5. Follows through with commitments.

Indicators of Ability — The individual . . .

1. Has experience in the activity.
2. Has skills in related activities.
3. Is intelligent and can think through problems.
4. Can find and use resources effectively.
5. Is self-directed.

17-3. Daring activities may be unsafe for a leader or member. Leaders must constantly assess situations to determine the appropriate actions. (Courtesy, Texas Tech University)

PERSONAL LEADERSHIP POTENTIAL

In our society, where most people live their lives in groups, there is a continuous need for leaders. We live in a rapidly changing world with ever expanding new technology, new threats, and new information. (It is estimated that the knowledge base now doubles every two years and by the year 2000, should double every six months.) With each development comes the need for a leader to emerge, but who can be a leader? Too often we come to believe that "leaders are born, not made." ANYONE has the potential to lead, but leadership development must occur first. Leaders must then have an opportunity to use their skills.

ELEMENTS OF LEADERSHIP

There are certain elements of leadership that allow a person to become a leader. The misconceptions of becoming a leader were listed in Chapter 1 and are reviewed here.

Leadership misconceptions:

- A person inherits leadership ability.
- Leaders have certain traits in common.
- Leaders must have a perfect physical make-up.
- Only exceptionally intelligent people will become leaders.
- Given the opportunity, anyone can lead.
- Everyone desires to lead.

These ideas are false! It may seem that some leaders are born with leadership traits, but this is mainly due to their development and circumstances.

Three elements of leadership which leaders must put to use to develop their potential are:

- Heredity—Heredity is a person's potential ability to lead. Everyone has the potential to become a leader. The association between leadership and the elite led many people to feel that leadership was an inherited trait. Soon, those supporting the hereditary theories of leadership gave way to other theories as people of all classes became leaders. To date, geneticists have not discovered a gene that they could label the "leader" gene.

- Opportunity—Opportunity is the availability of a situation to lead. The opportunity to lead will allow the person with experience to practice their leadership skills. These two elements (opportunity and experience) do not always coincide!

■ Experience— Experience involves the development of leadership skills and activities. Learning and developing these skills requires leadership training at schools, camps, and seminars.

Experience and opportunity are environmental elements. They are more subject to control when compared to heredity. Of the three elements, experience and opportunity are the most limiting. An "experienced" or skilled person may never have the opportunity to lead. On the other hand, the opportunity to lead may occur with an "inexperienced" or unskilled person. Each element alone cannot make a leader. The experience of all three must occur together.

To better understand the relationship of these elements, consider the following examples.

Example 1: A person assumes a leadership position, but has no prior experience or skills in leading a group. This individual will probably not achieve a high level of accomplishment. The individual must rely on experienced members to show him/her what to do if the group is to achieve its goal.

Example 2: The individual who has the leadership skills, but does not have the opportunity to lead. This may be due to never being selected as the leader or not being in the right place at the right time.

To realize maximum leadership potential, all three elements, heredity, experience, and opportunity, must occur together. Given the proper experience and the opportunity, *ANYONE* can become a leader should they so desire.

17-4. Developing leadership abilities for changing times may require considerable study. (Courtesy, Texas Tech University)

EMERGING AS A LEADER

For any group to be effective and achieve its goals, successful leadership must occur. Within a group, which member is most likely to become its leader? Three types of individuals who emerge as leaders of groups are:

- Member Oriented—The ***member-oriented leader*** will emerge when they perceive a conflict within the group and feel they can solve the difficulty. This leader feels they can mediate or referee a disagreement (conflict) between two sides.

- Goal Oriented—When the group's goals and rewards look good, the ***goal-oriented leader*** will emerge as the leader. This type of leader thrives on task accomplishment. In the event their leadership attempt fails, this leader will probably not attempt to lead again.

- Self-Oriented—***Self-oriented leaders*** emerge when such action is prestigious, or provides a direct reward to themselves. This type of leader enjoys the recognition a position of group leadership entails.

Members who emerge will usually exhibit all of the types to some extent. Those persons who emerge as a group's leader are willing, motivated, energetic, and goal-oriented. They tend to be more intelligent and exhibit originality and initiative.

IMPROVING LEADERSHIP ABILITY

Three approaches are used to improve group leadership. These are:

- Selection—***Selection*** is the quickest approach to improving a group's leadership. The group simply selects the person who has those skills most needed by the group. To be effective, perform an analysis of the group's needs first. Next, assess each candidate's leadership record, and, finally, select a leader. For example, a group might be in need of improving its meetings. This group should select someone with experience in parliamentary procedure and consensus building.

- Training—The ***training*** approach is the most widely used method of improving leadership. Usually, groups work with the individuals they have rather than select someone new. Businesses and other groups send employees and members to seminars, workshops, and camps to improve their leadership skills. Training can include improving technical, conceptual, and human relations skills.

Technical skills involve "doing" leadership skills. An increase of technical skills may occur with the use of computers, textbooks, and simulators. Delegating, using parliamentary procedure, and completing a report are examples of "doing" skills. This technique is most easily obtained and retained of the three.

Conceptual skills involve placing individuals in situations they might face as leaders of their groups. These are the "thinking" skills. They are harder to develop than technical skills. However, the use of "think" games to solve problems, forecast events, and make decisions make them easier to learn.

Human relations skills relate to the ability to work with others. These are the "people" skills. Leaders receive training in working effectively with others within groups. People are the foundation of all groups; leaders must be able to effectively deal with members.

■ Situation Engineering—***Situation engineering*** matches the situation with a leader. Some manipulation (or engineering) may be done before facing a situation to ensure the success by the leader. Leaders avoid placing individuals in situations in which failure is likely. For example, the increase or decrease of the leader's authority could depend on the situation they are about to experience. If the individual is capable, the leader can leave more of the decisions to the individual.

17-5. Leaders need good human relations skills to work effectively with other people. (Courtesy, Texas Tech University)

REVIEWING

MAIN IDEAS

As times change, the needs of leaders also change. A common model of leadership based on the maturity of the followers is situational leadership. The style of leadership to use varies with the needs of the followers to achieve a goal. Four styles are used with situational leadership: telling, selling, participating, and delegating.

To develop as a leader, three elements should be used: heredity, opportunity, and experience. Some people question the merits of heredity in leadership and say that a "leader" gene has not been found. Opportunity and experience are environmental elements and are more subject to control.

Leaders may be member, goal, or self-oriented. Member orientation focuses on the needs of members. Goal orientation deals with making accomplishments. Self-oriented leaders get involved when there is "something in it for me."

Leaders are obtained in three ways: selection, training, and situation engineering. Selection is the fastest way. Training assures that the leader has the proper skills. Situation engineering involves matching a leader with the situation to be handled.

QUESTIONS

Answer the questions using correct spelling and complete sentences.

1. What are the two major leadership roles? Explain each and how they combine.

2. What are the four categories of style in situational leadership? Briefly explain each.

3. What three questions should leaders ask before selecting a style? How do the answers influence the style selected?

4. What three elements must be developed to make a good leader?

5. What three types of individuals emerge as group leaders?

6. What are the major approaches to improving leadership ability?

EVALUATING

CHAPTER SELF-CHECK

Match the term with the correct definition. Write the letter by the term in the blank provided.

a. selection

b. self-oriented leader

c. task leadership role

d. situational leadership

e. relationship
leadership role

f. situation engineering

1. ____a leader who emerges for recognition.

2. ____the quickest way to get a leader.

3. ____the role of building positive relationships within a group.

4. ____the role of getting tasks done.

5. ____leadership based on the demands of the situation.

6. ____matching a situation with a leader.

EXPLORING

1. Research a leader of the past and compare them to a modern-day leader holding the same type of position.

2. Select a modern-day leader and write to them to ask about their most valuable leadership training and experiences.

3. Assess the members of your class based on the category of leadership style they would need on the following issues: raising funds for a field trip, setting up a plastic recycling program at school, and running a member of your class for student council president. Write a report that describes your analysis.

18

SYSTEMS THINKING

> *Leaders must communicate a vision in a way that attracts and excites.* **David E. Berlew**

When you hear the word "system" what image comes to your mind? A stereo system? The solar system? Each of these have several parts that work together.

A stereo system is one example. Without speakers, a receiver, a cassette deck, and a CD player, it is not a stereo system; it is just a radio, just a cassette player, or just a CD player.

Another example is a solar system. Without a sun for planets to revolve around, it is not a system. The planets interact with each other and the Sun to maintain orbits. They are interdependent.

How many other kinds of systems can you think of? How are the pieces interdependent?

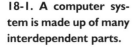
18-1. A computer system is made up of many interdependent parts.

OBJECTIVES

This chapter provides background information on systems thinking. It has the following objectives:

1. Explain systems thinking
2. Contrast models of organizational leadership
3. Explain elements of group dynamics
4. Describe techniques for team building and performance

TERMS

code of conduct
connected model
forming
group
group stagnation
norming
organization
performing
pyramid model
system
systems thinking
team mission
unity
value driven

SYSTEMS

A *system* can be defined as a whole made up of many interdependent parts. All of the parts are needed for the system to perform properly.

Just as a group of stereo components or planets can make up a system, individuals can combine to make a system. The system can be large or small. A large system is called an *organization*. On a smaller scale the system can be a group, team, or club.

Systems thinking is looking at an organization or team as interdependent parts that make up a whole. This is more than recognizing that one team member's actions affect the other members and the team as a whole. It requires an understanding of how those actions affect the team. Systems thinking focuses on the relationships component in the division of labor. It asks who does what, with whom, when, and where.

A leader's job is to make the system work. This is accomplished by looking at the relationships between jobs or roles and resolving conflict before it affects the whole. This requires the leader be sensitive to the interrelationships and be prepared to head off potential problems.

In the example of the solar system, it is not only important to understand that the interaction between the planets and the Sun exists, it requires an understanding of how gravity and the masses of the planets interact to maintain balance in the solar system.

MODELS OF ORGANIZATIONAL LEADERSHIP

Two primary models of organizational leadership are used. The traditional model is the *pyramid model*. It is also known as the military model of leadership. It is called the pyramid model because the organizational structure resembles a pyramid. The leader is at the top and various levels descend from there.

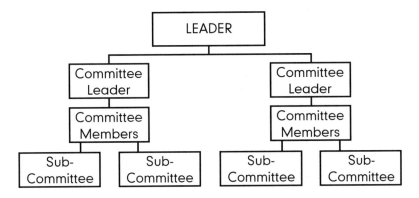

18-2. The pyramid model of leadership.

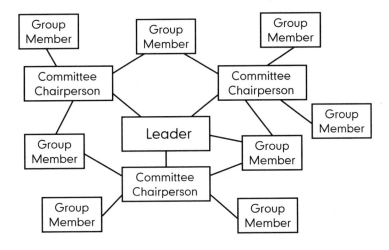

18-3. The connected model of leadership.

The second model of leadership, the ***connected model***, is most often represented as a web. The leader is at the center of the web, and other levels branch from there and are interconnected.

These two models have very different characteristics. Table 18-1 contrasts the important characteristics of each.

Table 18-1 Comparison of Two Leadership Models	
Pyramid Model	**Connected Model**
Focus is on the objective of control.	Focus is on interactive leadership with the objective being change.
Job performance consists of a series of transactions.	Leaders encourage participation by all.
Rewards are given for good performance, and punishment is given for inadequate performance.	Leaders share power and information.
Rank is important.	Leaders enhance other people's self-worth.
The leader issues orders, imposes discipline, and demands respect.	The structure is flexible and integrated.
The structure is rigid, mechanistic, and hierarchical.	

GROUP DYNAMICS

The types and characteristics of organizational leadership models can be used with groups or teams. If you are a member of a team where the leader makes all of the decisions and maintains a high degree of control, it follows the more traditional style. If, however, you are a member of a group where decisions are made by the group, with everyone having a part, you are following the connected model.

A ***group*** is two or more people working together to accomplish a goal. All of the elements in this definition must be present for it to be a group.

Obviously, you must have at least two people. One person does not make a group.

The people must work together and have a goal. If they are not working together to achieve a goal, they are not a group. People gathering to watch a house being built is an aggregation. If those same people gather to build the house, they are a group. A group must have a purpose.

GROUP CHARACTERISTICS

Success in a group depends upon the leader and the other members. The abilities each brings contribute to a group's success. Success also depends upon how adept the group becomes at solving its problems. Successful groups have at least three important characteristics:

- Unity—For a group to be successful, all of the members of the group must feel a sense of unity. **Unity** means that the members of a group feel connected, a part of the same whole. Establishing team goals and having a plan of execution are important beginnings. All members should have clearly defined roles and responsibilities within the group and be able to see how they make an important contribution to the overall success of the team.

- Relationships—In successful groups, members feel comfortable and free to contribute to and learn from the group. Clear and effective communication greatly enhances a group's performance. Members share personal relationships and exhibit supportive team behaviors.

- Work Together—Members of a successful group work together to achieve a goal. Individual differences can be put aside for the good

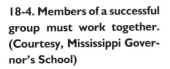
18-4. Members of a successful group must work together. (Courtesy, Mississippi Governor's School)

of the team. There are well-defined decision procedures and participation in the group when it is balanced and follows established ground rules. The group successfully uses the scientific approach to solving problems and achieving goals.

TECHNIQUES FOR SUCCESSFUL TEAM BUILDING

Team building is a three-phase process. The first phase, *forming*, includes all of the things necessary to get individuals together. During *norming*, the second phase, members take the steps necessary to develop team cohesion. The third phase, *performing*, includes things necessary for the team to conduct business and accomplish goals. Some models of team building also include a phase called "storming" since conflict is a natural part of the team development process.

FORMING

The formation phase of team building focuses on taking individuals used to acting on their own and making them into a cohesive unit that can progress and develop into an entity able to solve problems.

The first step in team building is the development of a mission. A *team mission* is what the team wants to accomplish. By formally establishing a mission, the team can concentrate on the things they need to do to meet their goal. It is the basis for having goals and outcomes that are measurable. A team must think as one in order to succeed, so every team member has to agree with the mission.

One important consideration in group formation is personal values. Whether you realize it or not, your values affect every decision you make. Human beings are *value driven*. This means they are motivated and act on things that are important to them. Differing values and beliefs are responsible for much of the individualistic behavior in people. It is also what is behind much of the conflict between people. That these differences exist is the most important reason a team must have a mission statement in writing and ensure everyone has a clear understanding. It should be what guides the team's actions.

Another important consideration during this phase is trust. Trust is the one thing that influences every aspect of human interaction. In the

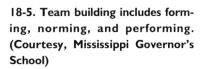
18-5. Team building includes forming, norming, and performing. (Courtesy, Mississippi Governor's School)

formation stage of group development, it should be the primary focus. The inability of team members to trust, and therefore get along, is the most common cause of team failure.

The team environment must be right for trust to develop. Trust is an outcome of a team's movement in a positive direction. It will grow or diminish based on team members' reactions to each other. Its development stems from members sharing information and believing they can influence decisions and exercise a degree of control over goal achievement. Consequently, it is very important that teams conduct trust-building exercises. The outcome of trust among members is an openness to learning from one another.

NORMING

The process of norm development will lead to a sense of cohesion among team members. Successful completion of this phase will lead to a highly productive team.

The norm development phase really focuses on the development of ground rules, or a way of doing things. Without conscious effort, teams will usually develop a way of doing things. However, it may not be the most effective way. Having guidelines and a code of conduct helps a team prevent misunderstandings and disagreements, and avoids wasting valuable time on resolving these types of issues. It is important to remember to include every individual in this process. The more team members share in the development of the group's norms, the more likely they will be to like each other.

This ***code of conduct,*** or way a team does things, should include the following:

- Everyone feels they are welcome and included.
- Members are not pressured to conform.
- Individual styles are accepted.
- Members share a sense of commitment to one another.
- Politics, favoritism, and other counterproductive acts play no part in decisions.
- The team has a method of self-evaluation.
- There are rules for handling conflicts that may arise.
- Decision making is consensual.
- Others are treated respectfully.
- There is a strong bond of caring.
- Teams should remain open to new ways of doing things.

PERFORMING

Once a team reaches the performance phase, there should be a close attachment between members. At this point, the team is characterized by a high level of productivity. This does not mean this is a period without evaluation or reflection.

Every team should have a way of reflecting on itself and its members. The team should verify adherence to its mission and norms established in the earlier phases. This feedback should be a way of facilitating continued learning and development and management of trust.

COMMON PROBLEMS TEAMS FACE

In an effort to avoid them, teams should be aware of some common problems teams face.

Inactivity

When a group stops striving to meet its goals, it is inactive. This problem can arise from different areas. Teams that begin with the wrong objectives or ignore parts of the development process are particularly susceptible. A team that does not continually build trust among its members and evaluate itself will not be productive. This lack of productivity can lead to inactivity.

Stagnation

Group stagnation is the result of a group set in its ways and resistant to change. Little happens in the group. This also can be a result of a team's failure to evaluate itself. When a team is newly formed, members are excited and creative. Teams must work to stay fresh and productive and not become dull and repetitive.

Poor choices

Selection of a team's goals and projects is important. Selecting projects that are outside a team's area of expertise or taking on too many projects can lead to problems. Also, setting unrealistic expectations, or being too vague when establishing expectations, can lead to team failure. All team members should help in making choices to assure the best possible choice for the team.

Lack of Accountability

Accountability deals with a group and its members fulfilling their obligations. Every team member must come to meetings fully prepared. When one person is unprepared, it affects the productivity of the entire team.

RESPONSIBILITIES OF GROUP MEMBERS

Every member should fulfill all of their team responsibilities. The following is a list of the responsibilities of all team members:

- *Prepare for the discussion*—A lack of preparation decreases team productivity.

- *Speak freely*—Every team member has different experiences and training. Different perspectives can increase the productivity of the group.

- *Listen thoughtfully*—Try to understand varying points of view; however, do not accept an unsupported idea.

- *Think straight*—Be alert for errors in thinking or facts. Also, watch for weak arguments, but be careful not to misinterpret what another is saying.

- *Speak up*—Present your ideas, but be careful not to monopolize the discussion. Let others talk, too.

- *Support your position*—Be prepared to give facts, examples, or authorities' opinions to support your statements. Be sure to quote accurately and concentrate on one or two important points.

18-6. All members of a grou should learn and fulfill their r sponsibilities. (Courtesy, Missi sippi Governor's School)

- *Do not argue over idea ownership*—Once you have presented an idea, it becomes group property.

- *Keep up*—If you do not understand something, say so. Remember, if you can relate ideas to your personal experiences, you can better understand.

- *Stay focused*—Digressions slow progress. Try not to repeat, and make sure all comments are relevant.

- *Be an attentive speaker*—Pay attention to other group members when speaking. Watch for signs of boredom or inattention. Arouse interests by involving others and giving examples.

- *Be pleasant*—Enjoy yourself and help others to do the same. Remember the Golden Rule. Accept criticism graciously.

REVIEWING

MAIN IDEAS

Systems thinking is looking at organizations and groups or teams as systems. A system is a group of interdependent parts which connect to make a whole.

Two basic models of organizational leadership are the pyramid model and the connected model. The pyramid model focuses on top-down leadership. The connected model focuses on the team effort, with the leader being part of the team.

Successful groups or organizations share similar characteristics. Members feel a sense of unity; they communicate clearly and work together to achieve a goal.

Team building can be seen as a three-phase process. The formation phase involves getting everything and everybody together. The focus of the norms development phase is on developing a code of conduct for the team. During the performance phase, the team is productive and continually evaluating its progress. A team's failure to continually evaluate itself can lead to problems, such as inactivity, stagnation, poor team choices, and lack of team member accountability. Every team member is responsible for the group's success.

QUESTIONS

Answer the questions using correct spelling and complete sentences.

1. What are the two primary models of organizational leadership? List three characteristics of each.

2. List and explain three characteristics successful groups have in common.

3. Define code of conduct. List five items that might be included in a team's code of conduct.

4. What is the three-phase process of team development?

5. Explain four common problems teams face.

EVALUATING

CHAPTER SELF-CHECK

Match the term with the correct definition. Write the letter by the term in the blank provided.

a. organization   d. connected model   g. value driven
b. systems thinking   e. group
c. pyramid model   f. team mission

1. _____ two or more people working together to accomplish a goal.
2. _____ a group or organization is made up of interrelated parts.
3. _____ being motivated and acting on things that are important to you.
4. _____ what the team wants to accomplish.
5. _____ organizational model characterized by top-down leadership.
6. _____ a large system.
7. _____ a web-like model of organization leadership.

EXPLORING

1. Contact three organizations or clubs in your local area. Ask if they have written team missions and codes of conduct. Compare and contrast the three groups and report to the class.

2. Check out a book about trust-building from your local library. Select two trust-building exercises and perform them with your group or class.

3. In groups of four or five, develop a mission statement and a code of conduct for a project of your choice, such as the development of a community recycling program.

19

ENCOURAGING PERSONAL MASTERY

> *Believe in yourself as being capable of overcoming all obstacles and weaknesses.*
> **Norman Vincent Peale**

People have much potential. Some people use more of their potential than others. Potential that is unused is lost. Both the individual and society lose when potential goes unused.

Individuals can use more of their potential by searching inward and setting goals that make use of potential. Mastering goals is a big, important step. It shapes how people feel about themselves.

How do you feel about yourself? How do you help other people feel good about themselves? Both involve understanding our strengths and weaknesses.

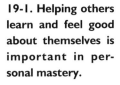

19-1. Helping others learn and feel good about themselves is important in personal mastery.

OBJECTIVES

This chapter is about helping people with personal mastery. It has the following objectives:

1. Explain the importance of personal mastery

2. Recognize personal strengths and limitations

3. List ways of developing a positive self-concept

4. Describe motivation and human needs

5. Explain the motivation of others

TERMS

biological needs
conceit
feeling
hierarchy of human needs
intuitive
intuitive-feeler
intuitive-thinker
motivation
personal mastery
self-concept
sensing
sensing-feeler
sensing-thinker
thinking

PERSONAL MASTERY

Personal mastery is using strengths and weaknesses to realize individual potential. Every individual has strong points and areas where they can improve. Personal mastery results when people know their strengths and weaknesses and use them to make personal accomplishments.

Personal mastery shapes two major aspects of leadership: the leader's mastery of himself or herself and the leader's approach in helping others understand themselves. Both help unlock human potential.

RELATIONSHIP TO SELF-CONCEPT

Self-concept is how an individual feels about himself or herself. It begins with an appreciation of who you are and respecting yourself. Personal mastery includes having a good self-concept.

Developing self-concept begins with an awareness of your weaknesses as well as your strengths. You must believe in yourself and accept yourself to have a positive self-concept.

With a positive self-concept, you can accept mistakes or setbacks without shame, guilt, or blame. You will learn to accept the weaknesses and mistakes of others.

As you develop a positive self-concept, the feeling that you need to prove yourself to others will lessen. You can approach tasks without fear of failure or defeat and help other people to do the same. Relationships with others will become stronger. More people will want to be around you. You will be capable of facing all kinds of situations!

19-2. Self-concepts are often evident when people work together.

IMPORTANCE OF PERSONAL MASTERY

Personal mastery is essential to becoming a well-rounded person and a good leader. Having a positive self-concept is a major part of personal mastery and allows an individual to be a success.

Individuals avoid playing false roles when they develop positive self-concepts. These false roles include trying to convince others everything is going well or blaming others for the way you feel. Striving for a positive self-concept brings out the potential for leadership. All people need to assess themselves in developing personal mastery.

Mastering oneself is a major part of building a positive self-concept. It can lead to many rewards:

- More confidence

- More trust in ideas, skills, and knowledge

- Ability to turn opportunities into realities

- Use mistakes to learn and improve

- Fears and obstacles will not stop progress

- More dynamic and interesting person

- Gain social approval

- More emotional security

- More inner courage

- Ability to control your destiny

- Learn to handle success (If your head is in the clouds, keep your feet on the ground.)

- Will have positive feelings for and from others

SELF-CONCEPT OR CONCEIT

Confusion sometimes exists between having a positive self-concept and being conceited. **Conceit** is the excessive feeling of one's own worth. Although self-concept is feeling good about one's

19-3. Does this person have a positive self-concept or is the person conceited? Why? (It is hard to make judgments without good information.)

worth, the key difference is excess. Excess refers to frequent and open displays of worth. A conceited person is boastful and arrogant. This is unlike a person with a positive self-concept.

Positive people do not speak about their own personal worth. The worth of these people naturally shines through to others. The difference between conceit and positive self-concept is a fine line.

PERSONAL STRENGTHS AND LIMITATIONS

People who want to improve on their self-concept must determine their strengths and limitations. You can do this by identifying and building on strengths and areas where you need to make improvements.

One way to learn your strengths is to make a list of personal attributes of people—not just you, but all people. Check the ones that you have. Put a circle by those that you do not have but that you need to feel better about yourself. You need to recognize your limitations before you can overcome them. After this personal analysis, it will be easier to overcome your limitations.

Decide the importance of each attribute as related to your self-concept. Ask yourself, "How does this enhance or hinder my self-concept?" From that point, you should be able come up with a reasonable starting point in improving your self-concept.

As a leader, you can encourage the people around you to do the same thing. Identifying strengths and weaknesses is the first step in encouraging personal mastery.

DEVELOPING A POSITIVE SELF-CONCEPT

People can improve their self-concept if they make a commitment to do so. A good beginning is to build on successes. Start with situations where success is likely. When there is success, emphasize it. The following is a list of suggestions to help develop a positive self-concept:

- Begin positive self-talk; don't put yourself down
- Do quality work; then compliment yourself to yourself
- Set goals
- Be on time (being late detracts)
- Dress to be successful (You want to feel good about yourself and convey the proper image.)
- Speak up and let others know your views
- Tackle the things you fear; don't put them off or fuss over them
- Forgive yourself as you would others
- Continue to learn and be observant
- Change undesirable habits and develop productive habits
- Seize opportunities to learn new skills
- Stand up for others
- Maintain good physical condition—exercise regularly
- Appreciate what you can do rather than what you are unable to do

⇨ Don't compare yourself to others

⇨ Count your blessings

⇨ Go the extra mile to do your best

⇨ Believe in yourself

By following these suggestions, you can begin to develop a positive self-concept. You will quickly begin to feel better about yourself.

MOTIVATION AND BASIC HUMAN NEEDS

Being a leader requires knowing others as well as yourself. People have different backgrounds, abilities, and attitudes.

MOTIVATION

Motivation is energizing and giving direction to human actions. Some motivation is from within an individual; other motivation is from external forces. What people do is based on their motivation. Motivation is closely tied to the needs of people, as was presented in Chapter 14.

What motivates people varies. Achieving awards or good grades may motivate some people. Other people may be motivated by money, or being around friends motivates others. Still other people are motivated by the personal satisfaction they receive from doing the best they can do. Understanding others is important in being a leader.

HIERARCHY OF HUMAN NEEDS

Leaders must realize that people have certain basic needs. These needs are a part of motivating them for personal mastery. Five basic needs of humans have been identified by A. H. Maslow and placed in a **hierarchy of human needs**. Human needs are in five-levels, with the basic needs coming first. Once individuals meet the first level, the next level of need becomes the motivation.

- Biological Needs—***Biological needs*** are the basic needs. These include food, sleep, shelter, and air. The need to survive is a person's primary concern. If a person is hungry, their primary concern is getting food. Reputation means little to someone who is without food. They will do whatever is necessary to satisfy this need.

■ Safety and Security—*Safety and security needs* represent freedom from fear. This can be in the physical sense (money, laws, property, etc.) or in the social sense (feeling at ease, knowing job duties, etc.). This level includes feeling secure about the biological needs that threaten survival.

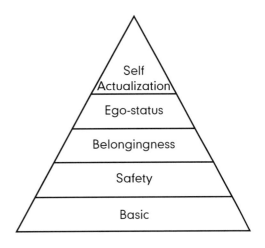

19-4. Hierarchy of needs.

■ Social Needs—*Social needs* relate to a feeling of belonging. The focus is on being accepted as an individual. These include feeling that others accept your ideas and that you have a sense of belonging with your peers. Families, social clubs, and organizations are important in meeting social needs. Being accepted by peers is a strong motivation.

■ Self-Esteem (Ego)—*Self-esteem needs* involve the desire for respect by others and a need to feel important. These relate to receiving recognition for your efforts. Being on the school's honor role or getting elected to a leadership position can help fill this need. Many other ways of meeting this need exist.

■ Self-Fulfillment—*Self-fulfillment needs* (also known as self-actualization) come when a person is reaching their potential. At this level, the person is striving for continued self-development. People who are self-fulfilled provide a service not for prestige but because they feel it is important and worthwhile.

Each level motivates people in different ways. For example, a person who is starting a new job receives their motivation from feeling accepted by others on the job. In this case, the physical needs and the security needs are no longer motives for the person. After meeting social needs, self-esteem needs might become the motivation. The individual would perhaps try to gain recognition for a job well done.

The level of needs serving as motivation to the individual can change any time. For example, if a storm damages an individual's home, security quickly becomes a concern and motivation.

MOTIVATION OF OTHERS

Motivation is a key to accomplishment. Effective leaders understand the role of motivation in being successful. Encouraging others helps motivate them to accomplish certain results or goals. Motivation is different for each person in a group.

MOTIVATION DIFFERENCES

Motivation differences are in two major areas: perceptions and judgment. Each of these has two subareas. Further, the two can be joined together in four categories.

Perception

People perceive almost everything in one of two ways: sensing and intuitive. **Sensing** is preferring action or concrete situations. Sensing people are motivated by real situations. They are contrasted with intuitive people. **Intuitive** means that associations or connections are most important. Their driving force is meaning.

Judgment

People also have two ways of coming to conclusions or making judgments: thinking and feeling. **Thinking** is when people fit judgments into a logical, analytical order. Their motivation is structure. **Feeling** is a more subjective way of making a judgment. Human values

19-5. People are motivated on the basis of perceptions and judgment.

and harmony interest these people. Care and caring is their motivating factor.

Combinations of Perception and Judgment

Perceptions and judgments can be combined to describe the driving forces of members of groups. Four categories are used:

- Sensing Thinkers—A *sensing-thinker* needs to know the planned results, the expectations of them, and how their contributions fit into the group effort. These people like to see progress being made toward group goals. They like to work within a clear chain of command and to see results.

- Sensing Feelers—A *sensing-feeler* needs a sense of belonging in the group. They must feel that no one objects to their presence and that they are to carry group purposes forward. These members like to share in planning a group's goals and know their ideas have had a fair hearing. They want results, but not at the expense of their relationship in the group.

- Intuitive Thinkers—An *intuitive-thinker* wants to know what the expectations of them are so they can work confidently. They like responsibilities delegated to them that are challenging and contribute toward the group's goals. These members need to be able to say at any given time, "This makes sense to me." They need to understand why something is to be done before they decide how to do it.

- Intuitive-Feelers—An *intuitive-feeler* wants to feel that the goals of the group make sense and are within reach. These members need to feel what they do contributes to the welfare of people beyond those in the group. Intuitive-feelers also need to have confidence in the leadership of the group with an assurance of consistent and fair treatment.

GROUP MOTIVATION

Differences among people can cause problems and conflicts in groups. Leaders need to be aware of this and use the differences to help the group. Effective leaders consider the type of differences and make assignments in planning activities and making decisions. This will keep the motivation of the group at a high level.

Other ideas that are helpful for leaders to keep in mind when motivating the members of a group are:

■ Recognition—Motivation increases when members receive recognition for their contributions toward the goal or project. A little praise can go a long way with some individuals.

■ Participation—People who have the opportunity to participate in the decision-making process will usually show more motivation. Effective leaders allow group members to help make decisions.

■ Communication—Communication helps increase members' motivation. When people understand something, they are more anxious to give their energy to accomplish it.

■ Concern—Showing a genuine concern for the members and their accomplishments will provide motivation and help the group be successful. Concern is often a two-way street—leaders have concern for group members and group members have concern for the leader.

Motivation with groups works very much like a battery in a car. If the car's battery is holding a charge, the car starts readily. However, if the battery has to have a jump every time, it loses it's effectiveness. Leaders who effectively use power and influence to start the group's motivation will not have to jump start the group constantly. Motivation will continue as the members rely on their past successes and move forward to new accomplishments and goals.

REVIEWING

MAIN IDEAS

Personal mastery involves realizing the potential of each human being. It involves self-concept—how an individual feels about himself or herself.

Building a positive self-concept involves personal mastery. Several rewards can result from striving to improve self-concept. Begin to make improvement by assessing your attributes in terms of what you feel you would like to be. Many approaches can be used to improve self-concept.

Motivation is an important part of personal mastery. A. H. Maslow has a widely accepted theory of "hierarchy of human needs." It is based on the importance of human needs in determining the level of motivation of an individual.

Differences in motivation are based on perceptions and judgment. These can be used in combination to describe individuals as sensing-thinkers, sensing-feelers, intuitive-thinkers, and intuitive-feelers.

QUESTIONS

Answer the questions using correct spelling and complete sentences.

1. Why is a positive self-concept essential to a person?
2. How does a positive self-concept differ from conceit?
3. According to Maslow, what are the five basic needs that people have?
4. How does a leader help fulfill the needs of the members of their group?
5. How do sensing-thinkers differ from intuitive-thinkers?
6. Evaluate what type of person you are and what motivates you.

EVALUATING

CHAPTER SELF-CHECK

Match the term with the correct definition. Write the letter by the term in the blank provided.

a. conceit
b. personal mastery
c. self-concept
d. biological needs
e. motivation
f. feeling
g. sensing

1. ____ energizing and directing behavior.
2. ____ excessive appreciation of one's own worth.
3. ____ how an individual feels about himself or herself.
4. ____ using strengths and weaknesses to realize individual potential.
5. ____ basic needs of a person to survive.
6. ____ perceiving situations on the basis of action or concrete examples.
7. ____ a subjective way of making judgment.

EXPLORING

1. Create an advertisement about yourself that sells your strong qualities.

2. Make a list of the items of jewelry and clothing you are wearing. In a column next to the list, write what each item says about you. Fold the paper so the second list does not show. Trade papers with a neighbor. Let them come up with their own list of what the items say about you. Get the paper back and compare the two lists. Think about what you might be trying to say with your clothing. This may show you that your appearance says a great deal about how you feel.

3. Volunteer to work two weekends at a food bank, community outreach center, or other related organization. Observe the needs of those people whom you encounter.

20

UNDERSTANDING
MENTAL MODELS

> *It's no exaggeration to say that a strong, positive self-image is the best possible preparation for success in life.*
> **Joyce Brothers**

Did you know that when certain species of birds hatch, they will follow the first moving object they see? They assume it is their parent, and for the remainder of their lives they show a preference for this object. Konrad Lorenz, a psychologist, conducted a study in which he demonstrated this phenomenon in ducks. He made sure he was the first moving object the hatchlings saw. Guess what! The ducklings followed him everywhere.

Though humans do not exhibit this type of behavior, there are patterns to their behavior. Researchers in the areas of psychology and sociology have studied human behavior and can offer us insight into them. Their models provide suggestions as to why we follow the people we follow and why people choose or are chosen for certain roles.

20-1. The leaders we choose are based on our mental models of persons in leadership positions.

OBJECTIVES

This chapter introduces mental models and their importance in leadership and personal development. It has the following objectives:

1. Describe the importance of perceptions

2. Explain how mental models are influenced by environment

3. Understand how roles/tasks are selected within a group

T E R M S

halo effect
member role
personality
role ambiguity
role conflict
selective perception
stereotyping

NOT EVERYTHING IS AS IT SEEMS

Have you heard someone say, "It isn't what exists but what we think exists that is important?" If so, you heard someone who was referring to perceptions being reality in the mind of the person.

PERCEPTIONS

How we perceive others affects how we treat them. Others' perceptions of how we treat them affect how they respond to us. In turn, our perception of their response affects how we perceive them. Confused? Perceptions are very complex. There are many factors involved.

We perceive, or become aware of things, through our senses of sight, smell, hearing, touch, and taste. Our perception, or knowledge obtained through the senses, is a mixture of information obtained from all of the senses. For example, think of eating an ice cream cone while sitting on a park bench on a beautiful spring day. You can probably imagine the sweetness of the ice cream, the freshness of the air, the brightness of the sun, the hardness of the bench beneath you, and the sound of the birds

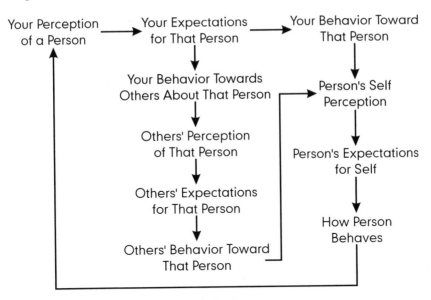

20-2. Perceptions and a person's performance are related.

in the trees as if you were really in the park. If you have had all of these experiences, your perceptions of them are stored in your brain. As you can see from this example, information often comes from more than one of the senses for a given perception. In this example, each sense was transmitting information to the brain.

Next, consider how different a person's perception would be if they did not like ice cream, had severe allergies, and could not go to the park in the spring when things were blooming, or lived in the desert where there was no park or trees. They would feel quite differently about the scenario presented.

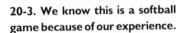
20-3. We know this is a softball game because of our experience.

Having negative perceptions, such as not liking ice cream, or have no perception, such as living in the desert, affects how a person feels about or interprets the world around them. The experiences a person has or does not have are affected by their environment.

We develop expectations and reactions based on experiences we have had. For example, when you see a fire blazing, you know the temperature around the fire will be higher. Or, when you walk across a street and a horn sounds, you know there is an automobile there. You have these expectations because of experiences you have had.

20-4. No two people share exactly the same interpretation of an event.

Individual Differences

No two people share the same interpretation of an event. Sure, we can agree on broader interpretations of events, but in the end, every person's interpretation is unique.

Have you ever participated in a discussion about an event and found others relaying details that you were not aware of? This is because people pay attention to different things in a given situation. The details you can most readily recall are those that you paid attention to—the things that were important to you or caught your eye. The things we pay attention to are determined by an interaction between our immediate needs, moods, cultural and societal influences, and attitudes.

Perceptual Limitations

Humans only sample part of the information available to them through their senses. To process all of the information available through the senses at any given time would waste energy and processing space in the brain. Those things we remember are the ones we pay attention to. This does not mean that other information we sampled is not in our memory. It is, but it is stored differently.

Also, our expectations lead us to see events, objects, people, and situations the way we want them to be. This theory of *selective perception* allows us to create our own world view. This world view is built upon our perceptions and beliefs. **Stereotyping** is the tendency to structure the world into a predictable pattern. We may treat members of a group according to our stereotypical perception. Sometimes, stereotyping is unfortunate. It creates biases that are incorrect. We need to keep an open mind to avoid stereotyping.

Perceptual Generalizations

Information from the various senses combines to influence our perceptions, whether we are aware of it or not. Suppose, for instance, you meet a person whose name is Jeff. Jeff has dark brown hair, and he is wearing a very distinctive cologne. During your meeting, Jeff offends you in a highly personal way. Your perceptions about dark-haired males, males named Jeff, and that particular cologne have all been negatively affected. The next time you smell that cologne, you may not like it. You probably will not even be aware that the reason you do not like it is its association with Jeff. The opposite is also true. Had the experience been a positive one—you and Jeff hit it off and became friends—your perceptions of these things on future encounters would probably be different.

How we see ourselves, and how others see us, affects our ability to establish relationships. If you do not have a clear understanding of who you are and what your standards are, it will be difficult for others to establish a close, mutually satisfying relationship with you.

Equally important is how you generally perceive others. Our evaluation of people we are not familiar with is often affected by the most obvious or salient characteristic that person possesses. Your perception of the school principal is not only affected by your perception of the individual but also by your perception of principals in general.

Also, if you think a person is superior in some important way, you will tend to allow that perceived superior ability to carry over to that individual's virtues. This is the **halo effect**. For instance, we are often surprised when a favorite television, movie, or sports star admits to some type of wrongdoing. Likewise, if a person has qualities you do not like, you may discount what they have to say.

20-5. We evaluate people based on salient characteristics.

PERCEPTIONS AND GROUP BUILDING

All of the factors involved in perception affect communication, conflict resolution, and group cohesiveness—important qualities for a successful group. You should remember that every member of a team or group has a lifetime of perceptions they bring with them. They have different values and belief systems. This is what we often refer to as an individual's **personality**. An individual's personality is how they deal with the world. We describe it in terms of behaviors and disposition, such as traits.

Leaders should remember three important aspects of perception when forming and leading groups:

- Members' own experiences and learned responses will affect their interpretation of events or messages.

- Members will interpret events and messages in ways that can resist any change to their personality.

- Members will group experiences so they can make whole patterns of life events.

Leaders should know their team members. Good leaders learn as much as possible about each member's frames of reference, needs, stereotypes, and other qualities. They also try to help team members overcome obstacles to their progress.

Personalities and Roles

One of the most challenging parts of team development is that of defining roles and responsibilities for members. A **member role** is a person's place on the team. It includes what the member expects to do and what other team members expect the member to do. It is important then to have clearly defined roles and to select people to fill roles very carefully.

All team members should have a clear understanding of all of the roles in a group. Understanding the jobs of other members increases the ability for everyone to work together. Every person has a clear picture of where they fit in the team and how their job contributes to its success.

Role ambiguity is when a person does not have a clear understanding of what is expected of him/her in their role. This can lead to **role conflict**. Role conflict is not understanding a role as related to other team members. When experiencing role conflict, a person can feel frustrated, helpless, and insecure. These feelings lead to a decrease in productivity, both for the person and for the team.

Also, to nurture the sense of teamness, every member must have a role, be aware of its importance, and be accountable for the work required by it. On a team, all roles are of equal importance.

Different roles are found on a group or team. All the team members should work together in deciding who will fill each role. Teams usually have eight roles. If the team has fewer than eight members, some members will fill dual roles. When deciding who should fill a role, personality and areas of expertise should be used.

The major roles in a group may include the following:

■ Leader—A team must have a strong leader to function. The leader must have a clear vision for the team, have other team members' trust, and help the team accomplish their goal. A leader cannot be imposed on the group. They must earn the right to lead. The leader's primary role involves keeping the group on task, leading discussions, ensuring all members have equal opportunity to participate in discussion, and resolving conflicts.

■ Recorder—The recorder should be a member who is organized, precise, and neat. Recorders should be good listeners and able to record what they have heard. They are responsible for recording all of the information from team meetings. Formal organizations elect secretaries to carry out the recorder role. Written records are prepared and kept in a permanent file.

■ Encourager—The encourager should be caring, tactful, and enthusiastic. Their role involves providing the team feedback on their team behaviors and motivating the team.

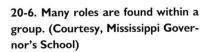
20-6. Many roles are found within a group. (Courtesy, Mississippi Governor's School)

- Time Keeper—The time keeper is responsible for keeping up with time and informing the team. In some cases, specific amounts of time may be allotted to a task. The time keeper must be organized and, of course, punctual. They must be able to operate the time-keeping equipment properly. (Have you been to a ball game where the time keeper failed?)

- Materials Specialist—The materials specialist is responsible for making sure the team has all of the supplies it needs to perform an activity. They should be resourceful and organized.

- Spokesperson—The spokesperson should be personable, articulate, and tactful. They are responsible for representing the team's thoughts to others outside the group. The duties of this role could also be assigned to the leader.

- Observer—The observer should be observant, tactful, and versed on group dynamics. They are responsible for providing the team feedback on how they are doing. This involves how well individuals are fulfilling their responsibilities and how well the team is functioning.

- Question Captain—The question captain should be neat, organized, and observant. They are responsible for seeing that questions raised but not answered in a team meeting are answered by the next meeting.

PSYCHOLOGY OF MEETINGS

Why is it that we need to have teams and team meetings. Why not just assign individuals tasks to perform and let everyone do their own things?

Teams fulfill some psychological needs. They are an intensive way of getting people involved. Some psychological needs satisfied by teams are:

⇨ the need to feel part of a group;

⇨ the need to feel togetherness, trust, and belonging;

⇨ the need to lessen the burdens of responsibility and loneliness; and,

⇨ the need to develop a sense of commitment among team members.

We are all part of many groups. It could be your class in school, church, community organization, or even the human race. But, by being part of

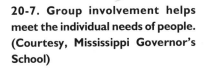

20-7. Group involvement helps meet the individual needs of people. (Courtesy, Mississippi Governor's School)

a smaller, more intimate group, we are better able to fulfill the psychological needs presented.

REVIEWING

MAIN IDEAS

Our perceptions are the result of complex psychological processes. They are affected by our experiences and are unique for every individual. Perceptions affect how we respond to others and how they respond to us. How we see ourselves and how others see us affects our relationships. It is important that we have a clear understanding of who we are and what our standards are.

Since groups consist of many different personalities, every member should be involved in the process of defining and designating roles and responsibilities. Involving every member of the group will help avoid role ambiguity and role conflict.

Groups or teams fulfill some important psychological needs. They are an intensive way of involving people and providing them with a sense of belonging.

QUESTIONS

Answer the questions using correct spelling and complete sentences.

1. Explain how perceptions affect behavior.

2. What is the relationship between attention and perception?

3. How does the halo effect shape perception of an individual?

4. How do perceptions affect group building?

5. Explain how role conflict can occur in a group? List the major roles in a group and briefly explain each.

CHAPTER SELF-CHECK

Match the term with the correct definition. Write the letter by the term in the blank provided.

a. stereotyping   c. member role   e. role conflict
b. halo effect   d. role ambiguity   f. selective perception

1. ____occurs when people do not have a clear understanding of what is expected of them.

2. ____allowing positive perceptions of a person's abilities to carry over to their virtues.

3. ____idea that what we experience is affected by expectations.

4. ____a feeling of frustration and helplessness that can be the result of role ambiguity.

5. ____the place a person fills on a team.

6. ____the tendency to structure our world into a predictable pattern.

EXPLORING

1. List the most important qualities you think people should possess. Next, think of a person you admire and list the admirable qualities that the person possesses. Compare the two lists.

2. Take a field trip or walk around the school grounds with several students. After returning to the classroom, write down everything you can remember. Compare your answers with the other students.

3. Get together with a group of other students. Practice assigning group roles. Explain why you think a person is or is not suited for a particular role.

4. What is the stereotype of the following: a football player? a debate team captain? a cheerleader? a winner of the state science fair?

21

BUILDING SHARED VISION

> Loyalty ... will cover a multitude of weaknesses.
> **Philip Armour**

Vision is important in being a successful leader. Good leaders need the ability to look into the future. After doing so, the leader can share what they see with others. Having good vision helps a person move ahead as a leader and in their career.

As a person develops vision, having sharing skills is important. Without sharing skills, the leader is unable to help others with thoughts, ideas, and feelings about the future. Building a shared vision helps others sense the future in similar ways to the leader. It builds a stronger team that is more likely to reach its goals.

21-1. Developing shared vision involves using materials that give all people the same information.

OBJECTIVES

This chapter introduces how a leader perceives the future and shares what they see with others. It has the following objectives:

1. Describe shared vision

2. List the benefits of shared vision

3. Explain how to develop a shared vision

4. Describe the role of a leader in the shared vision of a group

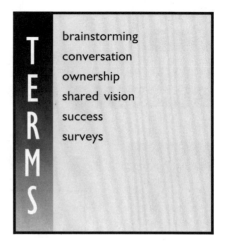

TERMS

brainstorming

conversation

ownership

shared vision

success

surveys

SHARED VISION: AN UNDERSTANDING

Building a shared vision is a part of our daily lives. We do it with our friends all of the time. Two examples are given here that help us understand shared vision.

THE APPLE OF MY EYE ... SEEING THE VISION

Take a deep breath, relax, and allow your mind to go blank. Clear your mind of all thoughts. Now that your mind is empty, you may think of anything you want to, except an apple. Whatever you do, do not think of a red, delicious apple. Don't do it now; don't think of an apple.

Not thinking of an apple as you were reading the preceding paragraph was impossible. No matter what you did, you found yourself unable to get that apple out of your mind. Some would say that was an unfair situation because you were asked not to think of something of which you were constantly reminded. However, this example is an excellent illustration of what it means to share the vision of one person with another.

FRIDAY NIGHT ON THE TOWN ... DEVELOPING A SHARED VISION

On Wednesday, you and two of your closest friends decide to get together Friday night, go to a movie, and cruise through the town. Over the next two days, you and your friends talk about the movie you want to see, where you will go to eat, and other places you plan to hang out. Finally, Friday night arrives and the plan that you and your friends have talked about happens. You start by going to the movie you have agreed upon, stopping at the local hamburger stand, and cruising the town just as you had talked about for two days.

Now what has this Friday-night-on-the-town got to do with a shared vision? Think about how the idea for going out on a Friday night started. Think about the process you and your friends went through in deciding which movie you would see, where you would eat, and other details. This is, in essence, the process of building a shared, mutually agreed on, vision for Friday night. A simple, yet true, example of what it means to build a shared vision.

21-2. Developing shared vision involves good communication.

SHARED VISION: A DESCRIPTION

Effective leaders have the ability to create a shared vision. By blending ideas from themselves and from those they serve, they create a vision in their mind of the direction the group should take. This image is much like the apple example earlier in the chapter. Just as you can imagine the apple, the effective leader can create a vision in their mind of what "can be."

Describing shared vision is not easy. It is not a physical object that can be felt. The best way to express the meaning of shared vision is to think of a jigsaw puzzle. If you had a jigsaw puzzle that had ten pieces and you were to give ten people a different piece, you simply have scattered pieces of the puzzle. However, if you were to bring the ten people together and have them put the puzzle together as a team, with each person helping equally, their shared effort would result in a complete puzzle. The complete puzzle is a picture that all ten people can enjoy not only because of what they see, but also because they each had an equal part in creating the finished product.

Vision, as covered in chapter 6, is an individual's mental picture of the future. It is based on the best information available. The vision will need to be continually revised as new information becomes available. One should never be set in their ways and unable to change their vision.

21-3. People work together better when they have a shared vision.

Shared vision is a group's mental picture of the future. A leader may help a group develop a common view of the future. Shared vision evolves among group members. It is not something that the leader can dictate to them. Having similar experiences and backgrounds makes it easier to develop a shared vision. Knowing as much as possible about the members of a group before attempting to develop shared vision is essential for a leader.

Leaders see each person they serve as valuable. Leaders want the ideas of the people they serve. Effective leaders gather the ideas of individuals and create a shared vision. If a vision is truly shared, it is developed with input from every member of a group. The shared vision inspires everyone to work hard to achieve a common goal.

SHARED VISION: THE BENEFITS

As a leader, creating a shared vision is important. It is important because of the benefits for you and the people who look to you for leadership. Several benefits are gained from shared vision:

- Involvement—The process of creating a shared vision requires involvement. This is based on active participation by the people you serve. It can take place in a variety of ways. You may seek input simply by asking people what they want to do. Involvement may occur through brainstorming, written surveys, committee meetings, open discussion, and in other ways. The way you choose to get input and involve others will vary from one situation to another. A leader must make a strong commitment to getting the ideas of others.

- Ownership—Creating a shared vision requires that many people have input and share their ideas. One important outcome of this process is shared **ownership**. This means that the members of the group feel that they own the vision. It belongs to them. Having full support means that you are serving as a facilitator to lead group members to the realization of their goals and dreams. Ownership is a key benefit of the shared vision process.

- Inspiration—Shared vision inspires others to take action. A leader may find himself or herself in situations where they are asked to serve as team captain, club officer, or committee chair. Regardless of the position, the leader cannot expect, nor should they be expected, to do all the work by themselves. Good leaders know that by creating a shared vision in which everyone is involved and has ownership will result in the group being inspired to take action. It is often said that 20 percent of the people end up doing 80 percent of the work in an organization. The reason for this is that only 20 percent of the people have been inspired to take action. If a person is to be successful as a leader, he or she must find ways to inspire everyone to get involved. The shared vision process can go a long way in making this happen.

■ Loyalty—Seeing the benefits of a shared vision is obvious. However, what are the personal benefits for the leader? Group members? The answer is loyalty. Loyalty is belief in someone else. Loyalty includes being faithful to another person. The loyalty and belief in the leader will grow as the members get involved. As the people around a leader succeed, the leader succeeds. This means you, as a leader, are only as successful as the group members. Loyalty of the group to you—the leader—results.

21-4. Loyalty results when followers and leaders are faithful to each other.

■ Success—Success results from shared vision. Shared vision is a part of being successful. **Success** is achieving worthy goals. Shared loyalty includes setting goals for a group and developing ways and means of achieving the goals. The members are active in many ways. Success results through shared vision and using the contributions of everyone in the group.

HOW TO CREATE SHARED VISION

Shared vision begins with you—the leader. As a leader, you must commit yourself to serving those who look to you for leadership. Shared vision will not occur if you do not want it to happen. Further, long-term success will not occur if you do not create a shared vision.

The important focus for you—the leader—is to get the input of others. This is most valuable as you go about developing shared vision. Several techniques of creating shared vision can be used. Three are included here: brainstorming, conversation, and surveys.

BRAINSTORMING

Brainstorming is bringing a group of people together to surface ideas or answers to questions. It is an open process where the ideas presented are not critiqued. No one is criticized for an idea, regardless of how silly it may sound. Being critical stops creativity.

Brainstorming is a good technique to use with committees and officer teams. It helps to solve problems in a way that all members of the group share. Successfully using brainstorming is based on the notion that there are no wrong answers. The possibilities are endless.

21-5. Brainstorming may occur in a variety of situations.

As the leader of a group, you will need to sort through the ideas. Identify the areas that everyone tends to agree with or feels comfortable about. Once this occurs, the group can focus on an agreed-upon answer to the problem. This results in a shared vision and shared implementation.

CONVERSATION

Conversation is informal spoken communication. All people communicate through conversation. Some people wonder how conversation creates shared vision. It does so by providing the opportunity for people to express themselves and to hear what others have said.

As a leader, maintaining contact with followers is important for you. Listen to the people you serve. By listening to people, you can learn their ideas, interests, and what they expect from their leaders. It also helps the leader understand what people want out of their association or organization.

21-6. Conversations among people are good ways to get information that leads to a shared vision.

By sharing the ideas you have collected with others, you get reactions that are both positive and negative. This input can be very helpful to a leader. It helps decide and select a course of action. Conversation allows the leader to determine the key elements needed in a shared vision. Open discussion is an important element while creating a shared vision.

SURVEYS

A *survey* is a formal way of collecting information from people. Surveys may use questionnaires or checklists for use in providing suggestions to the leader. Surveys are based on the simplest way of getting information: asking questions.

Good leaders recognize that they do not have all of the answers. They must ask the "right" questions to get the needed information. This gives better understanding of the people that a leader serves.

After the answers to questions have been collected, the answers must be organized to provide meaning. Look at what more people are saying. Cluster the answers and draw meaning from them. This provides valuable information for use in developing shared vision.

YOUR ROLE AS A LEADER

Being a leader is not easy. Sometimes, being a leader is fun, and sometimes, it is hard. Leaders get glory, but often their efforts go unnoticed. The important thing to remember is that as a leader, the people are depending on you. They have put their trust and commitment in you and are expecting you to represent them in a positive way. No matter how small or large your leadership responsibility may be, you must always remember that people are depending on you and you must do everything you can to be the leader they expect.

One of the most important roles you have as a leader is to create a shared vision. A shared vision inspires hope in those who follow you. Shared vision causes other people to get involved. A shared vision encourages others and motivates the leader to work hard and give top effort.

Leaders recognize four important roles in creating a shared vision. These roles are:

- Listening—Listening is often overlooked, yet it is an important leadership tool. If you are to create a shared vision for the people you serve, you must listen to them first. You must seek to understand their needs and find out what they are looking for from you and the organization. It is critical that a leader does not confuse listening and hearing. Each of us hears a great deal of information; however, what we hear is not nearly as important as what we understand. Leaders must listen carefully to the needs of the people they serve. Remember, hearing equals noise, listening equals understanding.

- Communicate—Effective leaders effectively communicate! It is your responsibility as a leader to have good communication skills. Communication is both verbal and nonverbal. Developing skill in both areas is important. Perfecting the skills is a lifelong process. However, your ability to communicate effectively will enhance your efforts to inspire others to take action in a shared vision.

- Action—Everyone has heard the expression, "actions speak louder than words." This is especially true of leaders. People are looking for their leaders to be action-oriented. As you help others develop a shared vision, they will look to you to take action—to live the vision! The example you set will set the tone for others. If you are slow to act, people will lose their enthusiasm for the vision. You must be proactive in your actions if you are to inspire a shared vision in others.

■ Encouragement—Everyone needs to be encouraged from time to time. If you expect others to stay focused on and excited about the vision, you must continually and sincerely encourage those who follow your leadership. Encouragement is often overlooked by leaders. It is essential if vision is to become reality.

21-7. Taking action is important for a leader.

REVIEWING

MAIN IDEAS

Creating a shared vision is the core of being an effective leader. It is an essential part of personal development. Just as other skills, the ability to create shared vision is learned. You can learn to do it if you want to be an effective leader.

Several techniques can be used in creating shared vision. Three techniques are brainstorming, conversation, and surveying group members to gather information. With each, the leader is trying to learn the ideas of the group.

A leader's role includes listening, communicating, acting, and encouraging. Members want to know that their concerns are heard. They want to see a leader who takes action in a timely manner. Along the way, members need encouragement and this is a prime responsibility of the leader.

QUESTIONS

Answer the questions using correct spelling and complete sentences.

1. What is shared vision?

2. How does a leader create shared vision?

3. What are the benefits of shared vision?

4. What is the role of the leader in creating shared vision?

5. How will understanding shared vision improve you as a leader?

EVALUATING

CHAPTER SELF-CHECK

Match the term with the correct definition. Write the letter by the term in the blank provided.

a. conversation   c. brainstorming   e. shared vision
b. success   d. survey

1. ____used to collect information from people.

2. ____an open session to surface ideas and concepts.

3. ____the feeling experienced when a goal is attained.

4. ____informal oral communication.

5. ____having members of a group with a similar vision.

EXPLORING

1. Make an appointment with the president and/or owner of a local business with 30 or more employees. Ask the person to share with you their vision for the future of their business. Write a report on what you learn. Give an oral report in class.

2. Make an appointment with the principal of your school. Conduct an interview to learn about the vision of the school administrators. Follow-up by asking how they involve teachers, community citizens, and others in building a shared vision. Prepare a report on what you learn.

3. Use brainstorming in a committee or officer team meeting to surface ideas to help improve the group. Assess how this helps develop a shared vision. Prepare a report on what you observe.

22

SHARED DECISION MAKING

> *Surround yourself with the best people you can find, delegate authority, and don't interfere.*
> **Ronald Reagan**

We make many decisions every day. Sometimes we make them ourselves. Sometimes we make them with others, especially those decisions that are more difficult.

The process we use to make decisions varies. We might flip a coin, draw straws, or vote. Have you ever voted for something, whether it be a class leader or your favorite song? Were you always satisfied with the outcome?

Every year, people all across the United States vote for leaders to hold various offices in the government. Every four years, citizens elect a President. Have you ever watched the election coverage on TV as they continuously update the results of the voting?

22-1. Voting is an important way decisions are made in the United States.

OBJECTIVES

This chapter is about sharing decision-making with other people. It has the following objectives:

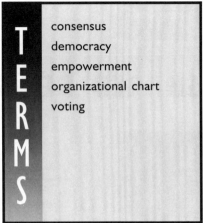

T
E
R
M
S

consensus
democracy
empowerment
organizational chart
voting

1. Describe the ways groups make decisions

2. Explain the importance of delegation

3. Describe how to delegate

4. Explain the advantages and disadvantages of individuals and groups for accomplishing tasks

GROUP DECISION-MAKING PROCESSES

22-2. Leader decision-making is the leader making a decision and announcing it to a group. (A tap of a gavel may be used to add emphasis to the decision.)

Decisions affecting groups are made in several ways. Among the most common are: the leader makes the decision, the group votes, or a consensus is reached. You can probably think of times when each was used in a group in which you were a member. Each method has its advantages and disadvantages and must be considered when a decision is to be made.

LEADER MAKES THE DECISION

Leader decision-making is the leader making a decision and announcing the decision to others. The decision may be made with or without input from the group. An advantage to this type of decision-making is the decision can usually be made quickly. This type of decision-making may be used for less critical matters that do not require group ideas or when a decision must be made before all members can be contacted.

Sometimes a leader may feel, after receiving group ideas, that an unpopular decision is necessary. Here, the leader may decide—feeling that the group's interests will best be served by doing the right thing.

VOTING

Voting is used because it appeals to a sense of fairness. Everyone can have a say-so in making a decision. **Voting** means that everyone involved in a decision makes a choice from the available alternatives, and the one chosen by the most people wins. Sometimes, re-voting may be needed to assure that the winner has a simple majority of the votes.

The idea of the majority deciding is the essence of **democracy**, upon which our form of government is based. Democracy means that the power of making decisions rests with the people. In a democracy, voting is viewed as a right, privilege, and responsibility.

Voting also has the added advantage of being relatively quick. However, it can be no better than the information the voters use in deciding how they will vote. Voters need good information to make good decisions!

Making a decision by voting may lead to envy or anger among the losing side of the voters. The decision is a win/lose situation. The losing side may be less supportive when it comes time to carry out the decision. Therefore, many organizations have rules for decision-making, which limit the degree of loss for either side because of a vote.

Voting is the decision-making process used to elect representatives in our country. The winner gets to be a member of the government and the loser does not. Have you ever been involved in a political campaign? This can be a very educational way to learn about decision-making.

CONSENSUS

The **consensus** process usually takes longer because people must have enough information before an agreement can be reached. With a consensus, people do not vote. They discuss and gather information on an issue until an agreement is reached. Basically, everyone can say no, or veto, a proposal. However, besides "yes" or "no," each person has the choice of "acceptable." This means that the decision is not his or her first choice, but is good enough to agree and to support.

22-3. Considerable time for discussion and gathering information may be needed for a group to reach a consensus.

There are several advantages to building a consensus. Perhaps the most important is that it means the decision has the support, although possibly with varying degrees of enthusiasm, of all group members. By spending the time going through proposed solutions, members can combine ideas. This can lead to new and creative solutions.

Besides taking longer, another drawback of building a consensus is that it is possible to reach a point where no decision can be made. Since all group members must agree, a refusal to compromise by one member means a further decision must be made. Either the group will revert to voting, or the leader will decide. Some organizations will set rules ahead of time about what to do in this situation.

DELEGATION

Delegation is sharing decisions, work, and similar duties with other people. In any group, the leader must learn to delegate. They cannot do everything alone. Leaders need help. Good leaders know the strengths of the people in the group and use them in an effective manner. This shows value and respect for members.

Another way to look at delegation is it frees the leader to do other things. The leader can focus on issues that may be of high priority.

Another word similar to delegation, which stresses the role of the follower, is empowerment. *Empowerment* is used in today's business world to reflect the need for subordinates to be given the power to make decisions at the lowest level possible. This makes everyone feel they have a say in how things are done in an organization.

Models of leadership were discussed in chapter 18. The traditional models of leadership place leaders at the top, making decisions that affect those below. This model is based upon the way the military has been run throughout history.

Modern leadership stresses the importance of all individuals in an organization involved in the decision-making process. For an organization to run effectively, all members must be committed and motivated, and feel they have a significant contribution to make to the overall team effort. ***Organizational charts*** are used to show the relationships among all people in an organization. Some companies have organizational charts that appear to have been turned upside down when compared with yesterday's pyramid-shaped organizational charts. Still others have organizational charts that seem flat, reflecting the fact that everyone in the organization is important. Models of organizational leadership were discussed in an earlier chapter.

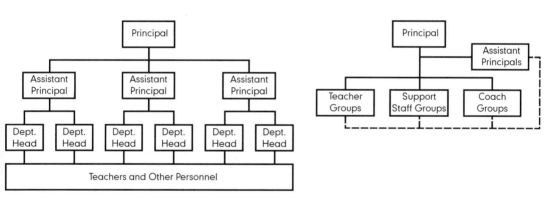

Traditional Line Organization   Newer Functional Team Organization

22-4. **Sample organizational charts. (In the line organization, a structure exists between the teachers and the principal. In the newer approaches, teachers and other staff members have direct access to the principal. Assistant principals fill supportive roles.)**

DEGREES OF DELEGATION

Delegation is not always all or nothing. There are degrees of delegation, from simply gathering information to acting without having to ask for permission.

Experts have identified five degrees of delegation. Each is suited for a particular type of group member. You, as the leader, must know members and decide which is appropriate.

Gather Information and Report Back

A group member gathers information and brings it to you. You take the information, decide, and act. This is appropriate when the member is new and inexperienced.

Gather Information and Recommend Action

A group member gathers information and recommends a course of action. You approve or disapprove the recommendation and take action. This is a good choice for a relatively new member when you want them to know that you value their opinion.

Gather Information and Inform Leader on Plan of Action

A group member gathers information and plans for action. This plan is approved or disapproved by the leader. Once approved, the member carries out the plan. This is appropriate when you are developing a rising leader and want them to be very involved in the entire decision-making process.

Gather Information, Take Action, and Inform Leader

This is almost complete delegation, except the individual is obligated to inform you of actions taken so you are aware of what is going on. This is appropriate when you can trust the member to act responsibly. It shows group members that you trust them.

Gather Information and Take Action

This is full delegation. The group member is trusted and given the power to decide and take action. It implies great trust in individuals and faith in their capabilities. This is appropriate for highly experienced and trustworthy group members.

GUIDELINES FOR DELEGATING

As a leader, your goal should be complete delegation as often as possible. Complete delegation, however, does not mean the leader is not involved. Some guidelines to consider when delegating are:

■ Provide Expected Results— When you delegate, share with the group member your expected results. Do not dictate how to go about getting those results. Otherwise, you are not really delegating. Dictating how to do something suggests a lack of trust in individuals and their abilities.

22-5. Delegate to individuals who have the skills to perform the task.

■ Set Deadlines—Usually, leaders should set deadlines by which the work being delegated should be done. The deadlines are "target" dates for completion of the work. People are often more productive and on-task if they have a deadline to meet.

■ Share Information—Share with the group members any information you have about the task. Allow them access to sources of information they need to accomplish the task. Give them the best possible shot at succeeding.

■ Don't Delegate Too Soon—Do not delegate too much to someone not ready for the responsibility. Often, an individual may need training before being ready to tackle tasks alone. Be sensitive to this and do not pile on too much too soon.

■ Show an Interest—Establish some way of keeping up with what is going on. This should be done in a non-threatening way. It should not appear that you are interfering in matters that you have delegated. However, since you are probably the one who will be held accountable for the results, it only makes sense to keep up with the progress.

WHAT TASKS TO DELEGATE

When you are ready to begin delegating, take a few moments to organize the tasks your group or organization is responsible for. These tasks can be broken down into three groups: Tasks only you can accomplish, tasks that can be delegated when someone is ready, and tasks that can be delegated immediately.

■ Leader tasks—Tasks that only you can accomplish include things assigned to you due to your role as leader. An example is running a group meeting. Another is deciding which task to delegate and to whom.

■ Knowledge and skill—Some tasks require certain knowledge or skills. As a leader, you are responsible for ensuring that people have the skills they need to accomplish the tasks you delegate. When you are sure a member possesses the skills necessary to accomplish a given task, you can immediately delegate.

■ Strengths and Weaknesses—Determine which tasks should be given to which group members, considering both their strengths and their needs. If members want to do a particular task, they will more likely be motivated to do a good job.

Finally, delegate with enthusiasm! Sell the task to the individual. Help the person see the value of accomplishing the task. Provide recognition when the task is done.

GROUP OR INDIVIDUAL

Several factors should be considered when deciding whether a task should be given to an individual or a group. Table 22-1 lists factors to consider in delegating to groups or individuals.

Table 22-1
Deciding to Delegate to an Individual or a Group

Individual	Group
Small tasks	Large tasks
No consensus needed	Team consensus needed
Easier for an individual	Too complex for an individual
Possesses skills to do task	Group not interested
Not a routine task for a group	Duties of a group, such as a standing committee

REVIEWING

MAIN IDEAS

Groups make decisions in several ways. The most common are when the leader makes the decision, the group votes, or a consensus is reached. Each has advantages and disadvantages that should be considered when a decision is to be made.

Since leaders cannot and should not do everything themselves, they delegate tasks to group members. This shows members that you have trust in their abilities.

Varying degrees of delegation are used. These vary from sending a member to gather information to giving a member the power to act without getting permission first. The nature of the task and the abilities of the member should be considered when deciding which degree of delegation to use.

When a leader delegates, strive to ensure the success of the person in accomplishing the task. They should provide a clear picture of the expected results. They should also share any information pertinent to the task. Finally, they should show an interest and keep up with the progress of the member.

Delegating a task to an individual or group needs careful assessment. For small, simple tasks, an individual might be the perfect choice. For a large, complicated task, a group may be necessary. In any situation, the advantages and disadvantages of each should be considered.

QUESTIONS

Answer the questions using correct spelling complete sentences.

1. What are the three primary ways a group makes decisions and what are the advantages of each?

2. What are the five degrees of delegation?

3. Name three of the guidelines a leader should consider when delegating tasks.

4. Under what circumstances would you give a task to an individual? A group?

EVALUATING

CHAPTER SELF-CHECK

Match the term with the correct definition. Write the letter by the term in the blank provided.

a. voting   c. democracy   e. organizational chart
b. consensus   d. empowerment

1. _____a solution everyone can live with.

2. _____giving subordinates decision-making authority.

3. _____shows relationships between people in an organization.

4. _____decision-making process with a winner and a loser.

5. _____form of government where the majority decides issues by voting.

EXPLORING

1. Get involved in a local election campaign. Politicians always need help and the experience will help educate you firsthand about our way of voting persons into office. Tell the class about your experience.

2. Decide whether an individual or a group would be best suited for the following tasks. Be prepared to explain.

   a. solving a crossword puzzle
   b. building a treehouse
   c. writing a poem
   d. setting up a soup kitchen for the homeless
   e. finding a cure for cancer

23

PRESIDING OVER MEETINGS

Presiding over meetings is a challenging and rewarding experience. The success of a meeting is closely related to the skills of the person who presides over it. Of course, all members have responsibility for having a good meeting.

Participating in a club will make meetings fun. You may already belong to clubs in your school or community. Having a basic understanding of meetings will help you grow as a leader.

How meetings are conducted is continually changing. As a leader, you will want to keep informed. Today, members are given more say-so. The presiding officer's role is expanding to include member-friendly roles.

23-1. Presiding officers need good skills to have an effective meeting.

OBJECTIVES

This chapter is about having good meetings that meet the needs of members. It has the following objectives:

1. Explain the role of meetings

2. Describe the requirements for effective meetings

3. Describe how to preside over meetings

4. Explain how to use parliamentary procedure

5. Categorize main, incidental, subsidiary, privileged, and unclassified motions

6. Perform parliamentary procedure abilities

7. Describe the importance of consensus building

TERMS

ad hoc committee
ballot
bylaws
committee
incidental motion
main motion
meeting
minutes
old business
order of business
parliamentarian
parliamentary procedure
presiding officer
principle motion
privileged motion
quorum
roll call vote
salient point
secret ballot
simple majority
standing committee
subsidiary motion
unclassified motion
voice vote

ROLE OF MEETINGS

A *meeting* is a group assembled for a particular purpose. They are usually to conduct business or learn about some particular topic. Meetings are a part of our culture. We use meetings for many purposes. The benefits we get from meetings are related to how well the meetings are planned and carried out.

Meetings serve several important roles. Some roles relate to having a good club. Other roles involve serving the needs of members. The nature of a meeting is often based on the skills of the leader and the tradition established for the meeting.

Roles of meetings include:

⇨ conducting the business of an association or organization

⇨ providing educational opportunities for members

⇨ helping members develop leadership and personal skills

⇨ providing social activities or entertainment for members

⇨ recognizing the outstanding work of members

⇨ getting reports on events or activities that are being planned

All meetings should be designed to provide a way for members to be treated fairly. Democratic processes should be followed.

23-2. Getting involved in organized clubs can make meetings fun.

Joining an organization usually involves making a commitment to attend meetings. Each member has the responsibility to understand the purpose, guidelines, and rules of the organization they have joined. Organizations provide the most benefits to those who actively participate. All members must understand the purpose, guidelines, and rules of organizations.

Once you decide to join a school or community organization, you will attend meetings. Each group has its own set of meetings. Each club may meet once a month, twice a year, or as often as the group decides to meet.

REQUIREMENTS OF EFFECTIVE MEETINGS

Meetings will be more effective if they are carefully planned and carried out. A team of elected officers or a committee is usually in charge of an organization's meeting. The structure of meetings varies widely. Many young people prefer meetings with a definite structure. They also like for the structure to be flexible so individual needs and interests can be met.

SCHEDULE IN ADVANCE

Meetings should be scheduled and announced in advance. This allows people to work the meeting into their busy lives and for the leaders to plan a good program. Meetings called at the last minute often lack quality. Poor meetings cause members to lose interest.

ORDER OF BUSINESS

An *order of business* is the step-by-step plan for the conduct of a meeting. An order of business is sometimes known as an agenda.

A written order of business should be prepared well before a meeting takes place. The officers or other responsible people prepare the order of business. Most orders of business are one page or less in length. They contain a list of business items for the meeting. Copies of the order of business are often duplicated and given to members when they arrive at the meeting room. Sometimes, the members approve the order of business when the meeting begins.

A standard order of business might include:

■ Call to Order—The call to order specifies the individual who is responsible for beginning the meeting. It often shows a specific time for this to take place.

■ Action on Minutes—Many organizations keep minutes of meetings. *Minutes* serve as the official written record of business in a meeting. The minutes of the previous meeting are acted on at the beginning of a meeting. This may involve an individual reading the minutes, handing out written copies, or orally summarizing the events of the last meeting. Corrections, if any, are made and the minutes are approved.

Minutes of a Regular Meeting

_____
(Organization Name)

_____
(Date)

Call to Order: The Meeting was called to order at _____ (time) by the president, _____ (name).

Roll: _____ (number of members present)

Minutes: Minutes of the previous meeting were read and approved.

Treasurer's Report: The treasurer reported a balance on hand of $_____ in the checking account and $_____ in savings.

Committee Reports: _____ (name) gave the following for the Recreation Committee: (include a brief statement summarizing the report).

Program: Example—Jane Smith presented slides on Australia.

Old Business: Example—Members were reminded to bring toys to the next meeting for the "Toys for Tots" campaign.

New Business: Example—A motion was made by Jill Olson that the organization sell Christmas wreaths. Sam Carter seconded the motion, and the motion carried.

Adjourn: The meeting adjourned at _____ (time).

_____   _____
Signed: President   Signed: Secretary

23-3. Sample format for keeping minutes.

- Reports of Officers and Committee Members—Most organizations have individuals or committees that are working on various projects. A financial report is often provided by the office of treasurer. Time is often allocated for these reports.

- Old Business—*Old business* refers to matters remaining from a previous meeting. These are handled before new business is begun.

- New Business—New business includes items for action that have not been considered before.

Treasurer's Report

Balance on hand at date of last report . . . . $_____

Receipts since last report:
                Dues . . . . $_____
                Donations . . . . $_____
Total Receipts . . . . $_____

Disbursements since last report:
                Flowers . . . . $_____
                File Cabinet . . . . $_____
Total Disbursements . . . . $_____

Current Balance . . . . $_____

Signed: _____ Date_____
       (Treasurer)

23-4. Sample format for a financial report.

■ Program—Many meetings include an informative program. The program is usually on a topic of interest to the members, such as developments in technology, career or educational opportunities, and protecting the environment.

■ Adjournment—Adjournment is the time when the meeting is to end. In some cases, a specific time has been set. This assures that the meeting moves along and does not bog down in detail. Meetings held during the school day are often regulated by the length of class periods.

GOOD MEETING LOCATION

Meetings need to be held in a convenient and comfortable location. Those held at school will normally be in a classroom. Those held at locations away from the school should be in places that are convenient and safe for those who attend. The facilities should help the group to have the best possible meeting. Appropriate chairs, tables, and other facilities should be available.

Order of Business
Meeting of FFA Chapter
Clinton High School
March 18, 1999
10:00 a.m.
Agriculture Classroom

Call to Order: President—Margie Oswego
      Welcome
      Announcements

Minutes of Previous Meeting: Secretary—James Gonzales

Reports:
      Treasurer—Angelica Loviza
      Social Committee—Jason Sloan

Old Business:
      Completing plans for making tour of horticulture industry

New Business:
      Selecting delegates for the State Convention
      Planning escargot sale

Program:
      Introduction—Jay Smith
      "Agriculture in Our State"—Honorable Rick Perry, Commission of Agriculture

Adjournment: President—Margie Oswego

23-5. Sample order of business. (Note: With official meetings, the opening and closing ceremony may be used to begin and end the meeting.)

FOLLOW BYLAWS

Organizations usually have constitutions, bylaws, and other regulations. These may include information about their meetings.

Bylaws are the rules or laws of an organization. They are developed and voted upon by the membership. Bylaws provide for fair and impartial treatment of members.

OFFICER DUTIES

Most organizations elect officers to lead in carrying out the work of the organization. Officers commonly elected are: president, vice president,

23-6. Officers need to know their roles in meetings.

secretary, and treasurer. Officers need to know how to fulfill the duties of their office.

The president usually presides over a meeting. A gavel is used to signal to members by tapping. Two taps calls the meeting to order. Three taps of the gavel signals members to stand. One tap of the gavel signals that a motion has either passed or failed. One tap closes a meeting.

QUORUM AND VOTING

For an official meeting to take place, a quorum must be present. A *quorum* is the minimum number of members that are present for members to legally carry out business. The bylaws of an association usually prescribe the quorum, such as half of all members must be present for voting.

Voting is how people make their choices about issues or other matters. It takes place through four common methods:

■ Voice Vote—A *voice vote* is typically responding "yes" or "no" to a motion when the vote is called for by the presider. Voice votes lack precision because no counts are made. The presider makes a judgment based on the side with the most votes.

■ Rising Vote—In a rising vote, people are asked to stand to indicate whether they support or oppose an issue. A modification of this includes a show of hands. This is an easy method of voting, but does not allow privacy when the votes are cast.

■ Secret Ballot—A *ballot* is a piece of paper on which a voter makes a mark or writes words showing her/his preferences. Ballots handled so the public does not know how any individual voted is a *secret ballot*.

- Roll Call—A *roll call vote* is a method of voting in which the names of all members are read aloud and each individual indicates their vote. How a person votes is not a secret. Votes are recorded and could become a part of the records of an assembly.

Most decisions are made by a simple majority of those who vote. A *simple majority* is one more than half of all votes cast. In some cases, a two-thirds or sixty percent vote may be required. In elections, runoffs are held to assure that the winner has at least a simple majority.

QUALITIES OF A GOOD PRESIDER

The person who presides over a meeting should exhibit qualities of a good presiding officer. Officers and individuals who aspire to leadership positions often study how to be a good presider.

Here are a few characteristics of a good presider:

⇨ Speaks clearly and distinctly

⇨ Has a professional personal appearance

⇨ Is fair to all people

⇨ Carries out business in a deliberate manner

⇨ Begins and ends meetings on time

23-7. Good presiders must be confident and impartial. (The exchange of the gavel is the symbol of passing duties from one officer to the next.)

⇨ Knows the rules associated with the association

⇨ Knows parliamentary and consensus procedures

⇨ Plans well ahead of time

⇨ Admits to mistakes and corrects errors

⇨ Uses correct grammar

⇨ Practices common courtesies and shows respect for other people

It is the duty of the **presiding officer** (president) to enforce the rules and orders of the assembly. For the process to work effectively everyone needs to know the basics of parliamentary procedure.

USING PARLIAMENTARY PROCEDURE

Parliamentary procedure is a method of conducting meetings in an orderly manner. It is based on the rules first set by the British Parliament hundreds of years ago. All individuals are given the opportunity to participate in debating issues and making decisions.

Clubs or organizations will be more effective if parliamentary procedure is properly used. Parliamentary procedure provides rules for an organization to use to conduct its meetings. Everyone needs some skills in parliamentary procedure. Most people will find themselves participating in a business or community meeting at some point. Parliamentary procedure is a democratic process. It is important to know and understand these basic procedures.

Each parliamentary procedure motion has a set of salient points. These **salient points** are basic descriptions of each motion. Salient points indicate if a motion requires a second, if a motion is debatable or undebatable, and type of vote it requires.

PRINCIPLE MOTION

The **principle motion** is the main motion. This is the motion from which all business of a group is transacted. To place a motion on the floor, a member asks for recognition by saying "Madam/Mister Chairperson" and must be called on by the chair (presider). He or she will wait for recognition and proceed with the motion by saying, "I move . . . "

Main motion is a motion that brings business before the assembly. A main motion requires a second, is debatable and amendable, and requires a majority vote. No main motion is valid unless it has been seconded, which shows that someone else favors bringing the motion to the floor. If no second is provided, the motion dies for lack of a second. If it is seconded, the chair then states the motion for the group and the motion is ready for consideration. Discussion is offered supporting and opposing the main motion. If no amendments are offered, the motion is voted on as proposed. Based on the vote, the motion either passes or fails.

PRIVILEGED MOTIONS

Privileged motions are those motions not related to the main question. These motions are used to help the meeting go smoothly. They help keep the meeting on track. Privileged motions include:

- Fix the Time at Which to Adjourn—*Fix the time at which to adjourn* is a motion to set the time for another meeting to continue business of the meeting. It requires a second, is not debatable, is amendable to time, and requires a majority vote.

- Adjourn—*Adjourn* is a motion to close the meeting. It requires a second, is not debatable, is not amendable, and requires a majority vote.

- Recess—*Recess* is a motion that allows the group (assembly) to take a short break in the meeting. It requires a second, is not debatable, can be amended as to time, and requires a majority vote.

23-8. "Fix the time at which to adjourn" is one of five privileged motions.

- Raise a Question of Privilege—*Raise a question of privilege* is a motion that allows a request relating to the rights and privileges of the assembly or any member to be brought up for immediate consideration. It does not require a second, is not debatable nor amendable, and no vote is needed. Action on the question of privilege is a decision of the presiding officer.

- Call for the Orders of the Day—*Call for the orders of the day* is a motion that allows a member to require the assembly to stay within the adopted agenda or order of business. It requires a second, is not debatable nor amendable, and no vote is taken unless there is a two-thirds vote taken to suspend the orders of the day to consider an item not on the order of business.

INCIDENTAL MOTIONS

Incidental motions are used to provide proper and fair treatment to all members. They have no particular precedence. They are usually handled as they arise during a meeting. Incidental motions include:

- Appeals—An *appeal* is a motion that a member uses when he or she disagrees with the ruling made by the chair (presider). It allows the assembly (group) to have the final say on all matters of procedure within the organization. An appeal requires a second, is debatable only if the pending motion is debatable, is not amendable, and requires a majority vote to reverse the decision of the chair.

- Division of the Assembly—*Division of the assembly* is a motion used when a member doubts the results of a vote. This motion requires a standing vote. It does not require a second, is not debatable nor amendable, and no vote is required—a single member can demand a division of the assembly.

- Point of Order—A *Point of order* is a motion that a member can use when the rules of the assembly are not being followed. It does not require a second, it is not debatable nor amendable, and no vote is required.

- Object to the Consideration of a Question—*Object to the consideration of a question* is a motion used if it would be inappropriate for a motion to even be presented before the assembly. A second is not needed. It is not debatable and not amendable. A two-thirds vote is required.

- Division of the Question—*Division of the question* is a motion used to divide another motion into two or more parts. This is done so each part can be discussed and voted on separately. It requires a second, is not debatable, can be amended, and requires a majority vote.

- To Modify or Withdraw a Motion—*To modify or withdraw a motion* is an ability to permit the withdrawal of a motion from consideration by the assembly. No second is required. It is not debatable nor amendable. A majority vote is needed for passage. The motion cannot be withdrawn after voting has started.

- Nominations—*To nominate* allows members to present the name of a candidate for an office or position. It is appropriate only when nominations have been requested by the presider. It does not require a second and is not debatable nor amendable. A majority vote is needed to elect. Nominations may be made by a committee or from the floor by a member. Candidates are usually voted on in the order in which they were nominated.

- Suspend the Rules—*Suspend the rules* is a motion that sets aside an established rule because it interferes with what the assembly wants to do. It requires a second and is not debatable nor amendable. A majority vote for standing rules (rules not related to parliamentary procedure) and a two-thirds vote for rules of order (rules related to parliamentary procedure) are required.

■ Open (or Close) Nominations—*Open (or close) nominations* directs nominations to be closed. A second is required. The motion is amendable and not debatable. A two-thirds vote is required to close nominations.

■ Reopen Nominations—*Reopen nominations* directs nominations to reopen. It requires a second, is amendable, and is not debatable. A majority vote is required.

■ Method of Voting—*Method of voting* is a motion used to direct a manner of voting on a motion by a method other than voice vote or by a division of the assembly. A second is required. It is amendable, not debatable, and requires a majority vote.

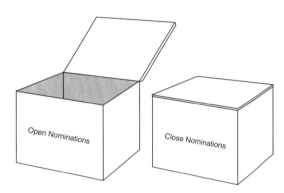

23-9. "Open (and close) nominations" are motions that assist in directing the nomination process.

■ Request for Information—*Request for information* is a motion used to allow a member to obtain further information about the business being discussed. No second is required. It is not debatable nor amendable. No vote is required. The chair answers the question or directs the question to a member of the assembly.

■ Parliamentary Inquiry—*Parliamentary inquiry* is a motion used to get information about parliamentary procedure. No second is required. It is not debatable nor amendable. No vote is required. The chair provides his or her opinion or asks the group's parliamentarian for assistance. (A **parliamentarian** is a person who has considerable knowledge of parliamentary procedure.)

SUBSIDIARY MOTIONS

Subsidiary motions are motions related to the main question. They are applied to main motions to alter them, to dispose of them, or to stop debate. All subsidiary motions have precedence over main motions. Eight subsidiary motions are commonly used.

■ Lay on the Table—*Lay on the table* is a motion that allows the assembly to set the pending motion aside temporarily for more urgent business to

23-10. "To lay on the table" allows a group to set a pending motion aside.

be discussed. It requires a second and is not debatable nor amendable. A majority vote is required for passage.

■ Call for the Previous Question—*To call for the previous question* is a motion designed to immediately close debate and prevent any other subsidiary motion except lay on the table. It requires a second, is not debatable, is not amendable, and requires a two-thirds vote.

■ Limit or Extend Debate—*Limit or extend limits of debate* is a motion to alter the limits of debate. It requires a second, is not debatable, is amendable, and requires a two-thirds vote.

■ Postpone—*Postpone to a certain time* (also known as *postpone definitely*) is a motion used to delay action on the pending motion to a definite day, meeting, or until after a certain activity. It requires a second and can be debated and amended. It requires a majority vote.

■ Refer—*Refer* is a motion to direct the pending motion to a committee for further information or action. To refer requires a second, is debatable, and is amendable. It requires a majority vote.

■ Amendment—To *amend* is a motion used to adjust a main motion by changing the wording of the motion before a vote is taken on the motion. Three basic methods of changing a motion are: by adding words, by striking out words, and by substituting words. An amendment requires a second and is debatable if the motion being amended is debatable. An amendment can be amended. To amend requires a majority vote.

■ Amend an Amendment—*Amend an amendment* is a motion used to adjust an amended motion by changing the wording of the amended motion. Three basic methods of changing a motion are: by adding words, by striking out words, and by substituting words. An amendment to an amendment requires a second and is not amendable nor debatable. A majority vote is required.

■ Postpone Indefinitely—*Postpone indefinitely* provides extra time to consider the motion being debated. It may be used as an attempt to eliminate the motion entirely. To postpone indefinitely requires a second, is debatable, and is not amendable. It requires a majority vote.

UNCLASSIFIED MOTIONS

Unclassified motions are those motions that bring questions back before the assembly. Five examples are presented here.

- Take from the Table—To *take from the table* is a motion used to bring a motion back that was laid on the table for further discussion. It requires a second, is not debatable, and is not amendable. It requires a majority vote.

- To Reconsider—*Reconsider* is a motion that allows a majority of the assembly to bring back a motion that was already voted on for further consideration. To reconsider requires a second and is debatable only if the motion being reconsidered is debatable. It is not amendable and requires a majority vote.

- To Reconsider and Enter in the Minutes—*Reconsider and enter in the minutes* is a motion that allows a majority of the assembly to bring back a motion for further consideration that was already voted on. It requires a second and is debatable if the motion being reconsidered is debatable. It is not amendable. A majority vote is required. The motion to reconsider can only be made by a member who voted on the prevailing side (the side that won the vote).

- To Rescind—*Rescind* is a motion to cancel action taken by the assembly. To rescind requires a second. It is debatable and amendable. Two-thirds majority vote is needed if notice of the motion to be proposed has not been given at the preceding meeting or in the call of the meeting.

- To Ratify—*Ratify* is a motion that, if passed, will approve an action already taken by the organization that was not previously voted on. To ratify requires a second and is amendable and debatable. It requires a majority vote.

CONSENSUS BUILDING

Many times during meetings, debatable issues arise. Members need to arrive at a consensus or group decision. Parliamentary procedure allows discussion of issues. By discussing issues, members can become aware of view points from both sides. Some members may be for the issue and some against. Discussing the issue in an organized manner will assist in building consensus. This form of consensus building will keep the meeting orderly. This is another benefit of parliamentary procedure. (Consensus was previously presented in Chapter 22.)

USING COMMITTEES

A *committee* is a group appointed to carry out specific functions. Committees are subgroups of a larger group. Using committees is a method of delegating that allows a few individuals the opportunity to investigate a matter. Their work is carried out at times other than the regular meeting of the entire group.

An organization may assign members or have members sign up to work on various committees. Special committees may be appointed by the president or presiding official of a group.

Organizations typically have two types of committees: standing and ad hoc. A *standing committee* exists because it is required by the bylaws or has a longstanding tradition.

An *ad hoc committee* is a special committee formed to handle matters not a part of the work of standing committees. Members of committees may volunteer or be appointed by the president. Ad hoc committees work much the same way as standing committees, but are disbanded after doing their work.

Examples of standing committees may include:

- Finance Committee—The finance committee is responsible for organizing fund-raising activities.

- Scholarship Committee—The scholarship committee is responsible for organizing activities that promote scholarship. The committee may also recognize individuals who have top grades in school.

- Recreation Committee—The recreation committee is responsible for planning recreational activities, such as bowling, volleyball, or skiing.

- Public Relations Committee—The public relations committee is responsible for carrying out public relation actions.

- Membership Development Committee—The membership development committee is responsible for developing methods designed to increase membership.

These are just a few examples of possible committees that can be developed within an organization.

Committees help an organization in completing work activities more efficiently, as long as everyone does their share.

REVIEWING

MAIN IDEAS

Meetings are important for clubs and other organizations to carry out their business. Meetings are more efficient if planned and an order of business is used. Every organization should have a set of bylaws and an elected group of officers. A quorum must be present to transact business legally.

Parliamentary procedure makes the rules used by an organization to conduct business. In parliamentary procedure, the principle motion is the main motion. Privileged motions include: To Fix the Time at Which to Adjourn, Adjourn, Recess, Raise a Question of Privilege, and Call for the Orders of the Day.

Incidental motions include: Appeal, Division of the Assembly, Point of Order, Object to Consideration of a Question, Division of the Question, To Modify or Withdraw a Motion, To Nominate, Suspend the Rules, Close Nominations, Reopen Nominations, Method of Voting, Requestion for Information, and Parliamentary Inquiry.

Subsidiary motions include: Lay on the Table, To Call for the Previous Question, Limit or Extend Time for Debate, Postpone to a Certain Time, Refer, Amend, Amend an Amendment, and Postpone Indefinitely.

Unclassified motions include: Take from the Table, Reconsider, Reconsider and Enter on the Minutes, Rescind, and Ratify.

Orderly discussion during parliamentary procedure allows for consensus building.

QUESTIONS

Answer the questions using correct spelling and complete sentences.

1. Explain privileged, incidental, subsidiary, principle, and unclassified motions.
2. Why do organizations have meetings?
3. What are four items to follow to have effective meetings?
4. What is the purpose of the gavel?
5. What does one tap of the gavel signify? What does two taps of the gavel signify?
6. Define amendable and debatable.
7. What is the purpose of the main motion?

EVALUATING

CHAPTER SELF-CHECK

Match the term with the correct definition. Write the letter by the term in the blank provided.

a. parliamentarian
b. order of business
c. presiding officer
d. ballot
e. secret ballot
f. simple majority
g. roll call vote
h. minutes

1. ____a method of voting in which the names of all members are read one at a time and they indicate how they are voting.

2. ____the written records of meetings.

3. ____a person who knows parliamentary procedure and helps organizations follow the rules.

4. ____a method of vote in which an individual writes on paper.

5. ____a method of balloting used so the vote of an individual is secret.

6. ____one more than half of the number of individuals who vote.

7. ____written step-by-step plan for a meeting.

8. ____the individual who conducts a meeting.

EXPLORING

1. Attend a meeting of the city government, board of education, or other group that uses parliamentary procedure. Observe how they go about their work. Prepare a report on what you observe.

2. Organize a team in parliamentary procedure. Get the rules from your teacher and prepare for competition.

3. Observe a local election. Determine the following: issues or candidates being voted on, requirements to be eligible to vote, hours of balloting, and location of voting places. Follow up the voting by determining the outcome of the voting. Also, determine the percentage of eligible voters who voted. Prepare a report on your findings.

24

SPEAKING IN PUBLIC

> *Speech is power; speech is to persuade, to convert, to compel.* **Ralph Waldo Emerson**

Think of the best speech you have heard. What made the speech good? The speaker was probably well prepared, used interesting techniques, and focused on a few points. Giving the speech was probably a demanding experience for the speaker.

Being good at speaking in public is a valuable skill. Like all skills, being a good speaker is a learned skill. Learning to speak in public will benefit you for a lifetime. Most fears of public speaking can be overcome by practicing good public speaking skills.

Communicating with others is very important. Communicating one-on-one or in a large assembly requires good communication skills.

24-1. An effective speaker confidently gives a carefully prepared message.

OBJECTIVES

This chapter covers the basics of speaking in public. It has the following objectives:

1. Identify the importance of public speaking

2. List characteristics of a good public speaker

3. Develop how to prepare a speech

4. Describe how to present a speech

TERMS

body
conclusion
eye contact
introduction
motivational speech
oral technical report
outline
podium
public speaking
realia
thesaurus

PUBLIC SPEAKING

Public speaking is a method of communication that uses oral methods of exchanging information. Spoken words are enhanced with nonverbal symbols, such as gestures and visuals. Good preparation is needed to be an effective public speaker.

People who give speeches need to understand the communication process. They need to use the process in preparing and making their speech. A good speech is focused on the audience—the listeners. The audience interprets the information. If members of the audience do not get the correct meaning from the speech, the speaker has not been successful.

KINDS OF PUBLIC SPEAKING

Public speaking is used to inform, motivate, and entertain. In preparing a speech, knowing your purpose is important.

A popular kind of informative speech is the oral technical report. An *oral technical report* is an informative speech that provides details of scientific or technical processes. They are often used at agricultural and scientific meetings. Oral technical reports involve careful attention to the accuracy of the information. Techniques are used to help the audience understand the information.

Motivational speeches are used to arouse people and encourage them to take a certain action. They are used to help people feel good about themselves and the world in which they live. Motivational speeches often use psychology in helping achieve their goals.

Speeches that entertain often contain motivational or technical elements. These speeches are designed to help members of the audience relax and enjoy a few laughs.

24-2. The oral technical report being given here is on a topic in forestry.

IMPORTANCE OF PUBLIC SPEAKING SKILLS

Being able to give a good speech is important for several reasons. It allows an individual the opportunity to emphasize strong ideas and ideals. What better way to publicly express yourself than through an organized and meaningful speech? Public speaking skills can be used as you give a prepared speech, an oral report, an illustrated talk, demonstration, when introducing a guest, or as part of a panel discussion.

Giving the public an informative speech is helpful. You can inform and persuade others through public speaking. It is a way for you to be of service to your community. It helps you communicate better with others.

As you continue to speak in public, you will gain respect from others. Practicing good public speaking helps you prepare for the future. Public speaking helps you improve your communication skills. Communication is a skill you can and will use every day.

Career success is often tied to speaking ability. People who can effectively use oral communication skills are more likely to

24-3. Career advancement is often tied to speaking ability. (Courtesy, Merle Richter, Bloomer, Wisconsin)

advance up the career ladder. They are also more likely to hold positions of leadership and earn higher salaries.

CHARACTERISTICS OF A GOOD PUBLIC SPEAKER

A good public speaker will follow a set of guidelines. The following guidelines will help you, the speaker, in all public speaking assignments.

- Be Prepared—Being prepared is essential. Plan your speech well ahead of time. Always give time to preparing no matter the audience, subject, and length of time for the speech. Good preparation helps you do a better job.

- Be Organized—Being organized means that you plan and have all details in good order. Write an outline and follow three simple steps:
  1. Tell the audience what you are going to tell them.
  2. Tell the audience the message.
  3. Summarize what you told them.

- Stay Within Time Limit—Watch the clock! Following the allotted time is extremely important. If a time of ten minutes is allowed, plan your speech for that amount of time. When speaking, be sure to stay within the ten minutes. It is important to say what needs to be said and not anymore. Extra small talk will only lose the attention of your audience.

- Use a Good Introduction—An attention-getting introduction is important in alerting the listeners to the fact that you have something important to say. Use an introduction that is lively and one that will catch the attention of your audience. You may want to use an appropriate anecdote. Humor in the right form and place is always appreciated by the audience.

- Be Enthusiastic—Present yourself in an enthusiastic manner. You will hold your audience's attention longer. Being enthusiastic drowns out being nervous.

- Facial Expression—Your facial expression has an influence on your speech. Facial expressions can be used to emphasize certain points within your speech. A concerned expression can reinforce a serious point of your speech. Think positively and be positive, success will surely follow. Smiles always help the audience feel good about listening to you.

- Use Notes—Keep important notes and the outline of your speech close by (usually on a speaker's stand). This will help you stay on track with your train of thoughts. It will assure that you can refer to important facts without fumbling. You will find that the more you speak, the less you need to rely on notes and the outline.

24-4. Being enthusiastic as a speaker creates enthusiasm in the audience. (Courtesy, Texas Tech University)

- Maintain Eye Contact—*Eye contact* is looking at the audience and into the faces of its members. It is important in public speaking. Eye contact helps get and keep the attention of the audience. It conveys a message of "I am talking with you and not at you." Look at all areas of the audience, but do not stare at any one individual.

- Use Variety—Vary your voice. This will help keep the audience's attention. You can use your voice to emphasize certain points. It also makes giving a public speech more fun.

- Observe Other Speakers—You can learn a great deal by watching and listening to other speakers. Pay special attention to their method of delivery.

- Be Knowledgeable—Know your subject. Spend time reading and studying the subject. Have answers ready for typical questions. If you do not know the answer to a question, say so.

PREPARING A SPEECH

Preparation is the key to being a good public speaker. How you go about preparing depends on the occasion at which you are speaking. If you have been invited to speak to a group, you will likely be given some general guidelines about the topic, time allocation, audience, and other details.

24-5. Preparation helps overcome the fear of speaking. (Courtesy, Texas Tech University)

Failing to adequately prepare places the speaker at a disadvantage and lets the audience down.

How much preparation is needed? Some speeches are prepared in complete detail. The speech is delivered from memory or by reading the copy. Giving a speech from memory is usually okay, but forgetting a line can disrupt the speech. Reading the copy is boring and should be used only for official or scientific matters where accuracy is essential.

For most speeches, preparing an outline and accompanying notes that you can take to the speaker's stand with you is best. Refer to the notes occasionally, as needed. Learn to think on your feet and choose the wording as you go. You can adapt the speech to the audience as it is delivered.

Before preparing a speech, learn as much as you can about the audience. Determine their age, interests, education, social status, and other details. These influence the approach to use in delivering the speech.

SELECTING THE TOPIC

Select an appropriate topic. Make your speech timely with up-to-date information. Your topic will depend on the occasion of your speech. Take one phase of the topic and expand on it. You cannot give all of the details about most topics.

Pinpoint your topic. Trying to cover too much results in a speech that may be too long or that does not communicate sharply. If you are speaking on a controversial subject, present points from both sides. Facts should be accurate. Sources should be cited to give your facts credibility.

GETTING INFORMATION

You can get up-to-date information in several ways. Use materials that are current. Get books and magazines from the local library or book store.

```
┌─────────────────────────────────────────────┐
│  Resource Title: _____     │
│  _____   │
│  Author: _____     │
│  Copyright: _____      │
│  Source/Publisher: _____      │
│  Information Summary: _____      │
│  _____   │
│  _____   │
│  _____   │
└─────────────────────────────────────────────┘
```

24-6. Example of a note card used in getting information for a speech.

Obtain pamphlets and research reports from universities or research stations. Talk to people who know the subject.

Search the databases on Internet for information related to your topic. Information that you locate on Internet can be printed out for easy reference. Always assess the accuracy of any information you get from this source.

Use note cards or a computer word processing system to record information. Cards work well because they can be sequenced to fit the outline of your speech.

Doing original research is a good way to get information. For example, survey or interview selected individuals to get local information. Telephone interviews can be quickly made to several individuals to get information from them. Incorporating accurate information you have gathered will impress your audience.

DEVELOPING AN OUTLINE

An *outline* forms the framework for your speech. Most people prefer a topical outline that organizes the speech into three major parts:

- Introduction—The *introduction* is the first part of a speech. It is designed to get the attention of the audience and provide the purpose of your speech. The introduction should be developed with carefully chosen information and phrasing. The first few moments of a speech set the stage for its success.

- Body—The *body* of a speech gives the main information that you want to convey. This is usually limited to two to four main points. The points are major topics in the outline. Supporting information is included under each topic.

```
Title: Recycling
Purpose: To convey the importance of recycling and encourage
         people to recycle

  I. Introduction (importance of recycling)

 II. Body
     A. First Main Point (everyone can recycle)
        1. Subpoint number one (at home)
        2. Subpoint number two (at business)
     B. Second Main Point (Items to recycle)
        1. Subpoint number one (when)
        2. Subpoint number two (where)
        3. Subpoint number three (how)

III. Conclusion (recycling needs to be done...)
     A. Summary of main points
     B. Action to take
```

24-7. Example of a beginning outline for a speech on recycling. (More details will be added as the speech is developed.)

■ Conclusion—The *conclusion* summarizes and reviews the content of your speech. It ties the content together and offers application to members of the audience.

Using an outline helps organize the content of the speech. It shows relationships between points you wish to make. An outline also helps sequence the content and helps in covering the most important topics. The outline can become a part of your notes while delivering the speech.

DEVELOPING A SPEECH

Approaches in developing a speech vary with experience. Always follow the outline. Revise the outline if necessary. It is often a good idea for beginning speakers to write out their speech in detail. By doing this, you will be sure to include all important details. Experienced speakers may only need an outline.

As you develop a speech, use word processing. This will save time if you need to rearrange the sequence or add information. You can store the speech on a diskette for easy modification in the future if it is needed. You can also prepare the outline and supporting information in some computer programs and carry the computer to the speaker's stand. Caution: A failure of the system can disrupt your speech. Embarrassing!

The information you have collected can be sequenced into your speech. Note cards can be arranged to fit the outline. Computer recorded notes can be "cut and pasted" into the desired sequence.

Write your ideas when you think of them. Remember, write to express your thoughts, not to impress the audience. Ideas will be refined as you continue preparation. You will be more comfortable with a speech that reflects your own thoughts and ideas. Be sure to add any relevant personal experiences because these draw the attention of the audience.

Use illustrations in your speech. This helps the audience understand your message. Illustrations can be used in the introduction or body of the speech. Facts and quotations will dress-up a speech if not used excessively. Blending statistical information into your speech helps in making your points.

Including a challenging question in your speech can bring clearer focus to your topic. A question also challenges the audience to listen. Often, you will want to provide information that answers the question.

Use a logical, easy-to-follow sequence. This will help you in giving the speech and help the audience follow what you are saying. Communication will be improved.

In a written speech, choose the words carefully. Use a **thesaurus** to help have variety in your vocabulary. A thesaurus is a dictionary of synonyms (words with similar meanings) and antonyms (words with opposite meanings). Using a thesaurus helps you find a better way to say what you want to say. For example, if you are looking for words related to "enthusiastic," the thesaurus may provide the following related words: interested, fascinated, animated, willing, thrilled, pleased, excited, attracted, exhilarated, and eager. Selecting from the "related" words gives variety and helps add interest to the speech.

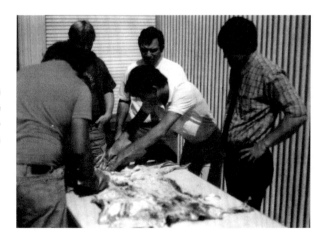

24-8. This oral technical report on preparing an animal skin was made easier by having a skin for the audience to see. (Courtesy, Texas Tech University)

Table 24-1 Examples of Realia Used in Public Speaking	
Category of Realia	**Common Examples**
Specimens (examples of real things)	fruits, nuts, flowers, food, animals, tools, products
Models (three-dimensional likenesses of real things)	cars, equipment, animals, animal systems, plant structures
Projected visuals	slides, transparencies
Audio materials	tape recordings
Interactive materials	computer simulations (may be projected onto a screen or with a large monitor)

USING SUPPORTING MATERIALS

Good speakers often use realia. **Realia** are real things or likenesses of real things. Models, specimens, audiovisuals, and hands-on activities are commonly used.

24-9. Practicing a speech helps make it better.

Realia should be selected based on the audience and the speaking environment. People must be able to see any realia that you use. The words on a transparency or other projected image must be large enough to be read from every part of the audience. Using small objects in a large room is not a good idea. In fact, poorly prepared or used realia detract from a speech. A good oral presentation can be destroyed with bad visual materials.

PRACTICING

Once you have prepared the content of your speech, it is time to practice. Give the speech in front of a mirror and to your friends. Use a video camera to record and review your practice. Strive to improve on every part of your speech.

In practicing, use note cards or the outline and any realia that will be a part of your speech. Learn to smoothly move from one point or item of realia to another. Fumbling with equipment—such as an overhead projector—is very distracting.

PRESENTING A SPEECH

Having a true desire to speak will help you with your public speaking. As you speak, use your audience as an inspiration. After all, you have something important to tell them. Be yourself as you present your speech, but do not get sloppy. There are many ways to develop and add meaning to your speech. Knowing what you can do to improve and practice good speaking skills will help you.

Avoid nervous actions or repetitive mannerisms. It will take away from the sparkle of your speech. You should have some nervous energy. It is perfectly normal. This energy will increase your enthusiasm towards your speech. Direct nervous energy toward the dynamics you use in your speech. If you are organized and prepared, you will be confident.

Maintain good posture when you are presenting your speech. Good posture will help you gain confidence. Your audience will notice and this will reinforce their respect for you.

Speak distinctly, clearly, and loudly. Use a pleasant tone of voice when you present your speech. If you have an opportunity ahead of time, become familiar with the area you are to speak in. Scope the size of your room and audience to be sure your voice volume will carry. Pronounce words carefully and accurately. Rehearse unfamiliar words ahead of time to avoid the embarrassment of stumbling on a word that is not familiar to you.

As you speak, do not forget to use eye contact. Eye contact will keep your audience's attention. Allow your movement on stage to be natural. Balance your eye contact with stage movement. These and other speaking abilities will be perfected with practice.

When presenting your speech, use brief intervals of silence. Pausing in silence emphasizes your message. It also allows time for your audience to think about what you are saying.

If you have a podium in front of you, your notes or the entire manuscript can be there. However, when you present your speech, refer as little as possible to these materials.

If giving a memorized speech, the notes will be helpful in case of a lapse in memory. Memorize your speech so you do not have to rely on your manuscript. Many people feel they need to have their manuscript there as a security blanket. Practicing is advisable so you do not have to rely on this type of security blanket.

A **podium** or speaker's stand may not always be there. Do not rely on podiums. Practice without a podium. If available, however, they are good places for your notes. Never lean on a speaker's stand or allow your hands to nervously "fiddle with" its attachments, such as a microphone or light switch.

Gesture naturally. A *gesture* is a body movement that can emphasize certain points. For example, moving hands and arms can provide emphasis to major points. Gestures also convey attitudes and help express thoughts and feelings. Avoid repetitive gestures. When not gesturing, leave your hands naturally at your sides.

Dress and groom appropriately for your speaking occasions. Be attentive to details. It is better to be overdressed than underdressed. Arrange your hair attractively, but out of your face and neatly placed.

Be sure to smile and enjoy your opportunity to speak. As a speaker, you are projecting an image. Let this image be a confident and happy image. Allow your smiles to come naturally. One continuous smile throughout your speech would not be natural.

When it is appropriate, allow time for questions. Be prepared and gain knowledge ahead of time about your subject so you can provide good answers. Knowing your subject will improve your self-confidence. Have answers ready for typical questions. You may not know the answers to every question. If this is the case, do provide helpful resources.

CONFIDENCE

Be confident in your ability as a public speaker. Think and act confident. Confidence will help generate a desire to continue your public speaking opportunities. You can public speak if you think you can. Here is an often shared poem, perhaps it can be used in one of your speeches.

> *If you think you are beaten, you are.*
> *If you think you dare not, you don't.*
> *If you'd like to win, but think you can't,*
> *It's almost a cinch you won't.*
> *Life's battles don't always go*
> *To the stronger or faster human;*
> *But sooner or later the human who wins*
> *Is the one who thinks he/she can.*
> *Anonymous*

You will need to search a variety of sources to find a variety of quotes and other information to use in your speech. Often, the best resource we can use is ourselves. Allow your speech to be an extension of your own creativity. Public speaking is an art that you can appreciate and perfect.

REVIEWING

MAIN IDEAS

Public speaking is an important form of communication. Skills in speaking will serve you for a lifetime. Always keep the following guidelines in mind when preparing for public speaking: be prepared, be organized, watch the clock, provide a catchy introduction, be enthusiastic, use facial expression, outline your speech, maintain eye contact, use variation, listen to other speakers, and be knowledgeable.

When preparing a speech, be selective of your topic. Keep your information up-to-date. Make your speech sparkle with action verbs, illustrations, quotes, and questions.

When researching, stay organized and your speech will be organized. This will help you in practicing delivery or the memorization process. Be confident and your confidence will build.

When presenting your speech, use important gestures and avoid nervous mannerisms. Speak clearly and loudly, use eye contact, stand erect with both feet on the floor, and gesture naturally. Dress appropriately, smile, and have fun. Public speaking will be a positive experience when you practice and prepare.

QUESTIONS

Answer the questions using correct spelling and complete sentences.

1. Why is public speaking important?
2. What are the basic parts of an outline?
3. Why are action verbs important to use in a speech?
4. List three guidelines of public speaking.
5. How can public speaking increase your self-confidence?
6. How can you keep your information organized when researching for your speech?
7. How can a thesaurus be helpful when preparing your speech?

EVALUATING

CHAPTER SELF-CHECK

Match the term with the correct definition. Write the letter by the term in the blank provided.

a. thesaurus   d. realia   g. conclusion
b. podium   e. outline
c. public speaking   f. eye contact

1. _____general framework of a speech.

2. _____method of communication that uses oral methods of exchanging information.

3. _____ending of a speech.

4. _____dictionary of word choice.

5. _____speaker's platform.

6. _____examples or likenesses of real things.

7. _____allows you to talk individually to your audience.

EXPLORING

1. Select a topic that is of interest to you and prepare a speech on it. Develop research cards following the format in this book. Research your topic and record the information on the research cards. Develop a detailed outline from the material gained through your research. Organize the material into a speech. Deliver the speech in your class or for another group.

2. Review the literature books in your local library. Find a speech already written. Become familiar with the contents of the speech. Ask a friend to videotape your speech. Then, critique yourself on your speaking habits.

3. Ask your local librarian for videotapes that have recorded speeches from other speakers. View and listen to another speaker. Make a list of do's and don'ts related to public speaking.

4. Challenge yourself by entering a speaking contest. Plan ahead and apply your newly acquired public speaking guidelines.

APPENDIXES

Appendix A

OPPORTUNITIES IN STUDENT ORGANIZATIONS

Many different organizations are available to students. The kind and nature of these organizations varies from one school to another. Being active in a student organization can be highly educational. Benefits from membership in an organization are in direct proportion to the efforts you put into it. Be an active member and not a passive member!

Some student organizations are closely tied to the curriculum and have national identification. Students with many areas of interest can find opportunities to get involved. For example, students with interest in science can join a science club, or those interested in drama can join a drama club. Students in career-oriented classes, such as agriculture and business, are fortunate to have vocational student organizations.

Vocational student organizations (VSO) are designed as an integral part of the curriculum. The activities of the organizations are closely related to the instruction. Students are normally required to be enrolled in a class related to the organization to become a member. Activities are selected to make class instruction have greater meaning. The work may be carried out in class, during activity periods, and after regular school hours.

Examples of national vocational student organizations are:

- National FFA Organization (FFA)—for students enrolled in high school agricultural education classes.

- Future Business Leaders of America (FBLA)—for students enrolled in high school business, office, and computer technology classes. (Some students enrolled in these classes also join the Business Professionals of America organization.)

- Future Homemakers of America (FHA/HERO)—for students enrolled in family and consumer sciences classes (formerly known as home economics).

- Vocational Industrial Clubs of America (VICA)—for students enrolled in trade and industrial education classes. (In a few cases, agriculture students are members of VICA in schools where the agricultural education classes are offered by trade and industrial education programs.)

- Distributive Education Clubs of America (DECA)—for students enrolled in marketing education in high school.

NATIONAL FFA ORGANIZATION

The National FFA Organization is a student organization founded in 1928. This makes FFA the oldest of vocational student organizations. It is also the world's largest student organization with more than 444,000 members from over 7,200 chapters. Members represent the 50 states and Puerto Rico, the Virgin Islands, Guam, and Rota. Students enrolled in agricultural education programs in grades 7–12 are eligible for membership. This dynamic organization is dedicated to making a positive difference in the lives of young people.

The primary mission of FFA is to develop premier leadership, personal growth, and career success through agricultural education.

The FFA motto is:

The FFA emblem has important meaning to its members. (Emblem used with written permission of the National FFA Organization, Alexandria, Virginia.)

> *Learning to Do,*
> *Doing to Learn,*
> *Earning to Live,*
> *Living to Serve.*

The organization changed its name from Future Farmers of America to the National FFA Organization in 1988. This was done to reflect membership stemming from science, business, and technology, in addition to production farming. It was also done to reflect membership from both rural and urban populations.

FFA truly is the ultimate experience, providing diverse opportunities for its members. There are many opportunities to meet members with diverse interests. These opportunities include:

- Gain Recognition—FFA programs recognize students for their efforts in learning and improving their communities.

- Learning—As a part of the school curriculum, FFA reinforces learning activities.

- Travel—As members participate in FFA activities, they are given the chance to travel. New sites are seen as members participate in local, district, state, and national activities.

- Earn Money—Each member develops a Supervised Agricultural Experience (SAE) program. Projects are based on student interest, and range from horticulture, the environment, floriculture, forestry, wildlife, to animal science, as well as a host of others. Members gain new knowledge and apply new techniques, along with earning and investing their money. Often, awards and recognition follow an individual member's success in a given SAE program.

- Fun—FFA is fun for everyone. Many chapters schedule recreational events. National and state chorus and band opportunities are also part of the fun. Opportunities in the FFA are nearly unlimited. You will also find much fun in making new friends through the FFA.

- Field Trips—In agricultural classes, members are provided field trips and tours to business and industry. These opportunities broaden members' horizons and help them in career planning.

- Individual Awards and Degrees—Awards are given at local, sectional, state, regional, and national levels. Members are given many opportunities to be recognized for their outstanding progress and success.

- Scholarship Programs—Scholarships are available through the National FFA Foundation for FFA members who plan to continue their education after high school. Educational choices may include colleges, universities, and technical schools. More than $700,000 is available through the FFA Scholarship Program each year on a competitive basis.

- Camps and Leadership Conferences—These opportunities may last from a few days to a week. Most often, they focus on personal leadership and communication skills. Nationally recognized programs include the Washington Conference Program and Made for Excellence seminars.

- International Opportunities—FFA also offers exchange programs through Work Experience Abroad (WEA). Exchange times range from three, six, or twelve months. Shorter travel seminars are also available from three to six weeks in length. FFA also provides members the opportunity to participate in the World

The National Agricultural Career Show is held in Bartle Hall in Kansas City, Missouri, during the National FFA Convention.

AgriScience Studies (WASS) program. Members who participate usually spend one year overseas or host an exchange student from another country.

■ State and National Conventions—Each state association holds an annual convention. It is at this convention that members and advisors gather each year. Activities include leadership workshops, contests, and state FFA business transactions.

Members are also able to attend the National FFA Convention. Over 37,000 FFA members, advisors, sponsors and guests travel to Kansas City, Missouri, for this major event. During the convention, business sessions are conducted and members can hear from motivational speakers. Educational tours and leadership conferences are also available. While attending the convention, members also attend the National Agricultural Career Show.

STRUCTURE

The FFA has local chapters in high schools throughout the United States. The members pay dues to become local, state, and national members. Each local chapter subscribes to the national constitution and participates in selected events. Chapters are chartered by state FFA associations.

Local chapters have an officer team. These individuals are responsible for providing leadership to the chapter. Chapters also have members organized into committees to carry out important work. The local chapter has an advisor who is an agriculture teacher.

Annual programs of work are developed at the local level. These are written documents that specify the important work of the FFA chapter for the year. All members are involved in accomplishing the program of activities through the committee structure.

At the state level, an adult agricultural educator serves as advisor. This individual may be helped by an executive secretary. Various activities are planned at the state level, including a state convention.

At the national level, the Board of Directors and the Board of Student Officers oversee the organization. A staff of professional agricultural educators organizes and delivers important information to members, such as the New Horizons magazine.

PROFICIENCY AWARDS

Proficiency Awards are individual member activities. The awards are designed to recognize excellence in supervised agricultural experience. Local, state, and national awards are given. The program is designed for individual members to set and achieve goals.

Two proficiency awards categories are used: placement and entrepreneurship. Placement is when a member works under the direction of another person, such as at a fish hatchery or in a flower shop. Entrepreneurship is when a student owns what he or she is involved with, such as animal production or lawn care service. To apply, you must be a member of the FFA and have completed two or more years of instruction in agricultural education.

The potential Proficiency Award areas are:

Agricultural Communications
Agricultural Mechanical Technical
   Systems
Agricultural Processing
Agricultural Sales and/or Service
Aquaculture
Beef Production
Cereal Grain Production
Dairy Production
Diversified Crop Production
Diversified Livestock Production
Emerging Agricultural Technology
Environmental Science
Equine Science
Feed Grain Production
Fiber Crop Production
Floriculture
Food Science and Technology
Forage Production

Forest Management
Fruit and/or Vegetable Production
Home and/or Community
   Development
Horticulture
Landscape Management
Nursery Operations
Oil Crop Production
Outdoor Recreation
Poultry Production
Sheep Production
Small Animal Care
Soil and Water Management
Specialty Animal Production
Specialty Crop Production
Swine Production
Turf Grass Management
Wildlife Management

CAREER DEVELOPMENT EVENTS

Career development events are designed for individual and team participation in demonstrating knowledge and skills. These events are to develop individual responsibilities, foster teamwork, and promote communication. Emphasis is on ethical competition and the importance of individual achievement.

Teams are typically made up of three or four individuals. The team works, learns, and competes together. The career development events and number of members who participate are:

Agricultural Mechanics, 3

Agricultural Sales, 4

Dairy Cattle, 4

Dairy Handlers, 1-2

Dairy Foods, 4

Extemporaneous Speaking, 1

Farm Business Management, 4

Floriculture, 3

Forestry, 4

Horse Evaluation and Selection, 4

Livestock, 4

Marketing Plan, 3

Meats Evaluation and Technology, 4

Nursery Landscape, 3

Parliamentary Procedure, 6

Prepared Speaking, 1

Poultry, 4

Team participation begins at the local level and advances through state and national competition. The top team in each state goes to national competition held during the National FFA Convention in Kansas City, Missouri.

FOR MORE INFORMATION

Exciting opportunities are available for every agricultural education student in the National FFA Organization. For more details on the exciting opportunities in the National FFA Organization, contact your local Agricultural Education Instructor or write to:

National FFA Organization
National FFA Center
5632 Mount Vernon Memorial Highway
P.O. Box 15160
Alexandria, VA 22309-0160
(703) 360-3600

Appendix B

PREPARING A RÉSUMÉ (PERSONAL DATA SHEET)

A résumé is a written summary of your education, experience, and other qualifications. Résumés are also known as personal data sheets or curriculum vitae. Some people prefer to use the term "personal data sheet" because it is easier to properly write. These written documents are used in applying for jobs, scholarships or awards, and in other ways.

The purpose of a résumé is to provide information when you cannot be personally present. The résumé also serves as a permanent record that can be put into a file or attached to a letter or application form.

A good résumé is easy to prepare. The contents should be accurate and reflect positively on your qualifications. The items to include are:

- Name and address, including telephone number
- Career objective or goal
- Education and training that qualifies you
- Work experience
- School or community activities
- Other items that reflect positively on you
- References (Including references is optional; however, a statement that references are available should be included.)
- It is also a good idea to date the résumé

A résumé should be attractive and represent you well. The résumé should be neatly typewritten on good quality white or buff-colored paper. Words should be spelled correctly. Slang and words that other people would not understand should be avoided. It is best to use computer word processing and a laser printer to have a clear, neat copy. Use a type face that is easy to read and widely accepted. Using a computer also allows the résumé to be saved on diskette and easily modified for future use.

Unless specifically requested, do not include a photograph with a résumé. Photographs can be used to discriminate against an applicant if the quality is poor or the applicant does not meet the stereotype of the reviewers of the résumé.

It is a good idea to keep an up-to-date résumé on file. Always take a résumé with you when seeking information about a job and going for a job interview. Having a good résumé demonstrates that you are sincere and competent.

A sample résumé is presented as a personal data sheet on the following page.

PERSONAL DATA SHEET

SUSAN ANN SLOAN

P.O. Box 580
Demorest, GA 30535
(706) 778–7464

OBJECTIVE: A position as a biotechnology technician with opportunities for increased responsibility and advancement.

EDUCATION:

1995–1997 North Georgia Tech, Clarkesville, Georgia
Associate Degree in Horticulture Biotechnology.
Graduated May 12, 1997, with a 3.4 GPA.

1991–1995 Central High School, Cornelia, Georgia
Graduated with honors. Class rank was 12 out of 392.

EXPERIENCE:

1995–present The Orchard Golf Course, Turnerville, Georgia
Part-time work included all areas of turf and landscape management.

1993–1995 Frank's Lawn Maintenance Service, Cornelia, Georgia
Part-time work included lawn care and landscape maintenance.

COLLEGE ACTIVITIES:

1996–1997 President, Horticulture Club
President, Student Government Association
Vice President, Scholarship Club
Member, Landscape Design Team
Member, College Ambassadors

1995–1996 Member, Horticulture Club
Member, Landscape Design Team
Representative, Student Government Association

HIGH SCHOOL ACTIVITIES:

President, Honor Society
President, CHS FFA Chapter
Member, Debate Team
Member, CHS Marching Band
Delegate, State FFA Convention
Member, Principal's Honor Club

COMMUNITY ACTIVITIES:

Member and Captain, Community Youth Tennis Team
Active, Community Beautification Program
Member, Sunday School and Church

REFERENCES: Available Upon Request.

DATE PREPARED: May, 1997

GLOSSARY

acceptable risk—risk that can lead to above average success without disastrous or unacceptable consequences for failure

accessories—clothing items, including shoes, belts, ties, and jewelry, that complete an outfit

action language—actions or body movements that transmit meaning, such as walking rapidly

ad hoc committee—a special committee formed to handle matters not a part of the work of standing committees

aerobic exercise—physical activities that raise the heart rate of an individual for at least 20 minutes

appropriate attire—used to describe the correct type of clothing to be worn to an activity

autocratic leader—style of leadership in which the leader is directive and makes decisions for followers

ballot—a piece of paper on which a voter indicates preferences

being kind—trait that includes benevolence, sympathy, and gentleness toward others

biological needs—in Maslow's hierarchy, the most basic needs, including food, sleep, shelter, and air

blended fabric—fabric made from a combination of two or more different types of fibers

body—in a speech, the main information a speaker desires to convey

brainstorming—technique of creating a shared vision in which a group of people are brought together to develop ideas or answers to questions

bylaws—rules or laws of an organization

caring—trait that involves concern and interest for the welfare of others

channel—in the communication model, the linkage between the sender and the intended recipients of a message

charisma—used to describe personality characteristics that arouse enthusiasm and loyalty in others

citizen—a person who lives in a certain location

civic club—group formed to improve life in the local community

code of conduct—the way a team does things

commitment—a promise to give time and effort to a group, activity, or cause

committee—group appointed to carry out specific functions; subgroups of a larger group

communication—the process of exchanging information

communication model—way of describing the communication process

community service—performing activities that improve the quality of life in a community

community service campaign—an organized and intense effort to carry out an activity

compass—device used to determine direction

competent—believing that you are capable and have the ability to do something

compromiser—in a group, a person who tries to see all sides of an issue

conceit—the excessive feeling of one's own worth

conceptual traits—"thinking" skills used to evaluate situations and create new ideas

conclusion—in a speech, a summary and review of the content of the speech

conflict—a difference of opinion between two or more people

conflict resolution—using techniques that allow a peaceful resolution to disagreements

conflicting loyalties—when loyalty and commitment to more than one organization, cause, or set of values are at odds and one must be chosen over the other

connected model—a model of leadership most often depicted as a "web"

consensus—group decision-making process whereby a group gathers and discusses information on an issue until an agreement is reached

considerate—trait indicating a high regard for others and their feelings

constructive feedback—feedback that is evaluative or critical and offered in such a way as to not discourage the receiver

context—in non-verbal communication, all of the things in the environment that help determine the meaning of a cue

contributor—in a group, a person who likes to share information and initiate projects

conversation—informal spoken communication

cooperation—the act of recognizing everyone's contribution to the success of a project

courage—the ability to face difficult situations

courteous—trait that relates to being polite and gracious

credibility—describes a person who is accurate and honest in what they do

cultural diversity—awareness of the variation in races, beliefs, and practices of others

daily planners—time management tools in which the daily activities of an individual are scheduled into specific time slots

decision making—selecting one choice from several that are available

decoding—in the communication model, the process by the receiver of drawing meaning from the symbols used by the sender

delegation—sharing decisions, work, and similar duties with others

democracy—describes a group whereby the power of decision making rests with the members or people

democratic leader—style of leadership in which decision making is accomplished through input from the leader and followers

dilemma—problem to be solved

distractor—in a group, a person who does or says silly or foolish things in order to attract attention

dominator—in a group, a person who tries to control the group and set the rules

draped—describes clothes that do not conform to the body

elaborator—in a group, a person who wants to see every project plan in complete detail

emotion—a deep inner feeling or opinion

empathy—attempting to identify with the feelings of another person

empowerment—giving decision-making powers to subordinates

encoding—in the communication model, the preparation of a message for sending

encourager—in a group, a person who provides courage, hope, confidence, and support to the rest of the members

ethics—the principles behind behavior or conduct that are morally correct

etiquette—code of social behavior

extrinsic motivation—motivation that results from the desire to obtain an external reward

eye contact—in public speaking, looking at the audience and into the faces of its members

fair—a personal trait indicating that one does things in an unbiased and honest manner

feedback—in the communication model, the return channel from the receiver to the sender

feeling—category of human judgment characterized by caring, human values, and harmony

filtering—the group of perceptions that a message passes through when it is being exchanged

first impression—what others see the moment they first meet you

focused—maintaining attention on things that are important

follower—an individual who follows the ideas, goals, or tasks of a leader or group

forming—first phase of team building in which individuals are brought together and made a cohesive unit

gestures—body movements used in non-verbal communication

goal—something you wish to achieve

goal-oriented leader—leader who thrives on task accomplishment and emerges when the goals and potential rewards are appealing

gossip—talk about another's affairs without their knowledge or participation

group—two or more people working together to accomplish a goal

group stagnation—inactivity resulting from a group's resistance to change

habit—an action done a certain way so often that it is virtually automatic

halo effect—the tendency to allow an individual's perceived superior ability in an area to carry over to that individual's virtues

harassment—behavior that disturbs another, including name calling, unkind gestures, and threats

hearing—the physical process of detecting sound

hierarchy of human needs—theory by A.H. Maslow which classifies human motivation based on five levels of needs

honesty—an ethical value which indicates that one has high principles and does not lie, cheat, or steal

incidental motion—in parliamentary procedure, used to provide fair and proper treatment to all members

influence—when an individual motivates others to take action

information-giver—in a group, a person who attempts to answer questions and help the group solve problems

information-seeker—in a group, a person who seeks out facts and information pertaining to group issues

informed decision—decisions based on the best available information

intangible—characteristic of things that cannot be recognized by the sense of touch

integrator—in a group, a person who tries to bring separate ideas together to form a major goal or plan

integrity—personal characteristic which implies honesty and virtuous actions

intermediate goal—desired outcomes that fall between short-and long-term goals

internal traits—personal characteristics

interpersonal goals—goals that represent improvement of relationships with others

interpersonal traits—"people" skills used to work with others

interpret—to draw meaning from

intrinsic motivation—motivation that results from the inherent desire one has to feel competent and self-fulfilled

introduction—in a speech, the first part designed to gain the attention of the audience and inform them of the purpose of the speech

intuitive—category of human perception characterized by a preference for associations or connections

intuitive-feeler—category of human motivation characterized by an individual's need to know what is expected of them

intuitive-thinker—category of human motivation characterized by an individual's need to feel that goals make sense, are within reach, and contribute to the welfare of others

involvement—being an active participant in an activity or group

jealousy—behavior that results from resentment or envy of another

laissez-faire leader—style of leadership in which followers are given a major role in decision making

leader—person who helps an individual or a group in achieving their goals

leadership—relationship where influence is used to meet individual and group goals

leadership role—roles that leaders assume in providing leadership

leadership style—ways individuals act in their role as leader, such as autocratic, laissez-faire, or democratic

learning curve—a graphical representation of how quickly a person learns something new

listening—the active process requiring hearing, concentration, assimilation, understanding, and remembering of information

long-term goal—a desired outcome that usually involves many steps and will take a long time to achieve

love—concern for the well-being of others

loving person—one who possesses a combination of all the desirable social behavior traits

loyalty—characteristic of relationships based on mutual trust and respect; faithfulness of one person to another individual or group

main motion—in parliamentary procedure, the motion that brings business before the assembly

management—controlling and directing others, including domination by the person in charge

manipulator—a person who uses other people for selfish reasons

manners—used to describe a way of behaving that is polite

meeting—an assembly of a group people for a particular purpose

member role—a person's place on a team or in a group

member-oriented leader—type of leader who attempts to mediate or referee disagreements within a group

mentor—an individual who has influence and helps guide others in the right direction

message—in the communication model, the idea or information that is to be exchanged

minutes—the official written record of business in a meeting

mission statement—a document that expresses the values and desires of one's life

moral ethics—knowing the difference between right and wrong and applying that knowledge to daily life

motivational speech—a type of speech used to arouse people and encourage them to take action

motivation—energizing and giving direction to human actions

motive—internal forces that direct our conscious behaviors toward satisfying our needs or achieving our goals

natural fiber—type of fabric made from animal and plant products

noise—interference in the communications process, including sound and visual images

non-negotiable limits—the areas in your life on which you will not compromise

non-verbal communication—exchanging information without the use of words

non-verbal cues—signals used to tell others about one's emotional state, attitudes, or other personal information

norming—second phase of team development in which members take necessary steps to develop team cohesion

no-show—in a group, a person who does not show up for events or group activities

object language—physical items that convey messages

old business—matters remaining from a previous meeting

open door policy—policy held by leaders which means that subordinates can discuss issues with them at any time

openness—in a group setting, implies the leader and group members are able to communicate and share information effectively

opinion-giver—in a group, a person who provides an opinion on every matter or issue that arises

opinion-seeker—in a group, a person who ask others for their opinion and may seek the opinion of an expert on an issue

oral technical report—an informative speech that provides details of scientific or technical processes

order of business—the step-by-step plan for the conduct of a meeting

organization—a large system

organizational chart—visual representations of the relationships among all people in an organization

outline—framework for a speech

ownership—relating to a group's shared vision, means that the members of the group feel the vision belongs to them

paralanguage—the vocal sound that influences the expression of spoken words

parliamentarian—person who has considerable knowledge of parliamentary procedure

parliamentary procedure—a method of conducting meetings in an orderly manner that is based on the rules first set by the British Parliament

patterns—the particular, distinctive weaves and printed shapes found in fabrics

people skills—skills used to get along with others and to help others work together

perception—how people view or feel about something based on knowledge obtained through the senses

performing—third phase of team development in which team business in conducted and goals are accomplished

persistence—continuing an activity even in the face of adversity

personal comfort bubble—the comfortable distance for personal conversation, usually between 2 and 4 feet

personal conflict—type of conflict between people, usually based on a difference of opinion, that disrupts and impairs the achievement of goals

personal effectiveness—feeling as if you have a positive impact on the outcome of things you do

personal goals—goals that represent self-improvement

personal hygiene—the cleanliness and freedom of an individual from body odor

personal management—personal responsibility; the skills related to a strong work ethic, including positive self-esteem, self-motivation, and goal setting

personal mastery—using strengths and weaknesses to realize individual potential

personal responsibility—the inner you that is shown in the principles you live by, the decisions you make, and how much you can be trusted

personality—the collection of distinctive and individual qualities that a person possesses

plan of service—a written statement of a person's talents, skills, and ways of providing service

podium—speaker's stand

positive attitude—an approach to situations which focuses on seeing new experiences as challenging and opportunities to learn as opposed to chances to fail

positive reinforcement—the strengthening of a response to a stimulus through the presentation of some type of reward, such as praise or an award

power—the ability of a person or group to employ force on others in order to accomplish goals

presiding officer—in parliamentary procedure, the person (president) whose duty it is to enforce the rules and orders of the assembly

principle motion—in parliamentary procedure, the motion from which all group business is transacted

principle—a guiding rule that helps in setting limits of behavior

prioritizing goals—ranking goals from most important to least important

privileged motion—in parliamentary procedure, motions not related to the main questions which help meetings run smoothly

proactive behavior—type of behavior in which responses are chosen to a given condition

procrastination—delaying tasks until a later time

professional goals—goals that represent success in a job or group activity

protestor—in a group, a person who speaks out strongly against an issue

public speaking—method of communication that uses oral methods of exchanging information

Pygmalion effect—term used for self-fulfilling prophesy

pyramid model—tradition, top-down model of leadership

quorum—minimum number of group members that must be present in order for a group to legally carry out business

reactive behavior—behavior that is the response to a given condition

realia—real items or their likenesses, such as models, specimens, or audiovisuals, used as supporting materials in speeches

receiver—in the communication model, the individual for whom a message is intended

recognition-seeker—in a group, a person who wants to be recognized for any and all contributions made or goals achieved

reflective listening—conflict resolution technique in which the listener demonstrates understanding and acceptance of the sender's message

reinforcement—the strengthening of a response to a stimulus

relationship leadership role—leadership role that involves building, enhancing, and maintaining positive relations within the group

respect—providing the proper courtesy and acceptance of another person

responsible—used to describe one who fulfills his or her obligations

risk—the possibility of failure, loss, or injury

role ambiguity—occurs when a person in a group does not have a clear understanding of what is expected of him or her

role conflict—a result of role ambiguity in which a team member does not understand his or her role as related to other team members; can result in frustration, a sense of helplessness, and insecurity

roll call vote—a method of voting in which the names of all members are read aloud and each individual votes

safety and security needs—second level in Maslow's hierarchy; represents freedom from fear

salient point—basic description of a motion

secret ballot—type of voting which handles ballots in such a way that the public does not know how any individual voted

selection—quickest approach to improving a group's leadership; group selects a person who has the skills most needed

selective perception—the blockage of incoming information

self-concept—how individuals feel about themselves

self-determination—feeling as if you have control over what happens to you

self-discipline—controlling oneself in order to reach a goal

self-esteem—how you feel about yourself

self-esteem needs—fourth level in Maslow's hierarchy; includes desire for respect by others and need to feel important

self-fulfillment needs—highest level in Maslow's hierarchy; represents need for self-development and self-fulfillment; also referred to as self-actualization

self-imposed constraint—a limit one places on oneself

self-motivation—the mental desire to do something

self-oriented leader—leader who emerges when actions of the group are prestigious or provide them with direct rewards

self-respect—holding oneself in high regard

semantics—when the same words mead entirely different things to different people

sensing—category of human perception characterized by a preference for action or concrete situations

sensing-feeler—category of human motivation characterized by an individual's need to know planned results, expectations, and how his or her contributions fit into the group effort

sensing-thinker—category of human motivation characterized by an individual's need for a sense of belonging within a group

service—helping others through action

shared vision—a group's mental picture of the future

short-term goal—a desired outcome that can be achieved in a short period of time and usually involves few steps

sign language—those forms of communication that take the place of spoken words

simple majority—more than half of all votes cast

situation engineering—method of leadership improvement in which a person and the situation are matched; situations may be manipulated to ensure success

situational leadership—a model of leadership behavior that focuses on determining the demands of the situation

social behavior—behavior around other people, including manners and mannerisms

social needs—third level in Maslow's hierarchy; represents feelings of belonging and acceptance

source—in the communication model, the sender or initiator of the attempt to communicate

standing committee—in an organization, a committee that is required by the bylaws or has a long-standing tradition

stereotyping—the tendency to structure the world into a predictable pattern

stress—feeling nervous or frustrated when in a pressure situation

subsidiary motion—in parliamentary procedure, motion related to the main question that is used to alter, dispose of, or stop debate on it

success—achieving worthy goals

survey—formal technique of collecting information from people, i.e., questionnaires

synthetic fabric—type of fabric made from nylon, polyester, or other manufactured products

system—a whole made up of many interdependent parts

systems thinking—way of looking at an organization or team as interdependent parts that make up the whole and the relationship between those parts

task leadership role—leadership role that deals with getting tasks done

team mission—what the team wishes to accomplish

technical traits—"how to do it" skills, such as ability to follow directions

texture—in clothing, the qualities of roughness or smoothness of fabrics

theory of selective perception—theory that our expectations lead us to see events, objects, people, and situations the way we want them to be

thesaurus—a dictionary of synonyms and antonyms

thinking—category of human judgment characterized by a need for order or structure

time management—scheduling activities and commitments so that time is spent most productively

to-do checklists—time management tool which is simply a list of things an individual wishes to accomplish

total communication—describes the exact duplication of what the sender intends to convey to the receiver

Total Quality Management (TQM)—management style in which front-line employees are a part of the decision-making processes within an organization

training—most widely used method of leadership improvement; groups provide training to someone within

traits—the distinguishing characteristics about a person that make him or her unique

trust—having confidence that an individual will do the right thing

truthful—a personal quality of one who says and does things that conform to reality

unclassified motion—in parliamentary procedure, a motion that is used to bring questions back before the assembly

unity—feeling of connection between members of a group or team

value driven—idea that humans are motivated and act on things that are important to them

values—set of beliefs and standards that influence one's life and decisions

values clarification—the process of knowing and understanding your own values

violence—the use of physical force against others in an attempt to resolve conflict

virtue—moral excellence

vision—a well-developed mental image of a possible and desirable future

visionary behavior—set of actions undertaken in order to anticipate and plan for one's future

voice vote—typically an oral "yes" or "no" response to a motion when called for by the presider

volunteer—an individual who willingly performs a service without pay

volunteerism—giving one's time and talents without monetary benefits

voting—type of group decision-making process whereby everyone involved in the decision makes a choice from available alternatives

weekly planners—time management tool which allows an individual to schedule commitments for one week at a time

well-mannered—carrying out the basics of common courtesy

work ethic—the drive of an individual to begin and finish a task with high standards of performance

SELECTED BIBLIOGRAPHY

Aguayo, Rafael. *Dr. Deming: The American Who Taught the Japanese About Quality*. New York: Simon & Schuster, 1990.

Binkley, Harold R. *Be a Leader: Make Things Happen*. New York: Carlton Press, 1989.

Boyer, Bruce. *Eminently Suitable*. New York: W.W. Norton & Company, 1990.

Buhagiar, Marion, ed. *The Book of Secrets*. New York: Boardroom Reports, Inc., 1991.

Caraway, E. and M. Sanborne. *A Challenge for America—How to Live the American Dream*. Danville, Illinois: Interstate Publishers, Inc., 1986.

Cheek, Jimmy G., Larry R. Arrington, and Max B. McGhee. *Effective Oral Communication*. Danville, Illinois: Interstate Publishers, Inc., 1995.

Crunkilton, John R., Susan L. Osborne, Michael E. Newman, Edward W. Osborne, and Jasper S. Lee. *The Earth and AgriScience*. Danville, Illinois: Interstate Publishers, Inc., 1995.

Drache, Hiram M. *History of U.S. Agriculture and Its Relevance to Today*. Danville, Illinois: Interstate Publishers, Inc., 1996.

Gifford, Charles S. and Glenn A. Shiro. *Unlocking Your Potential*. Danville, Illinois: Interstate Publishers, Inc., 1995.

Hersey, Paul and Ken Blanchard. *Management of Organizational Behavior*. Englewood Cliffs, New Jersey: Prentice-Hall, Inc., 1982.

Hersey, Paul. *The Situational Leader*. New York: Warner Books, Inc., 1984.

Kouzes, James M. and Barry Z. Posner. *The Leadership Challenge*. San Francisco: Jossey-Bass, Inc., 1995.

Levine, Stuart R. and Michael A. Crom. *The Leader in You*. New York: Simon & Schuster, Inc., 1993.

Locke, Edwin A. *The Essence of Leadership*. New York: Lexington Books, 1991.

Manske, F.A. Jr. *Secrets of Effective Leadership*. Memphis: Leadership Education and Development, Inc., 1990.

Natemeyer, Walter E. and J.S. Gilberg, Editors. *Classics of Organizational Behavior*. Danville, Illinois: Interstate Publishers, Inc., 1989.

Oakley, Ed and Doug Drug. *Enlightened Leadership*. New York: Simon & Schuster, Inc., 1991.

Porter, Lynn, Jasper S. Lee, Diana L. Turner, and Malcolm Hillan. *Environmental Science and Technology*. Danville, Illinois: Interstate Publishers, Inc., 1997.

Roberts, General Henry N. *Roberts Rules of Order*. New York: Harper Collins Publishers, 1990.

Russell, Kenneth Lee. *The "How" in Parliamentary Procedure*. 5th ed. Danville, Illinois: Interstate Publishers, Inc., 1990.

Scearce, Carol. *100 Ways to Build Teams*. Palatine, Illinois: Skylight Publishing, Inc., 1992.

Schrumpf, Fred. *Peer Mediation Student Manual*. Champaign, Illinois: Research Press Company, 1991.

Schwarz, Roger M. *The Skilled Facilitator*. San Francisco: Jossey-Bass, Inc., 1994.

Tichy, Noel M. And Mary Anne Devanna. *The Transformational Leader*. New York: John Wiley & Sons, Inc., 1990.

____. *FFA Is*. Alexandria, Virginia: National FFA Organization, 1995.

____. *Agricultural Proficiency Award Handbook*. Alexandria, Virginia: National FFA Organization, 1995.

____. *Conflict Resolution*. Pleasantville, New York: Sunburst Communications, 1994.

INDEX